The Campus History Series

Mount Saint Joseph Academy

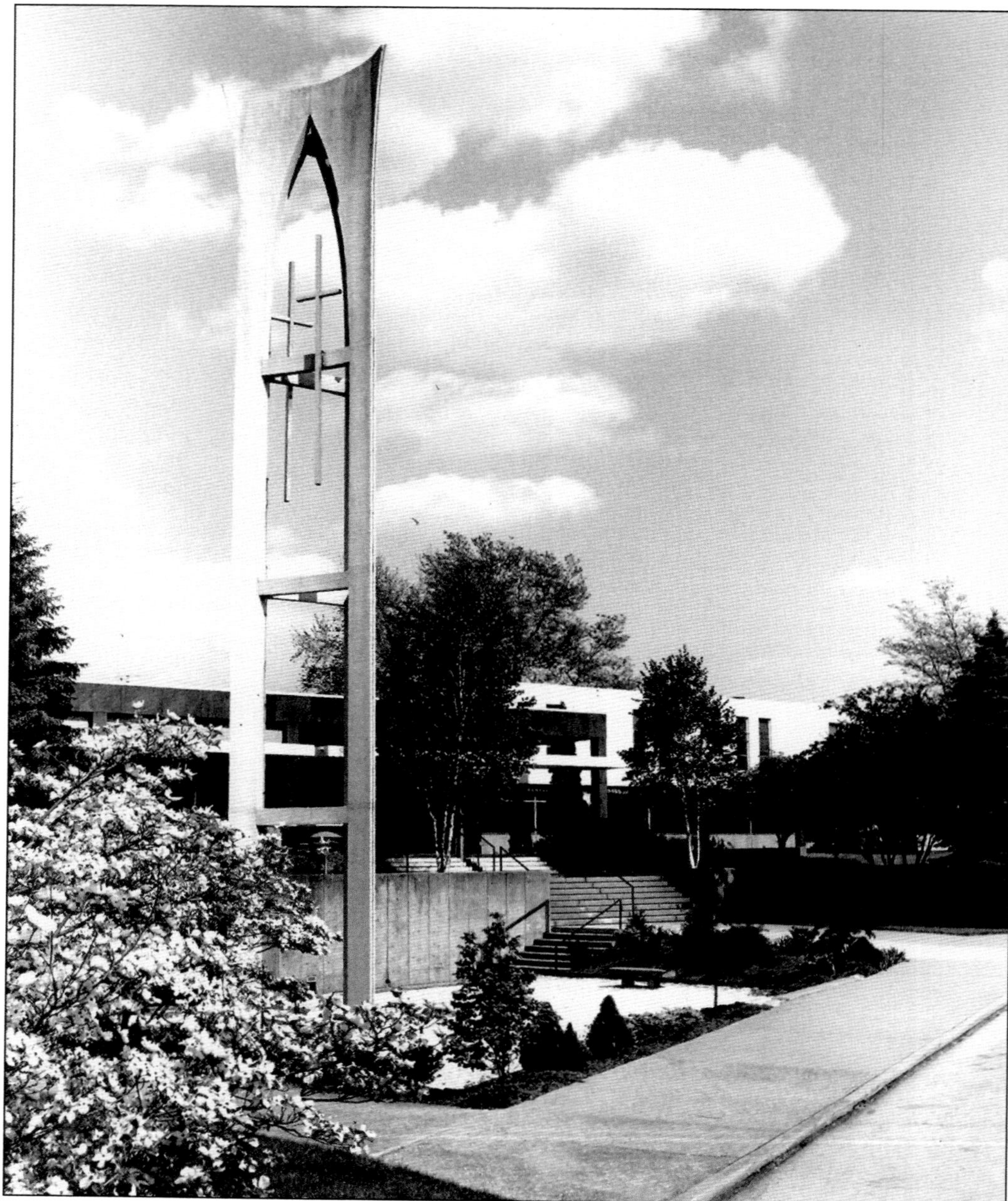

Erected in 1961, the campanile stands proudly as a symbol of Mount spirituality and rise to educational excellence. Located in the foreground of the Mount campus in Flourtown, it overlooks Saint Joseph's Hall and the first campus of "the Old Mount" one mile southwest in Chestnut Hill, Philadelphia.

On the cover: The class of 1904 was the first class to be graduated from Saint Joseph's Hall, which was home to Mount Saint Joseph Academy for 58 years. Since then, each class has worn the Grecian gowns and gold Juliet caps that are the hallmarks of the Mount graduate. (Courtesy of Mount Saint Joseph Academy Archives.)

The Campus History Series

MOUNT SAINT JOSEPH ACADEMY

MOUNT SAINT JOSEPH ACADEMY ALUMNAE ASSOCIATION

ARCADIA PUBLISHING

ISBN 978-0-7385-6254-4

Published by Arcadia Publishing
Charleston SC, Chicago IL, Portsmouth NH, San Francisco CA

Printed in the United States of America

Library of Congress Catalog Card Number: 2008932666

For all general information contact Arcadia Publishing at:
Telephone 843-853-2070
Fax 843-853-0044
E-mail sales@arcadiapublishing.com
For customer service and orders:
Toll-Free 1-888-313-2665

Visit us on the Internet at www.arcadiapublishing.com

This book is dedicated to the Sisters of Saint Joseph, whose spiritual leadership continues to inspire; to the Mount alumnae, who are the embodiment of their teachings; and to present and future Mounties, may they treasure the legacy now in their hands.

CONTENTS

ACKNOWLEDGMENTS

Laced in a legacy, nourished by a mission, seeding a harvest for the future, the Mount rejoices in 150 years.

This sesquicentennial chronicle would not have been possible without the generous support and guidance of many. We are indebted to Kim Rothwell '01, alumnae board member, who, undaunted by the task, graciously compiled the sports and arts captions. Our many nights spent combing through the school archives and dusting off hundreds of images were made easier knowing that Elizabeth Racine was there at every turn to work her scanning magic and dig up needed nuggets of history. Throughout the past year, we have been emboldened by the skillful leadership of Sr. Kathleen Brabson and Sr. Karen Dietrich, who have encouraged us along the way in this momentous task.

We are grateful to the members of the 150th committee, especially Sr. Mary Dacey, Angel Stout '83, Kate Groark Shields '93, Jill Gregori, and Theresa Moyer, as well as Kelly Clarke '05. Special thanks to Sr. Patricia Annas, archivist of the Sisters of Saint Joseph; and journalist Michael Klein for his copy editing.

We had only 128 pages to sing the Mount's praises and provide the text to this loving pictorial history. We know there are many still-untapped sources of school history and of course the personal memories that each Mountie carries with her. We have strived to be as factually accurate as possible, and thank the many former Mounties who shared their personal reflections and insights, especially Eugenia Cooper Comerford '37, Mary Merz Berko '48, Sr. Florence Edward Sullivan '49, Madge Mansell Keehn '50, and countless other members of the Mount community.

Except where noted, all images are courtesy of the Mount Saint Joseph Academy Archives. The sources of written history are *A Chronicle of Mount Saint Joseph Academy* by Sr. Marie de Sales Smith, class of 1904; *Mount Saint Joseph Academy: Centenary Year 1858–1958* by Kathleen M. Kugler '58; *Glimpses of the Past: A Jubilee Sketch of Mount St. Joseph 1858–1908* by the Sisters of Saint Joseph; *Centenary of the Sisters of Saint Joseph in Philadelphia 1847–1947*, published in 1947; *Sisters of St. Joseph of Philadelphia* by Sr. Maria Kostka Logue, published 1950; *Mount Saint Joseph Alumnae Record: 1895–1915* by Regina M. Fisher; plus many school yearbooks, handbooks, newsletters, and school newspapers.

All royalties from this book benefit Mount Saint Joseph Academy.

Foreword

Spes messis in semine, "the hope of the harvest is in the seed." It is my privilege, as the president of Mount Saint Joseph Academy, to invite you to page through this commemorative book that marks the 150th anniversary of a school whose seeds have spread far and wide and have yielded a harvest of women who possess a confidence and a conviction that the future is theirs to create. For 15 years, I have had the honor of witnessing the great harvest that is the Mount.

This book calls the reader to see and imagine what the founding Sisters of Saint Joseph, whose legacy of courage, ingenuity, and great love, did to nurture the soil and cultivate the seeds of hope in the women of the Mount. It was their dream of educating women that led them to open the hearts and minds of their young students as they began their studies at the Middleton Mansion, later in Saint Joseph's Hall, and currently at the Flourtown campus. Each picture and caption will draw you into the traditions and celebrations that are etched in the heart of each Mount graduate.

True to our mission of providing a holistic education, we have created an environment that has prepared our young women to realize their fullest potential. This book captures how we have done this in the academic program, including music and the arts, as well as our numerous athletic accomplishments.

As we celebrate 150 years, we are reminded, as our history states, "that we are rooted in the past with an eye toward the future." I believe that the Mount provides the seed bed for new growth, a place where the cultivation of new ideas and dreams can flourish. This is not only our legacy but also our responsibility toward what has now become the life of the world.

In 1895, the Mount Saint Joseph Alumnae Association was formed. The proud legacy of friendship and loyalty among its members serves as a foundation for the successes and relationships that existed in the past and continues today.

This book marks another milestone in the history of the Mount, and I am personally indebted to Jennifer Dorazio '90, Charlene Keller Fullmer '89, Erin McClafferty '96, and a number of other alumnae who have made this 150th commemorative book another fine example of why we continue to believe and sing with joy, "Spes messis in semine."

Enjoy the read!

Sister Kathleen Brabson, SSJ
President, Mount Saint Joseph Academy

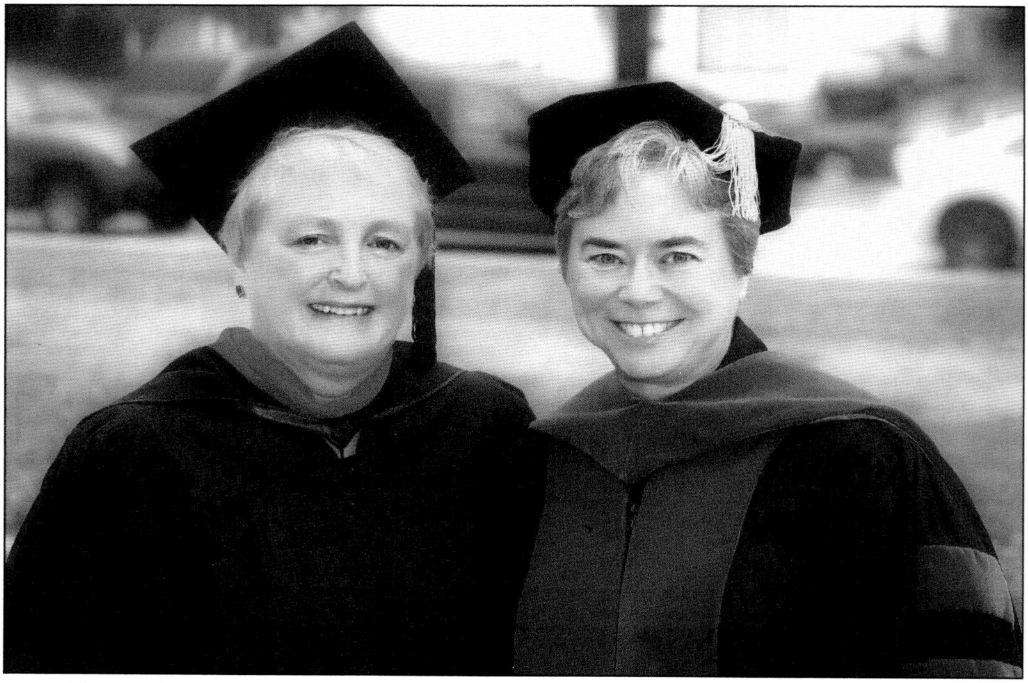

Sr. Kathleen Brabson (left), the second president of the Mount, and Sr. Karen Dietrich, the 19th principal, continue to lead young women into the 21st century during the Mount's sesquicentennial year.

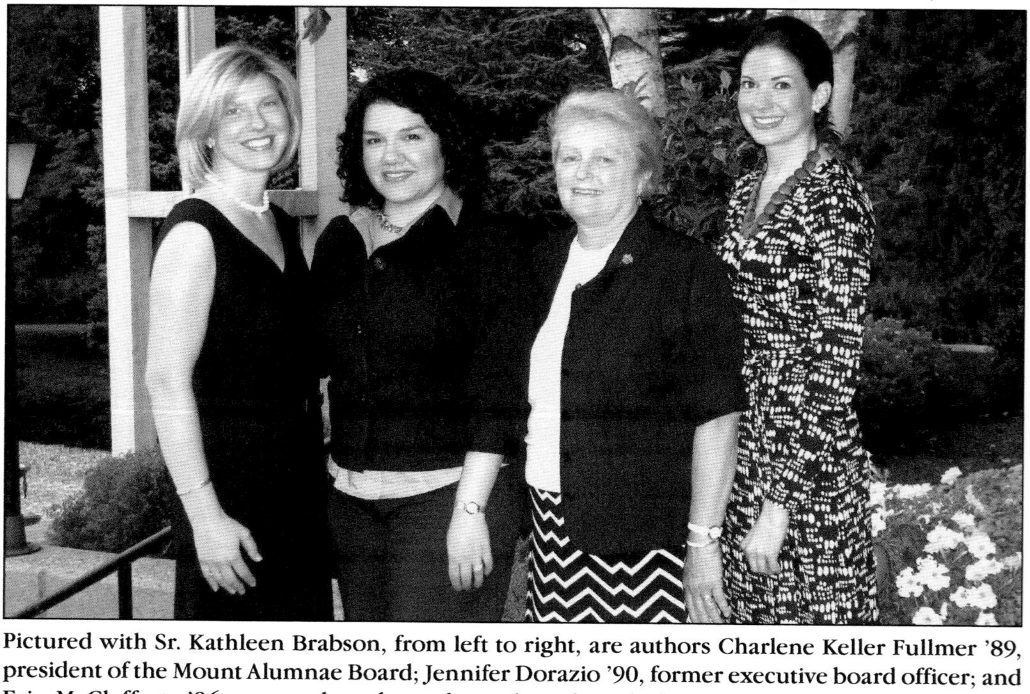

Pictured with Sr. Kathleen Brabson, from left to right, are authors Charlene Keller Fullmer '89, president of the Mount Alumnae Board; Jennifer Dorazio '90, former executive board officer; and Erin McClafferty '96, current board member, who selected photographs and illustrations from the Mount's archives and edited this book. They serve on the Mount's 150th Anniversary Steering Committee to plan events commemorating the history of the Mount.

One

The Founding Sisters

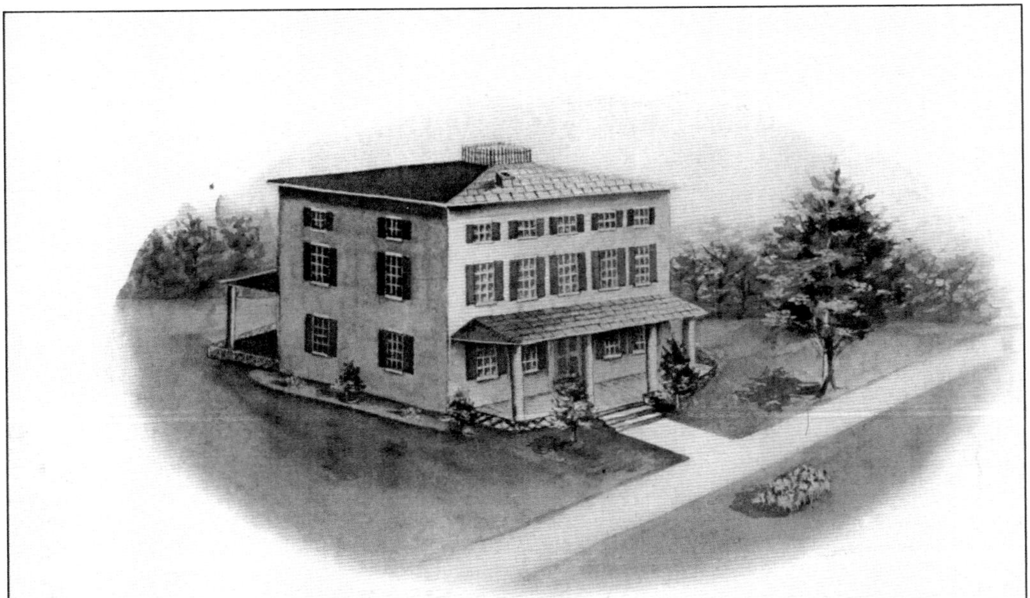

On August 16, 1858, Mother St. John Fournier, the first superior-general of the Sisters of Saint Joseph, surveyed a hilly stretch along the Wissahickon Creek in Chestnut Hill, on the northwestern edge of Philadelphia. The land, owned by Quaker convert Joseph Middleton, housed a stone mansion, Monticello. On the advice of Bishop John Neumann, the order purchased Monticello as the motherhouse. Mount Saint Joseph had a home.

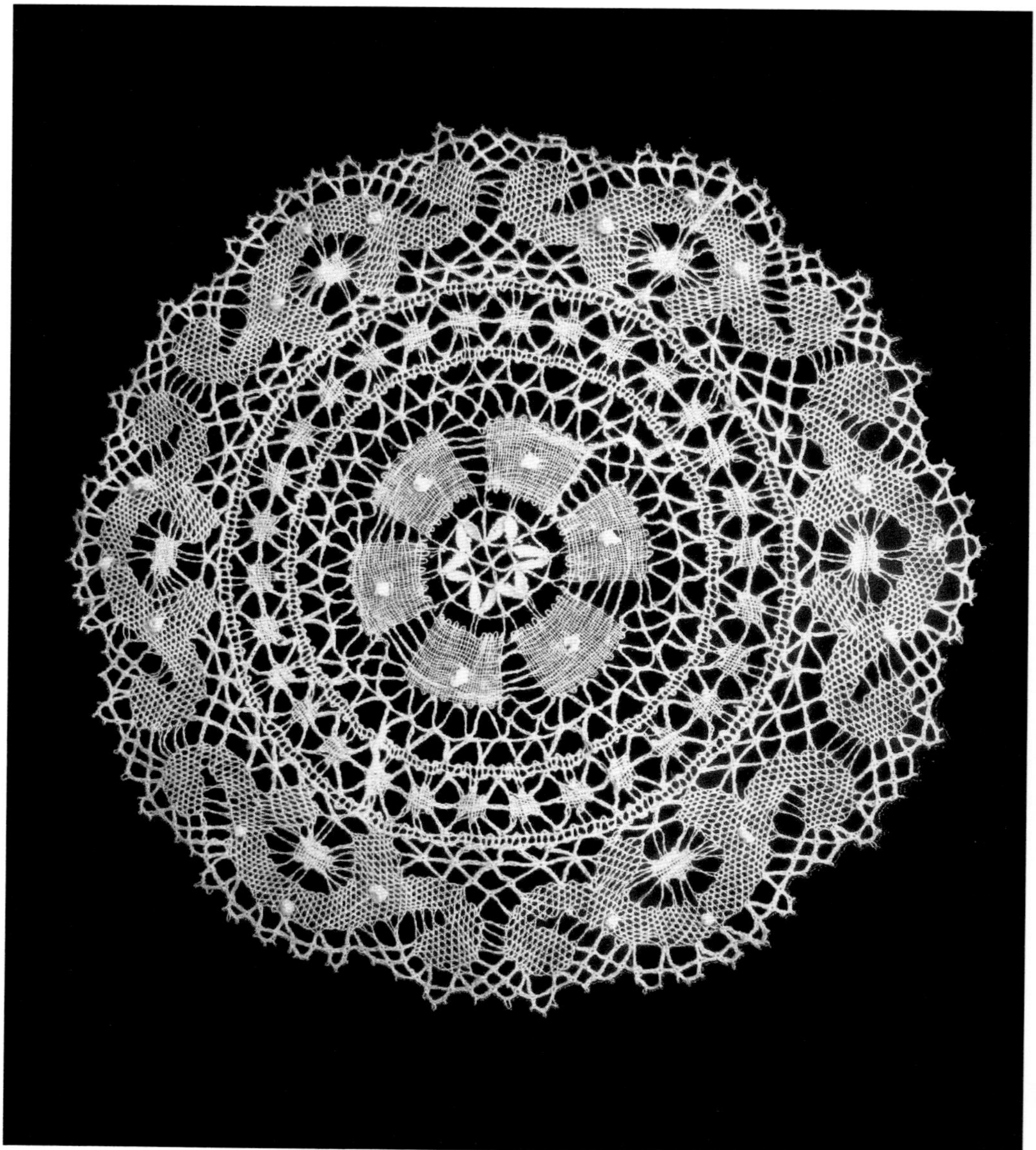

The roots of the order of the Sisters of Saint Joseph can be traced to Le Puy, France, in 1650. The first six Sisters of St. Joseph were lacemakers, using the craft to support the order. In the early 19th century, under Mother St. John Fontbonne, the sisters established academies for girls throughout France. In 1836, one group left for America and settled near St. Louis. In 1847, Mother St. John Fournier traveled to Philadelphia to manage St. John's Orphan Asylum. The sisters took on other ministries and in 1854, with the help of Bishop Neumann, acquired property near Gettysburg. But travel was difficult, and they relocated to Chestnut Hill, Philadelphia. Bishop James F. Wood proclaimed the new home Saint Joseph's Mount. On August 21, 1858, Bishop Neumann celebrated mass on an improvised altar in the front parlor, "and placed it under the patronage of the good St. Joseph." The 12 sisters and 5 postulants were joined on October 4 by boarding student Annie McCann of New Orleans. There were 21 students during that first year, including Lydia and Margaret Middleton, who had the privilege of attending school in their former home.

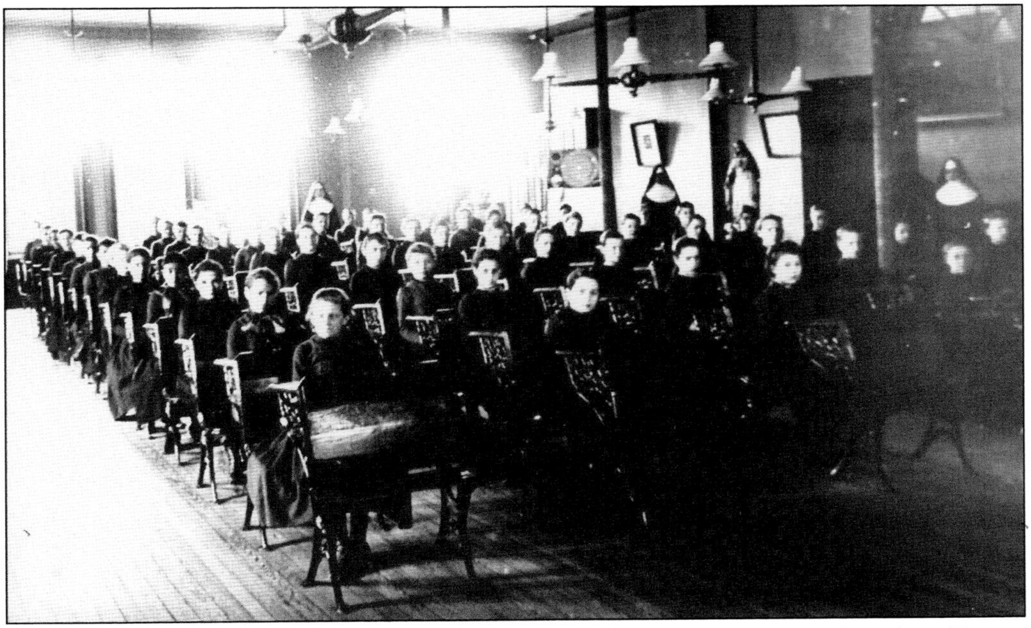

At the Mount's opening, the sisters and students enjoyed a close relationship in their shared home. Expenses for a term were $135—more than $3,200 in today's dollars. One large room served as study hall, assembly room, classroom, and sewing room; religion, English, music, French, and German were the chief subjects. Mother St. John Fournier taught French. Bishop Neumann presided at the first graduation in 1859 on the front porch. The sisters, who educated "young girls about to enter society to impress upon them a fear of God and to school them in Christian modesty and other virtues," believed that "on the education of women depends the future of society." In 1871, the Mount received its charter. In the lower photograph, students study under busts of Shakespeare and Yeats that now watch over today's students at Chestnut Hill College.

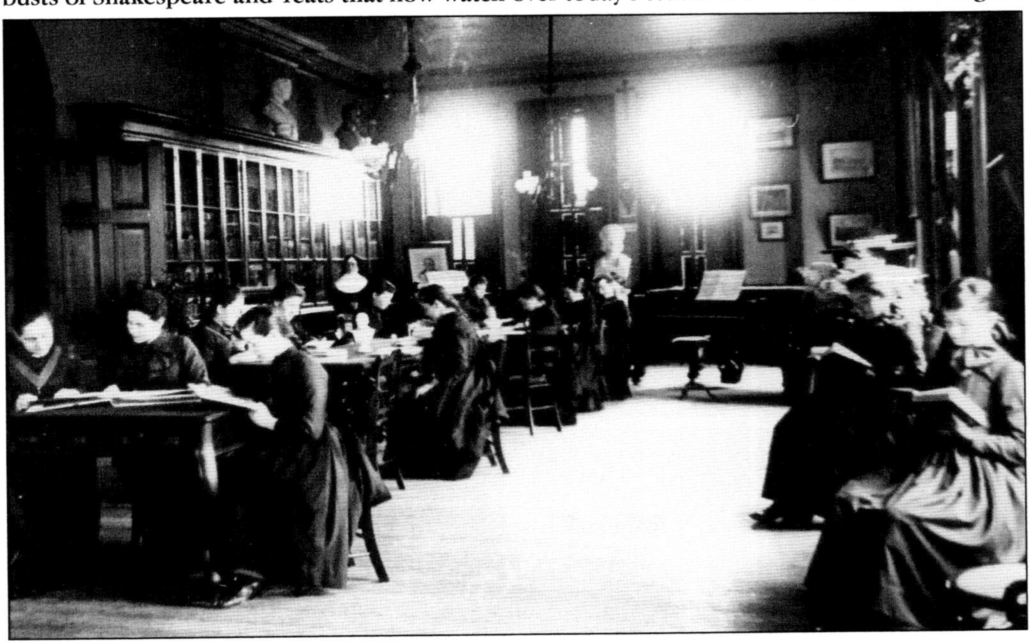

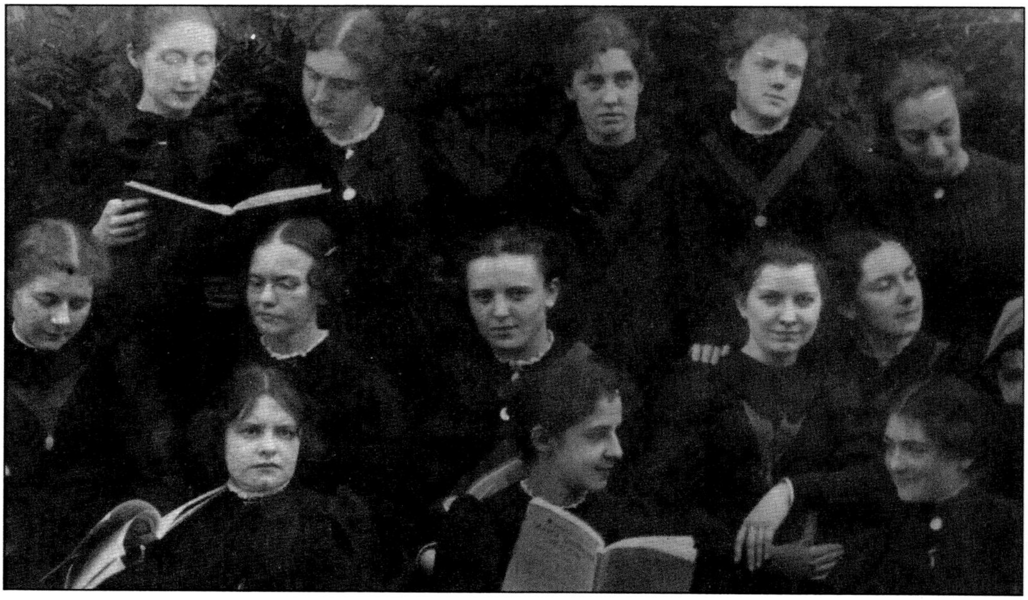

In 1890, when this photograph was taken, Mother St. Ephrem (directress, 1888–1909) established a division of the Columbian Reading Circle called the Queen Isabella Literary Circle, later known as Sedes Sapientiae, to interest the girls in Catholic books and authors. The motto of the club, which existed until 1909, was "The ways of wisdom are beautiful ways, and all her paths are peace." Shortly after the Mount's opening, Mother St. John Fournier saw the need to expand. Rev. Thomas Kyle gave sermons at surrounding parishes to raise money. On St. Joseph's Day 1860, Bishop James F. Wood blessed the addition (below), which included a chapel, a refectory (dining hall), and classrooms. For years, the wing was known lovingly as "Father Kyle's Extension." The Sisters of Saint Joseph and pupils still shared a dining room and chapel.

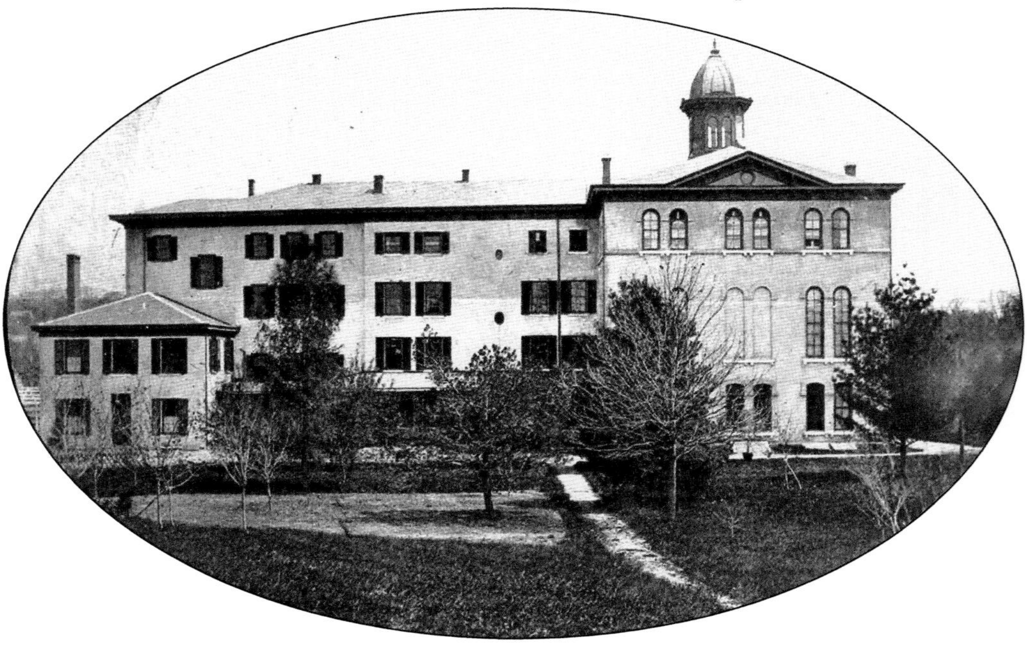

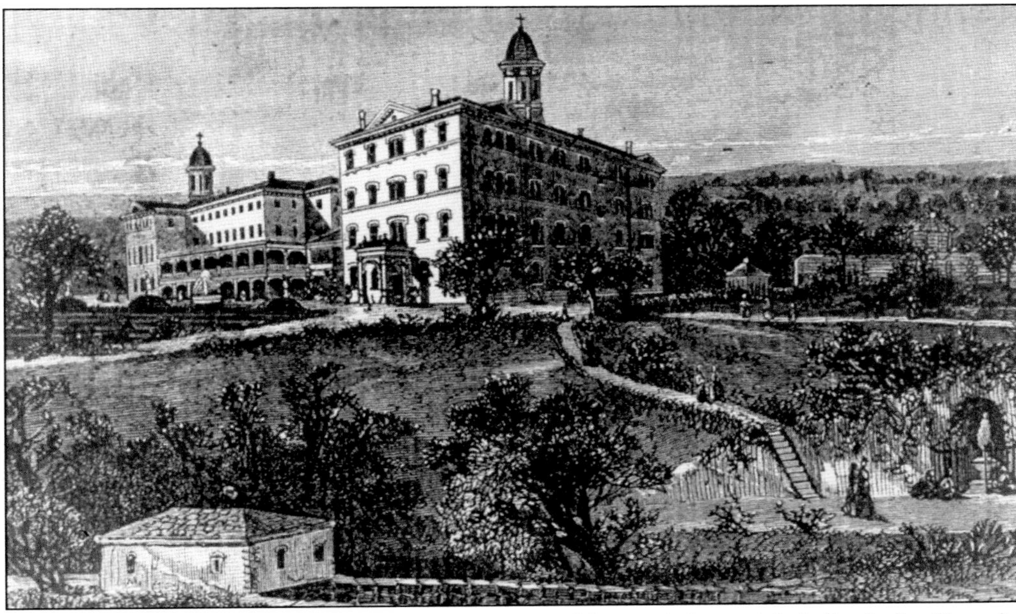

This *c.* 1875 artist's rendering (above) shows numerous additions. At lower right is Our Lady of Lourdes grotto. At lower left is a building housing a waterwheel, which may have generated electricity for the school's elevator. The student body doubled and the four-year high school program expanded to six years. Toward the end of the 19th century, a girl could attend for 10 years. American history and French history were part of the curriculum, along with Latin, Spanish, Italian, science, and elocution. Geography, mathematics, geometry, and mythology were added. The students enjoyed a sprawling campus, perfect for sleigh rides and snowball battles, boating on the Wissahickon, and rolling hoops. By 1890, when this photograph of the camera club was taken, the suffrage movement was in its infancy. The Mount was about to change with the times.

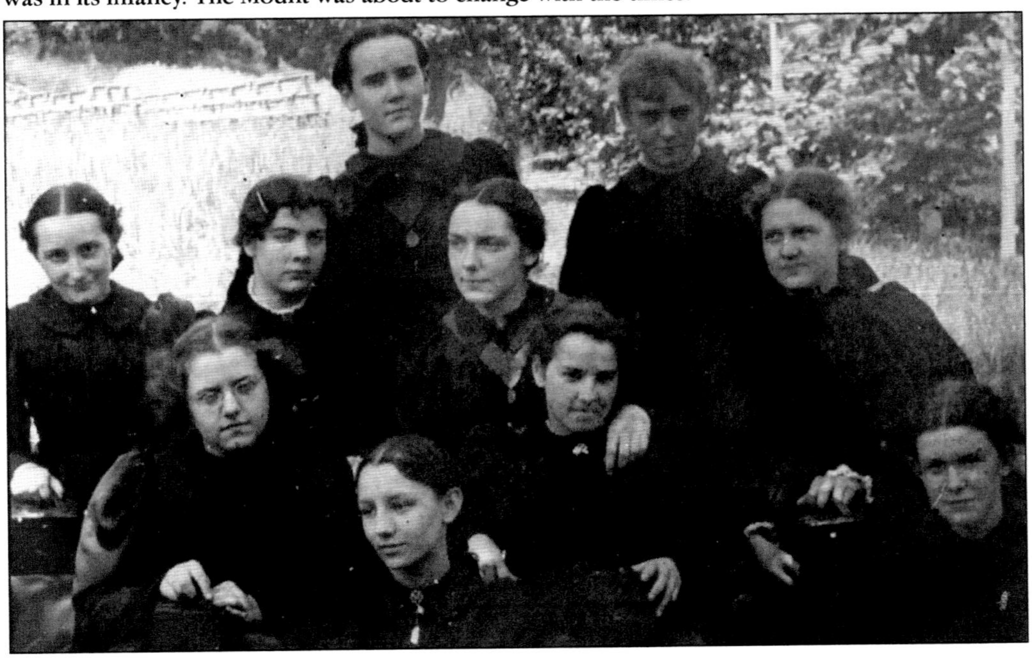

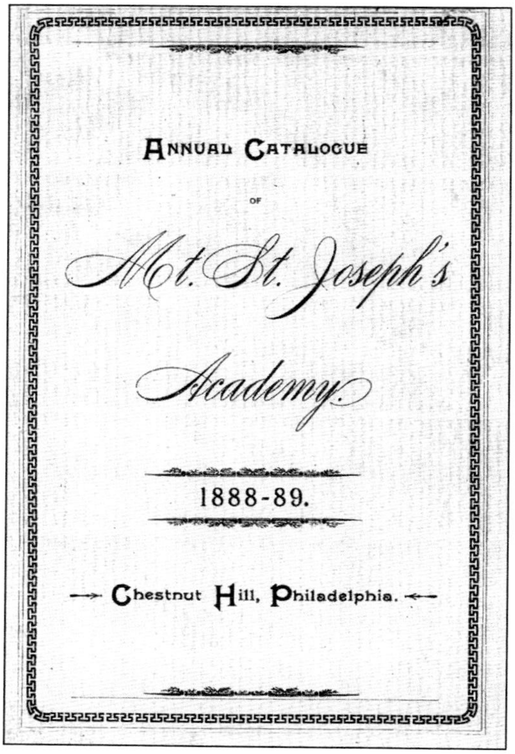
ANNUAL CATALOGUE

OF

Mt. St. Joseph's

Academy.

1888-89.

→ Chestnut Hill, Philadelphia. ←

Women achieved more economic independence during the Industrial Revolution. Secretarial work opened up, and the Mount—whose name alternately was presented as Saint Joseph and Saint Joseph's through the years—added a commercial course to the curriculum. The Sisters of Saint Joseph sought to widen the opportunities of women in business, and courses such as English became more practical. Below, superior-general Mother Mary John directed the building of a grotto—a replica of the shrine to the Blessed Mother in Lourdes. Our Lady of Lourdes Grotto, with kneeling statue of peasant girl Bernadette Soubirous and the words spoken to her by the Blessed Virgin ("I am the Immaculate Conception"), was erected on the same spot as the one on which Mother St. John Fournier placed a statue of Mary upon the sisters' arrival in Chestnut Hill.

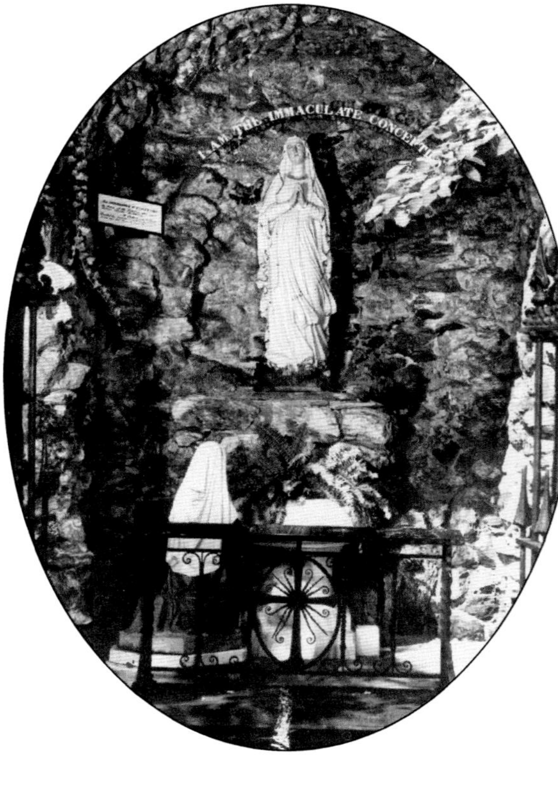

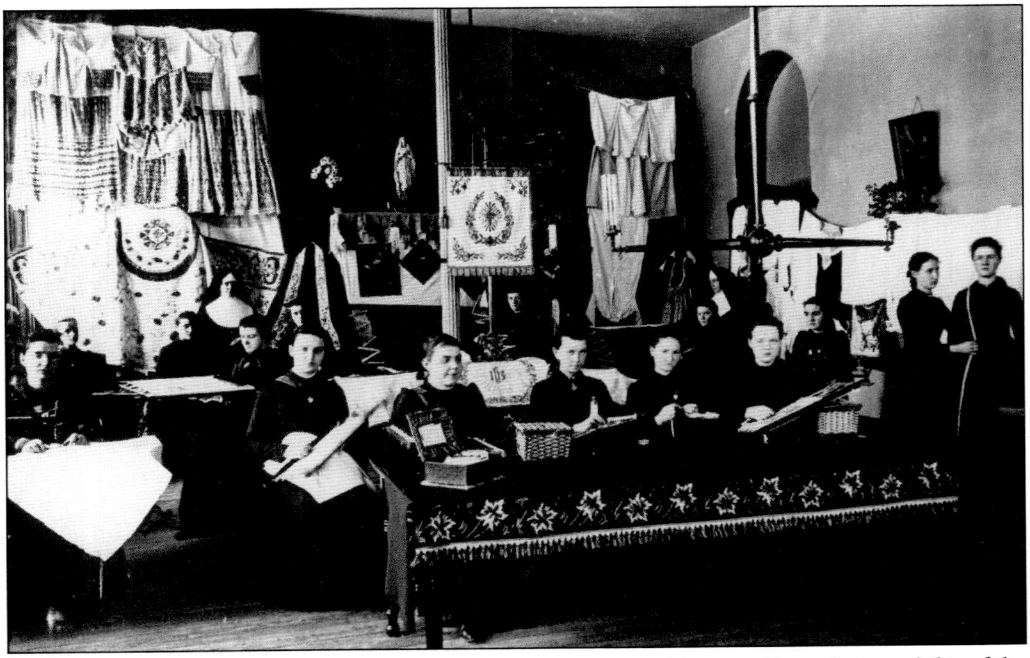

From the school's beginnings, much attention was given to teaching needlework. An exhibit of the girls' completed work, such as the church vestments and altar adornments in this 1893 display, was usually incorporated into commencement exercises. The nuns pictured here are Sr. Margaret Mary (at left rear) and Sister St. Anselm Jennings (right rear). Wax and shell work, along with gold embroidery, was studied in subsequent years. The girls would also display their paintings and drawings and demonstrate their abilities in music and drama. Others studied cooking—as this 1893 photograph of a cooking laboratory shows—the modern equivalent of home economics. Sister St. Margaret stands in the back.

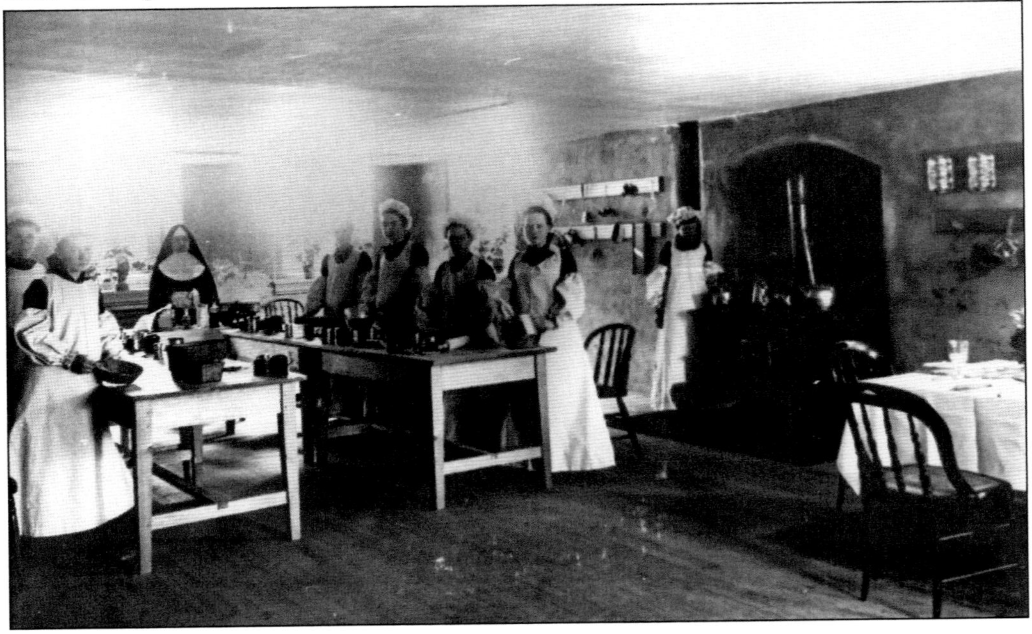

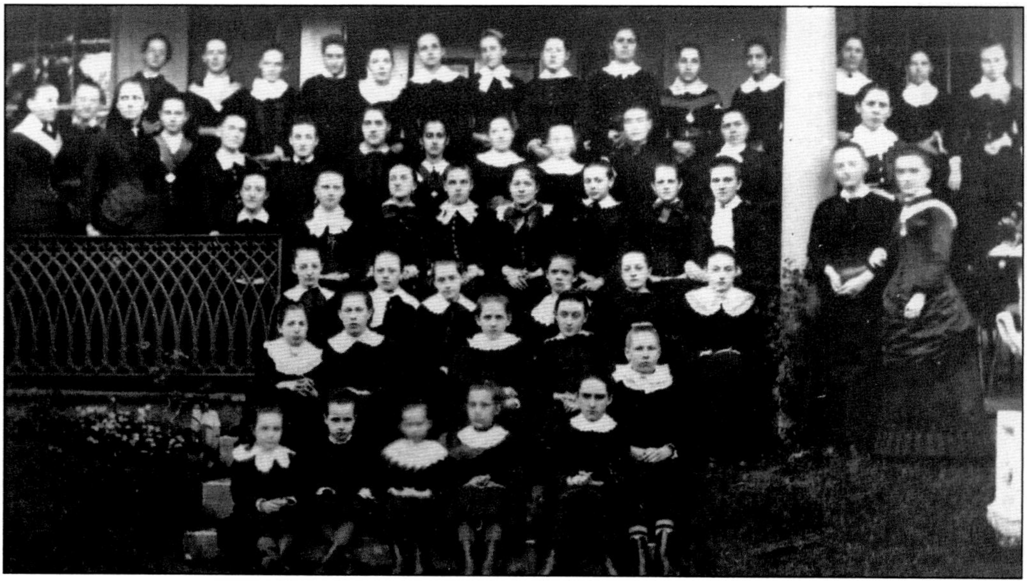

The Sisters of Saint Joseph took special care to tailor the Mount's studies to the changing needs of the era—a progressive educational policy that would earn the school accolades. By 1880, when this photograph was taken, about a dozen boys had been admitted, mainly out of economic necessity. In 1919, the sisters purchased property at 8891 Germantown Avenue, and Norwood Academy, Mount Saint Joseph School for Boys, opened in 1920. In 1924, 44 girls in the first six grades were transferred to the new house at 9001 Germantown Avenue, named Fontbonne Hall, Mount Saint Joseph School for Girls. The Mount remained a junior and senior high school until 1941, when Fontbonne became the home of the seventh- and eighth-grade girls. The Mount then became a senior high school.

CONGREGATION OF THE SISTERS OF ST. JOSEPH OF PHILADELPHIA

FOUNDED IN LE PUY, FRANCE, OCTOBER 15, 1650

At the request of Rt. Rev. Bishop Rosati, C. M., ot St. Louis, Mo., a colony of Missionaries was sent from Lyons to America by the Countess De La Rochejacquelin, arrived at Carondelet, Mo., March 25, 1836.

Mother House and Novitiate Established in Chestnut Hill, Philadelphia, Pa.

AUGUST 16, 1858

MOUNT ST. JOSEPH COLLEGE

CHESTNUT HILL, PHILADELPHIA, PA.

Germantown Avenue and City Line

A Residential and Day College for the Higher Education of Women

STANDARD COURSES LEADING TO DEGREES

ACADEMIC DEPARTMENT - - - - THREE DISTINCT COURSES:

College Preparatory, Secretarial, Home Economics

FONTBONNE HALL

PRE-ACADEMIC SCHOOL FOR GIRLS

(Resident and Day Pupils)

GERMANTOWN and SUNSET AVENUES

Chestnut Hill, Philadelphia, Pa.

NORWOOD ACADEMY

Elementary and Junior High School for Boys

(Resident and Day Pupils)

GERMANTOWN and SUNSET AVENUES

Chestnut Hill, Philadelphia, Pa.

(Gymnasium and Military Training in charge of Expert Master)

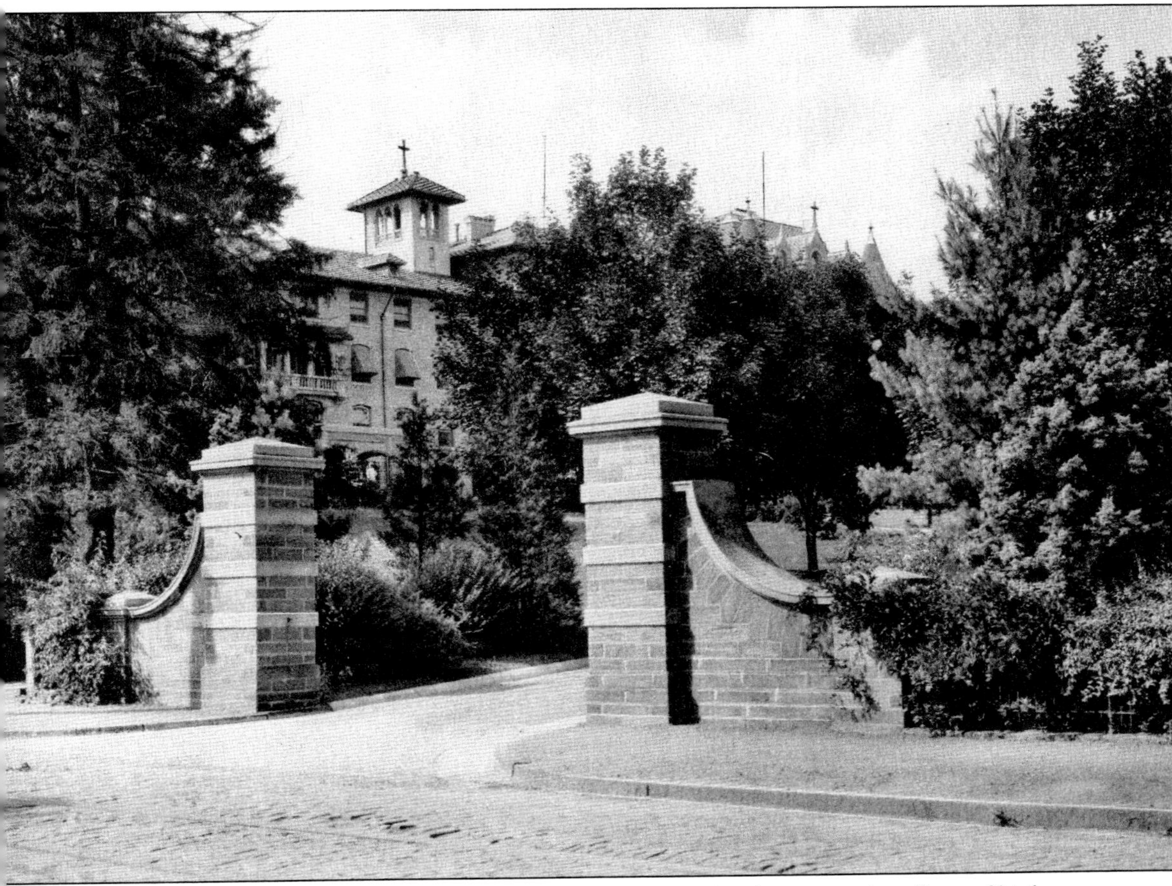

In 1924, in response to requests both within and outside the school, a women's college of higher education opened. Unfortunately, gaining full recognition, approval, and accreditation by the state was a slow and difficult process. Therefore, the college operated under the 1871 Mount charter, which allowed the sisters to confer degrees. The college was known as Mount Saint Joseph until 1938, when it was changed to Chestnut Hill College of the Sisters of Saint Joseph, to avoid confusion. Today the grounds of Chestnut Hill College encompass what is nostalgically referred to as "the Old Mount."

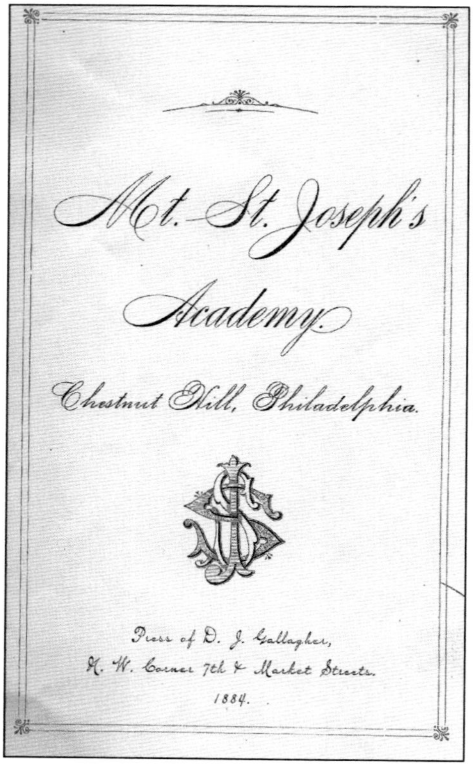

Mt. St. Joseph's Academy

Chestnut Hill, Philadelphia.

Press of D. J. Gallagher,
N. W. Corner 7th & Market Streets.
1884.

The academy's published catalog, like this one from 1884, was mailed to interested students and their families. The dictated memoirs of Katy Tracy, who attended the Mount from 1866 to 1870, shed light on the daily routine of those early Mounties. The girls were awakened by Reverend Mother Clement (directress, 1863–1888), clapping her hands as she walked through the dormitories, saying aspirations while the pupils dressed and went to mass. After mass, morning prayers, and breakfast, the girls went to class at 8:30 a.m. The school day included lessons, chapel, lunch, and a short recess. The remainder of the day included mending and sewing and three more hours of class before dinner at 6:00 p.m., accompanied by a spiritual reading. After dinner and a recreation period, the day was capped by more study. Bedtime was 8:00 p.m., or 8:30 p.m. on special occasions.

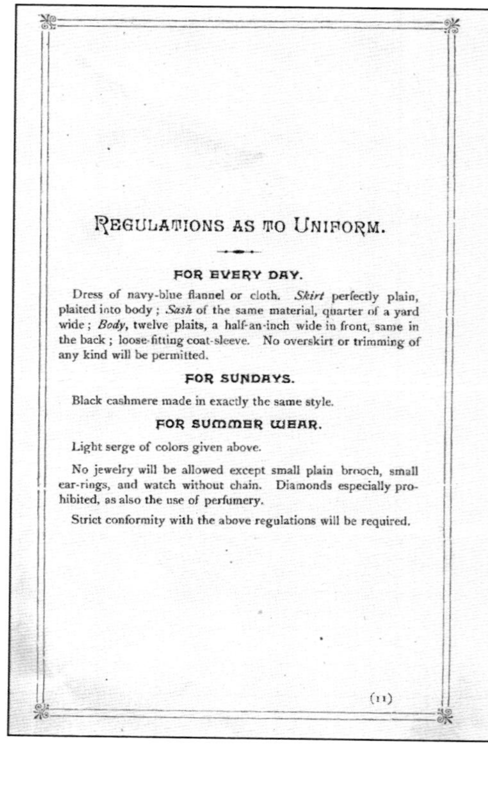

REGULATIONS AS TO UNIFORM.

FOR EVERY DAY.

Dress of navy-blue flannel or cloth. *Skirt* perfectly plain, plaited into body; *Sash* of the same material, quarter of a yard wide; *Body*, twelve plaits, a half-an-inch wide in front, same in the back; loose-fitting coat-sleeve. No overskirt or trimming of any kind will be permitted.

FOR SUNDAYS.

Black cashmere made in exactly the same style.

FOR SUMMER WEAR.

Light serge of colors given above.

No jewelry will be allowed except small plain brooch, small ear-rings, and watch without chain. Diamonds especially prohibited, as also the use of perfumery.

Strict conformity with the above regulations will be required.

(11)

Terms for Scholastic Year.

(Payable half-yearly in advance.)

Entrance Fee,	$5 00
Board, tuition, bedding, and washing, per annum,	200 00
Piano, with use of instrument, "	50 00
Organ, " " "	50 00
Guitar, " " "	50 00
Vocal Music (private lessons), "	50 00
" (in class), "	20 00
German, Drawing, etc.,	20 00
Painting in water colors and pastel,	30 00
Oil Painting, per annum,	50 00
Spanish and Italian, each per annum,	40 00
Gold Embroidery, Wax, Hair-work, each	10 00
Use of Library and Reading-room,	2 00
Board during Vacation,	40 00

French and Latin being included in the course, form no extra charge.

Physician's Fees and Stationery are extra charges.

Pupils pay each year for the *use* of books, according to class.

Pupils are received at any time, and are charged from date of entrance.

None are received, however, unless they intend to complete the session; and no deduction will be made in case of withdrawal, except for severe illness.

Bills of expenses are sent at the close of each session.

If parents wish clothing, materials for sewing, etc., to be procured by the Institution, they should leave a deposit for that purpose.

(12)

The "Special to Parents" also spells out the school's regulations. Principles of religion and virtue, it was said, were the girls' safeguards through life. The Sisters of Saint Joseph's method of rewarding and publishing the infractions of the rules was the "bank of one hundred points," allotted to each girl at the beginning of the school year. Excellence or failures in conduct, order, or "ladylike deportment" meant the addition or subtraction of precious points, the results of which were reflected on student report cards.

Special to Parents.

In placing your children under our care, you give us a mark of confidence, to prove ourselves worthy of which we deem a binding duty.

On your side, you seek their improvement in moral training, mental growth and physical development.

Our end is the same, and to labor for its attainment we have bound ourselves, not for a few years only, but for our whole lives.

The rules and regulations of the Institution are laid down in this little book. They are the outcome of varied experience and long years of observation, and all tend, we conscientiously believe, to the welfare of our children.

We then assume that they meet your approval, and that, so far as you are concerned, you will not encourage infractions of them.

We draw your attention especially to those which concern visits, dress, and punctual attendance. One day more or less may seem of trivial consequence, but the injurious effects of absence, tardiness, and the like, are known only to teachers. Children cannot be taught too early that pleasure must yield to the call of duty.

In order to avoid misunderstandings, we respectfully ask that you will give special messages as to health, wardrobe, studies, etc., not to the children, but to the Directress or Sister in attendance.

Your confidential suggestions regarding disposition, health, etc., of your children will be thankfully received.

To their health we promise the utmost attention, and should anything more than trifling indisposition be threatened, you will be immediately notified.

In conclusion, we can but hope that our mutual co-operation will be productive of good in regard to those whom we look upon not as *your* children alone, but ours also.

For further particulars, address

SISTER SUPERIOR,
Chestnut Hill, Philadelphia, Pa.

(14)

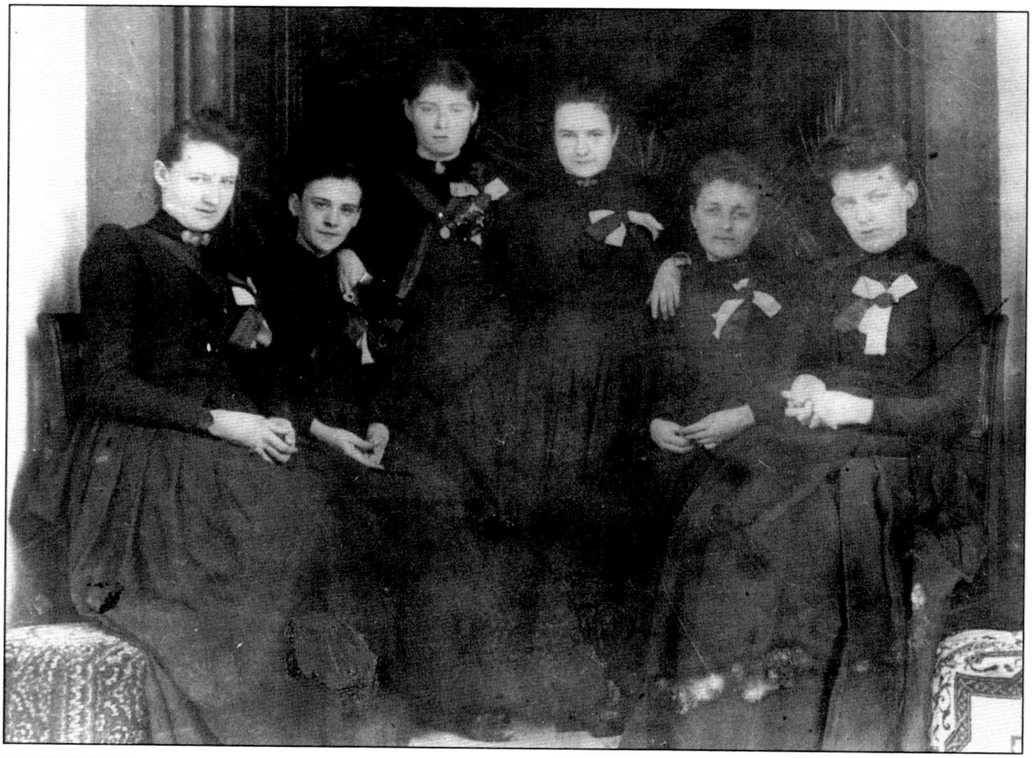

Wardrobe for Boarding Pupils

The uniform regulations must be followed in each detail. No concessions will be granted, and for the sake of uniformity we request the adoption of same by our Day Pupils during the school session.

1 Black and 1 Blue Uniform Dress (Acad. Dep't).
4 Sets Collars and Cuffs.
2 Blue Uniform Dresses (Elementary Dep't).
2 Blue Linen Dresses for summer.
2 White Aprons (Elementary).
2 Gingham Aprons (Elementary).
2 Black Sateen Aprons (Intermediate Dep't), long sleeves with cuff.
1 Black Gymnasium Suit.
All the above can be had at John B. Simpson's.

2 Dozen Handkerchiefs.
6 Changes of heavy and light Underwear (strong and serviceable).
4 Night Dresses (plain and strong).
1 Summer and 1 Winter Robe and 1 pair Bedroom Slippers.
3 Bath Towels, 3 Face Towels and 3 Washcloths.
3 Pair Black Shoes, with *rubber heels;* 1 pair Overshoes.
2 Black Underskirts (not silk, but washable).
3 Flannel or Outing Skirts.
1 Dozen pairs Good Hose (silk stockings may be worn on dress occasions only).
Hats and Coats suitable for season.

From the Mount's early days, the girls received grades on care of clothing and attention to polite deportment. Medals for ladylike deportment, order, and neatness were coveted. On Saturday, the girls took baths, after which they put on a kimono or "wrapper" and had their hair washed and brushed during private consultations with Sister Clement. All the while, the girls' friendship and affection with this nun strengthened. One pupil used a diamond ring to etch "Sister Clement is good" into a novitiate window. Through the years, the Mount uniform has undergone numerous reinventions, from dresses to jumpers to skirts of varying lengths. Uniform dress was introduced in 1864. The dark blue or black of the winter uniform has remained, as has the presence of a purple, white, and gold emblem on the sleeve or chest.

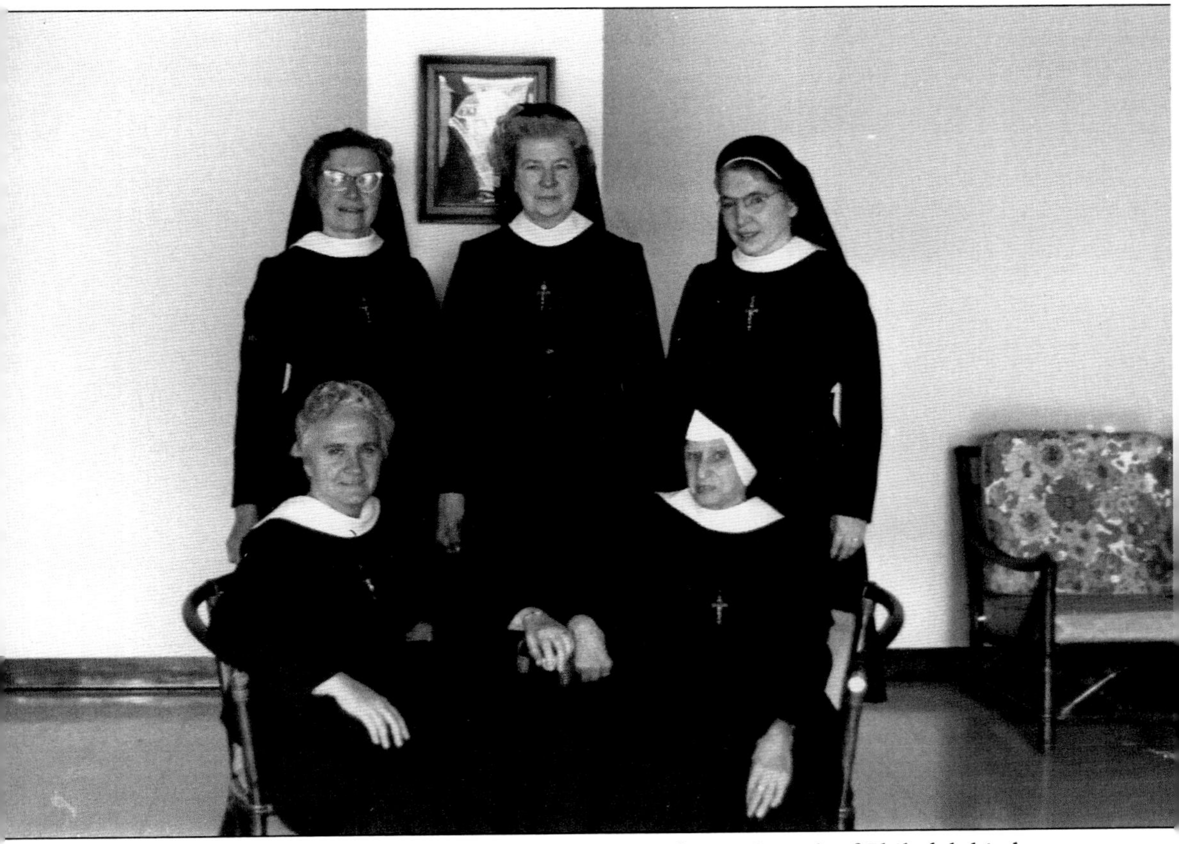

From the days of Mother St. John Fournier, the Sisters of Saint Joseph of Philadelphia have not only schooled, but also guided and prepared young girls of each decade with the spiritual enrichment and the tools to succeed in a changing world. This photograph, taken in the early 1980s in Fontbonne Lounge, shows four Mount leaders of the 1950s through 1980. From left to right are (first row) Sr. Elizabeth De Sales (principal 1972–1980) and Mother M. Sylvester (directress 1956–1967 and 1970–1971); (second row) Sr. Jane Matilda (principal 1969–1970), Rev. Mother Alice Anita Murphy (superior-general of the Sisters of Saint Joseph of Philadelphia), and Sr. Ann Elizabeth (principal 1971–1972).

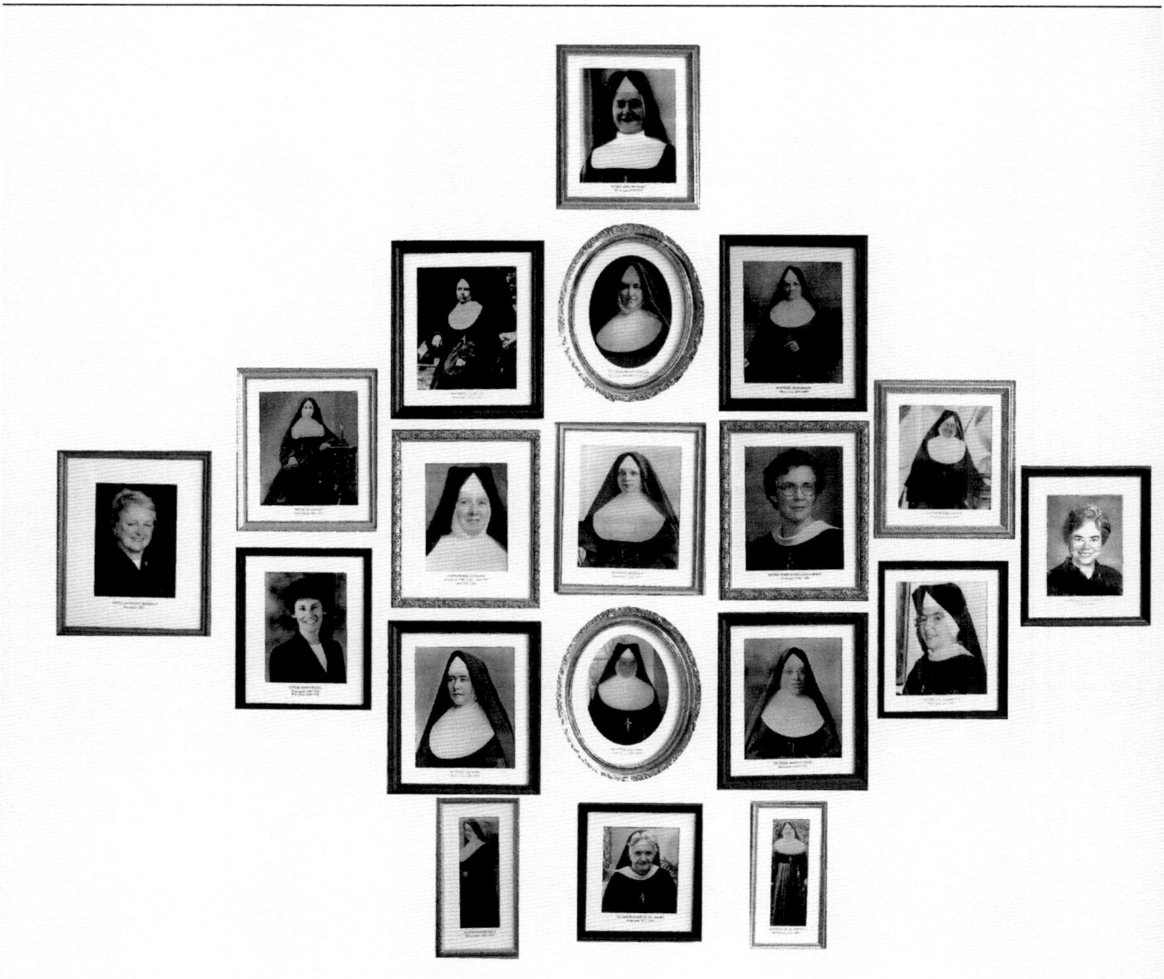

These portraits in the Mount's main stariwell watch over today's students as they race to and from class, whether upstairs to Fournier Auditorium or downstairs to Fontbonne Lounge. From far left to far right, then top to bottom are (first column) Sr. Kathleen Brabson (president 2005–present); (second column) Mother Xavier (directress 1861–1863) and Sr. Mary Dacey (principal 1988–1994, president 1994–2004); (third column) Mother Clement (directress 1863–1885), Mother Denis Marie (directress 1941–1947, 1950–1956, 1968–1969), Mother De Neri (directress 1920–1925), and Mother Carmela (directress 1947–1950); (fourth column) Sr. Jane Matilda (principal 1969–1970), Mother M. Sylvester (directress 1956–1967, 1970–1971), Mother Stephen Hesse (directress 1858–1861), Mother Aquinas (directress 1885–1888), and Sr. Elizabeth De Sales (principal 1972–1980); (fifth column) Mother St. Ephrem (directress 1888–1909), Sr. Mary Josephine Larkin (principal 1980–1988), Mother Mary Joseph (directress 1915–1920), and Mother M. St. Ursula (directress 1935–1941); (sixth column) Mother Mary Louis (directress 1923–1929) and Sr. Ann Elizabeth (principal 1971–1972); (seventh column) Sr. Karen Dietrich (principal 1994–present).

Two

Chestnut Hill Legacy

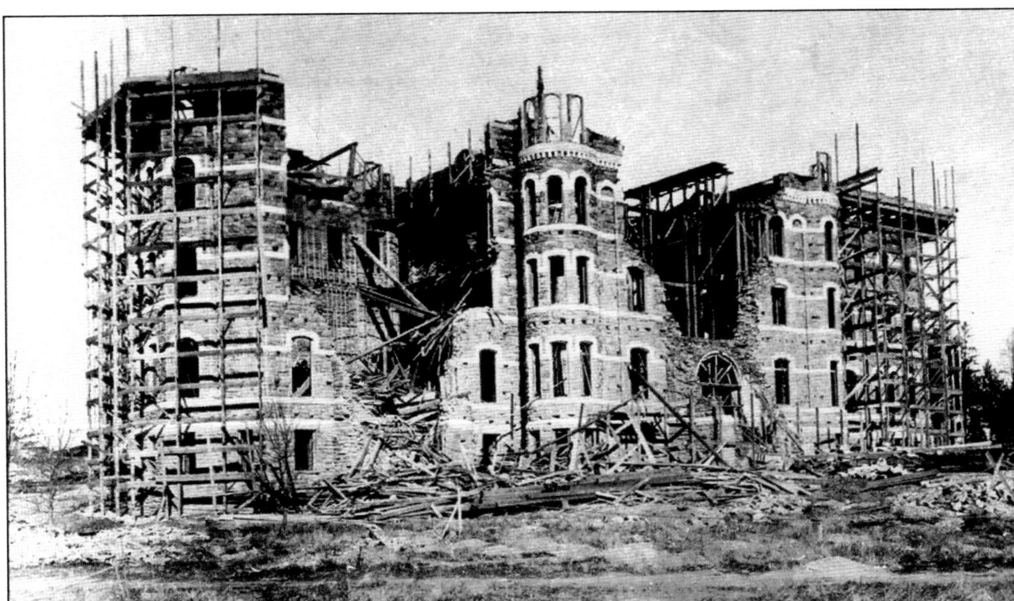

By the end of the 19th century, the academy needed a new building. The edifice was ready for roofing when, on the night of November 20, 1900, the rotunda and the concrete front of the building collapsed. What remained was torn down, and construction began again after Rev. Mother Clement and Sister St. Ephrem led a fund-raising drive. By fall 1903, the academy, referred to as the Collegiate Institute, was completed.

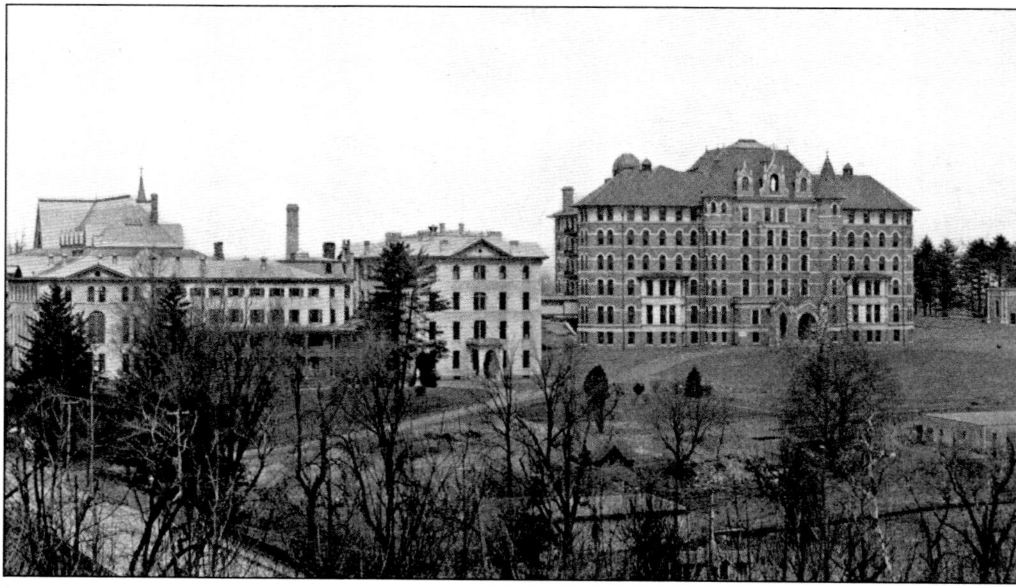

A new era at Mount Saint Joseph Academy began when students entered Saint Joseph's Hall on September 29, 1903, over two years after the first cornerstone of the new building was relaid on March 20, 1901. The formal opening of the school was on November 20, 1903, with Archbishop Patrick J. Ryan in attendance. Archbishop Ryan, celebrating the golden jubilee of his ordination, is remembered in the nickname "the Bishop's Stairs," referring to the grand staircase in the rotunda. Saint Joseph's Hall was the home of the Mount for the next 58 years.

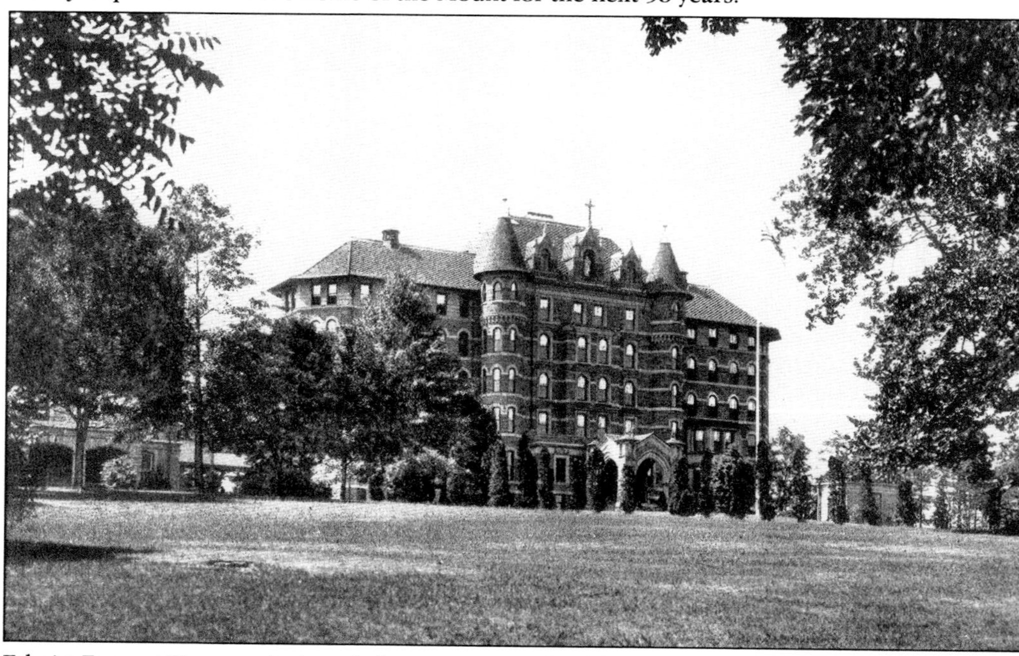

Edwin Forrest Durang designed the seven-story building with towered, Loire Valley facade and French Gothic porte-cochere. Red terra-cotta tile roofs, recalling the French roots of the founding Sisters of Saint Joseph, top the walls of Wissahickon schist rock. (Courtesy of Chestnut Hill College.)

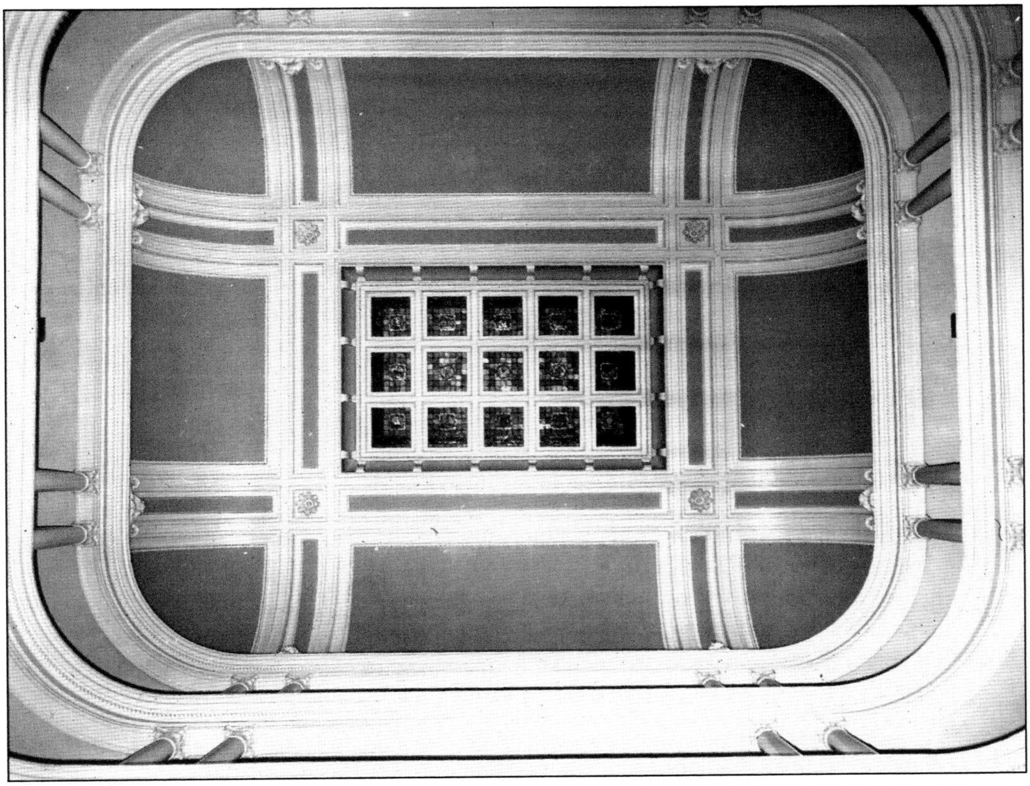

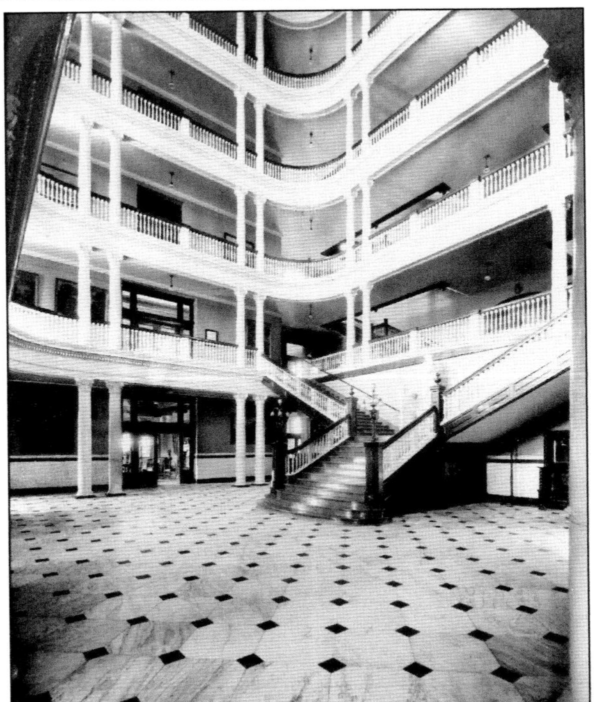

The rotunda is one of the most beloved features of Saint Joseph's Hall. With its Greco-Roman design, marble floors, grand chestnut staircase, and balconies, it rises six stories, crowned by a stained-glass skylight. Designed by H. J. Smith and Sons in Philadelphia, the skylight contains 15 sections of leaded glass, each a symbol of Jesus, Mary, or St. Joseph.

Mount St. Joseph Collegiate Institute

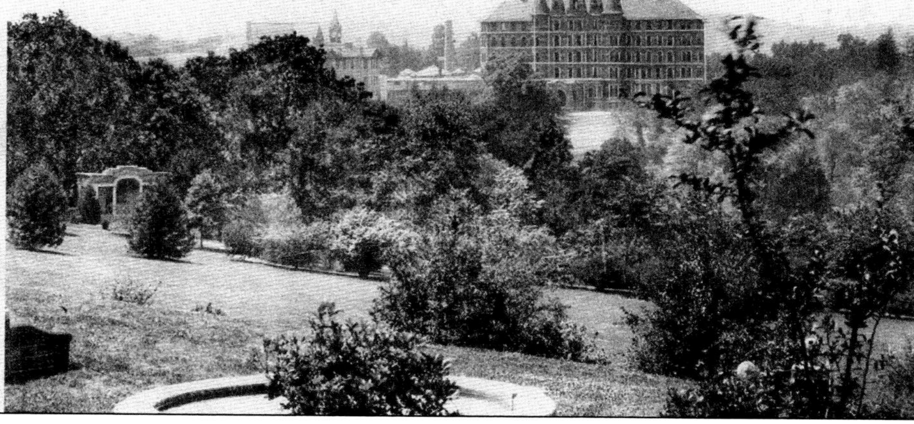

With the appointment of Mother St. Pierre as the first superior-directress in 1909, the school entered a new era of separation between the motherhouse and the school. The old convent school life had passed away, and a new academic life began at the Mount. The students were divided into various classes with one sister prefect in charge of each class. The last four years of study were called the collegiate department, with college preparatory, literary, classical, commercial and general, and special diplomas awarded. In an early catalog for the school, the Sisters of Saint Joseph offered college courses, which were dropped in 1906 due to the financial burden of the reconstruction.

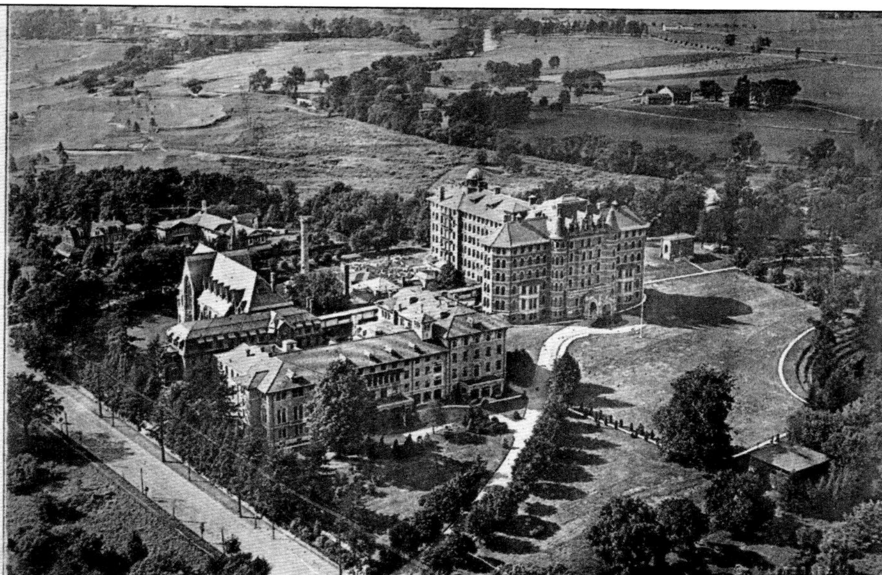

—"the dearest spot on earth" is Mount St. Joseph, where the Wissahickon's rippling waters glide.

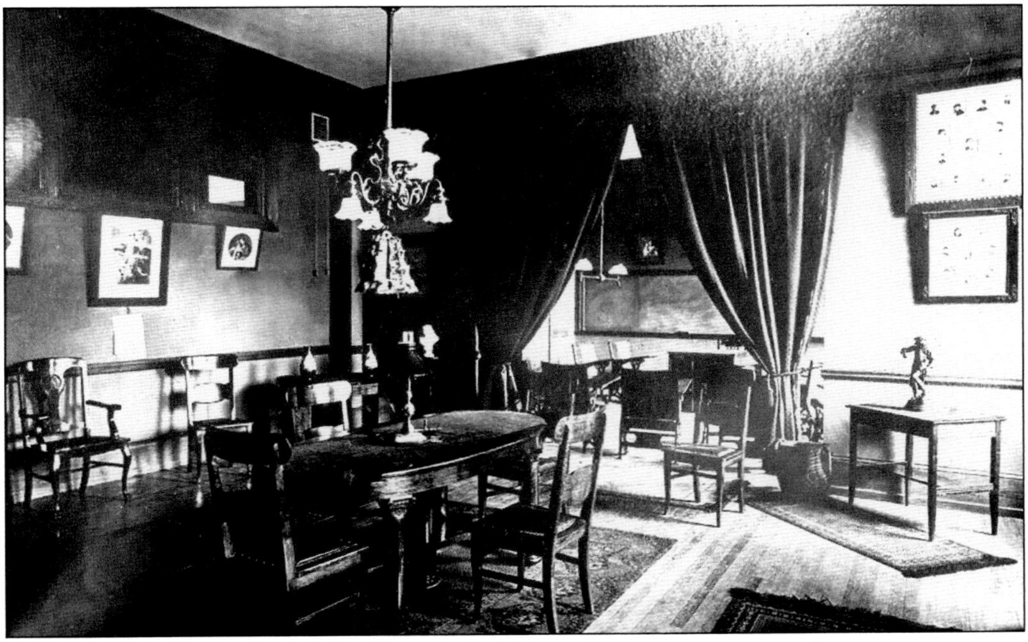

Adjoining the senior classroom in the new building and separated from it by portieres was an attractive parlor, known as room No. 46 (above). Located on the second floor, the graduates took turns entertaining classmates or a sister class. There is one record of the class of 1904 returning to the school and entertaining the class of 1905 at a dinner followed by a dance with refreshments. In the room adjoining the rotunda in Saint Joseph's Hall is the east parlor, or reception room (below). Pictured in front of the fireplace in the east parlor is one of the earliest classes to graduate from the new building.

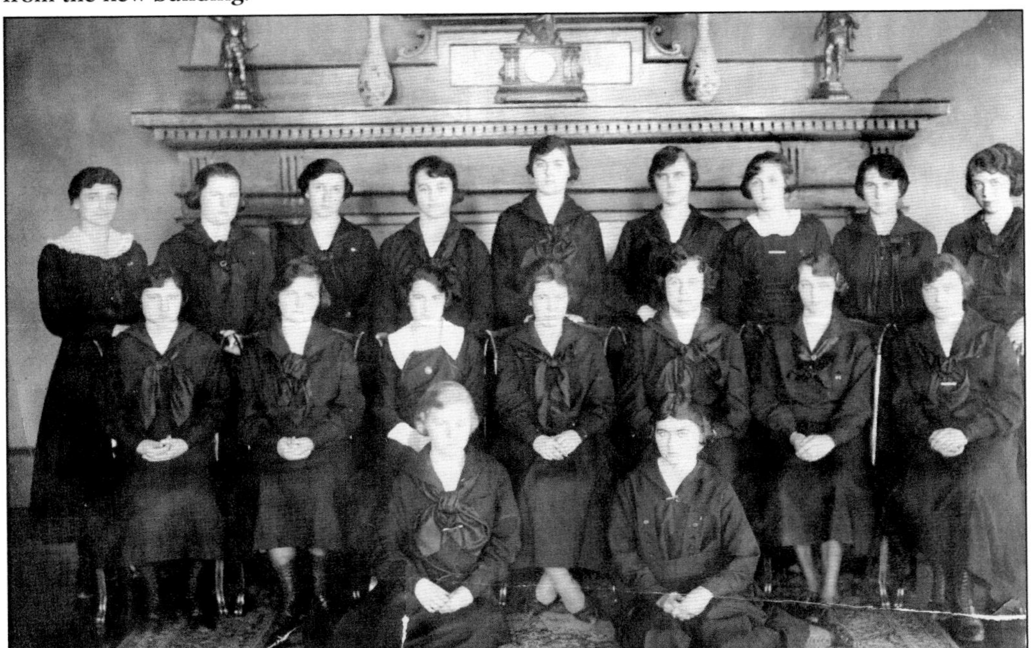

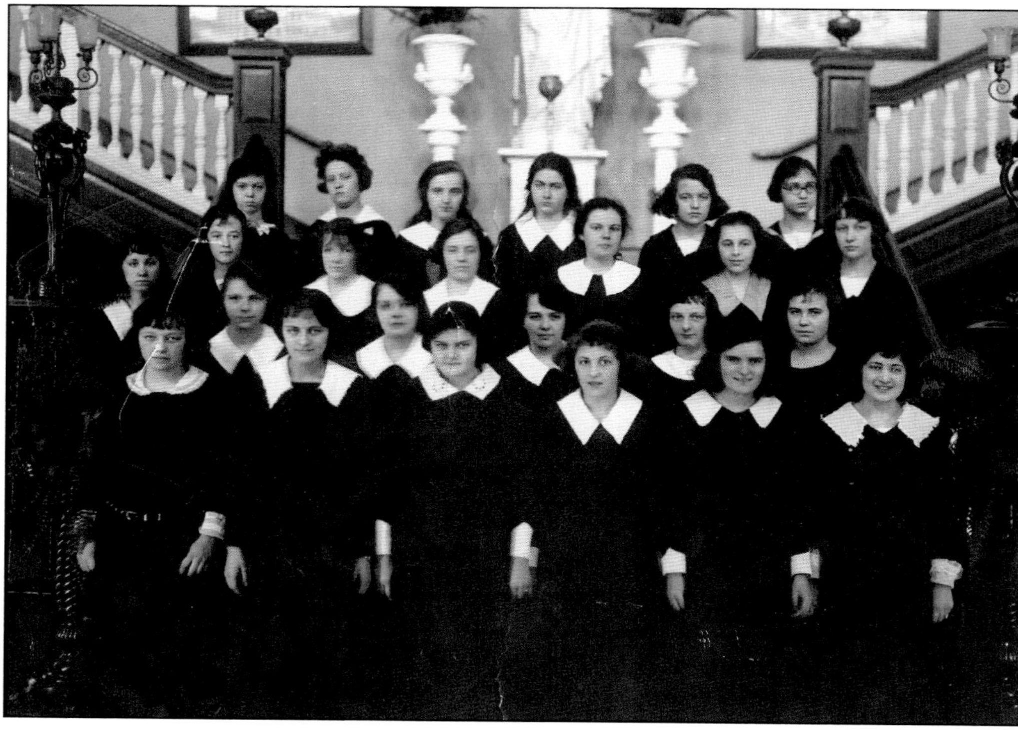

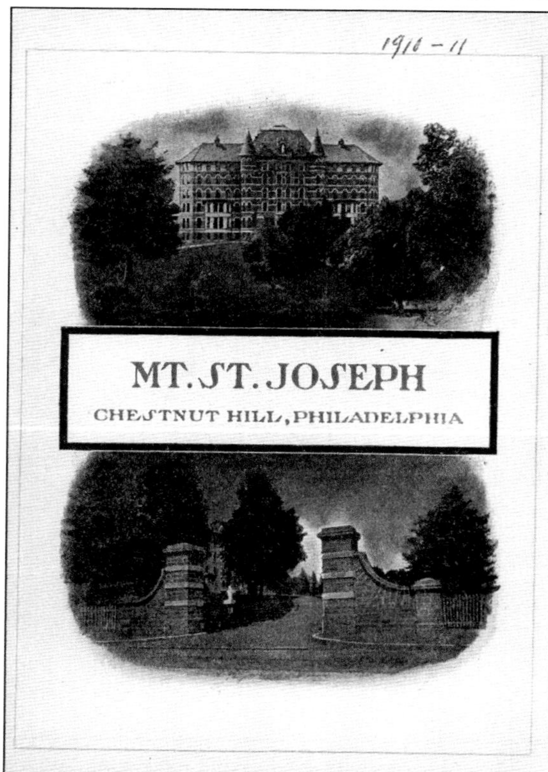

For the first few years, the new building came with restrictions, and many girls were nostalgic for the "Old Mount." Although the "Bishop's Stairs" in the rotunda (shown above) and front stairs of the school were always sacred territory, in the early 1900s the stairs were off-limits. A late study hour from 8:00 to 9:00 p.m. and long stretches of corridor to classrooms from the dormitory (an effort to spare the front stairs from wear) seemed among the greatest hardships. In 1910–1911, the Mount formally advertised itself as both a boarding and day school. The school admitted 14 day pupils, known as "day hops," during this year. There had been only a few nonresident students before this time, and they were selected because they lived near the school.

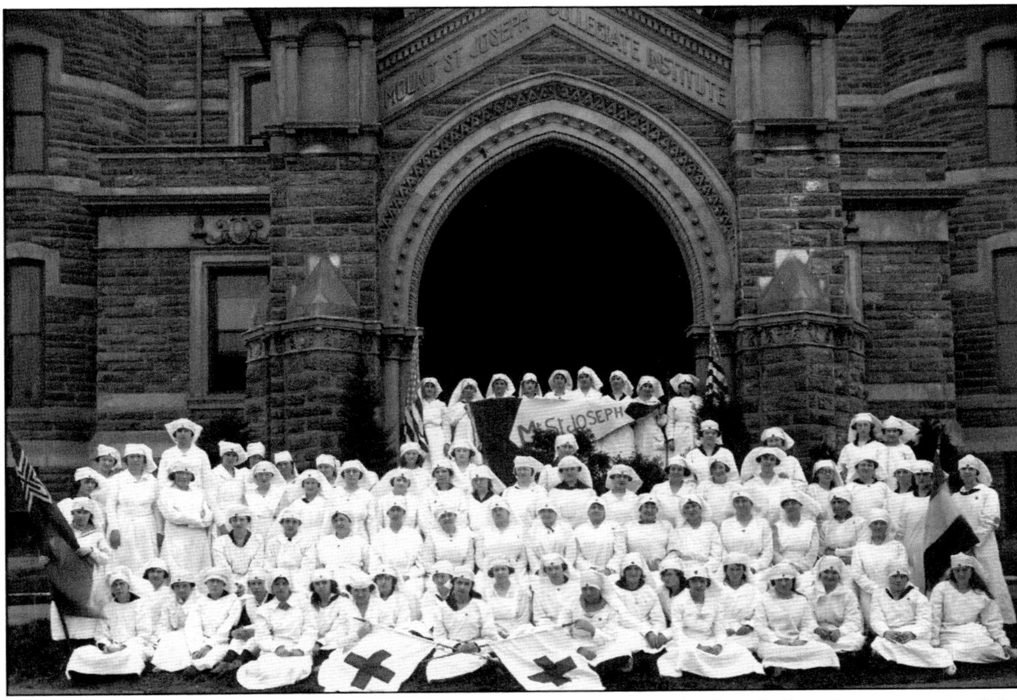

In spring 1917, "white-capped and white-aproned" students worked with the alumnae unit of the Red Cross, Auxiliary No. 138, to make about 9,000 comfort kits for American soldiers in France. Plays were performed, the proceeds of which were given to the Knights of Columbus for a war relief fund. Letters of appreciation poured in from James Flatery, supreme knight of the Knights of Columbus, and from Father Brady of the American Marines Club at the front in France.

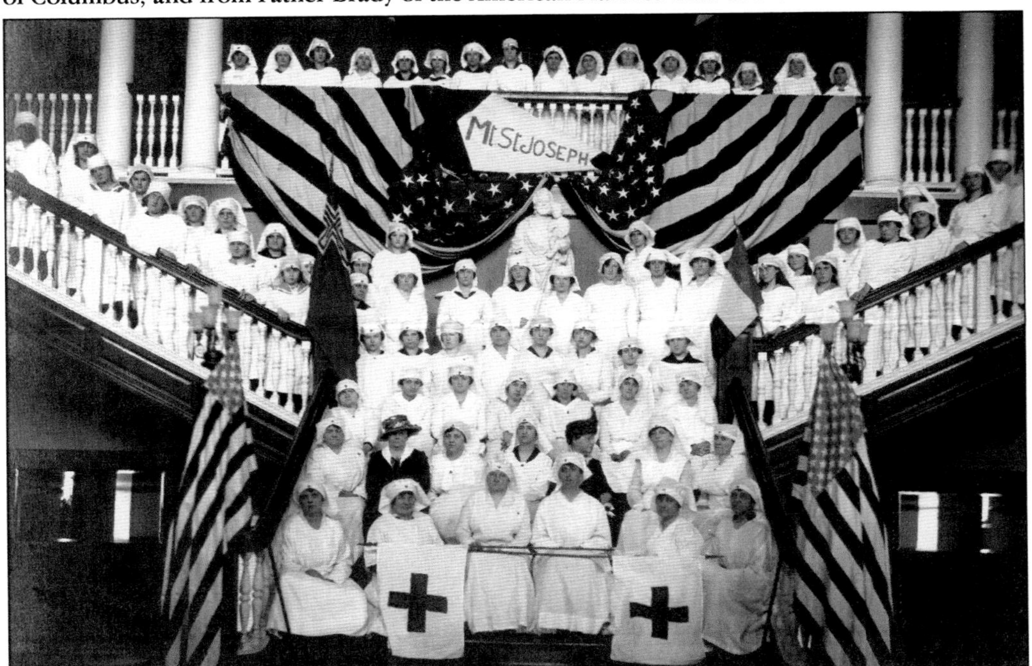

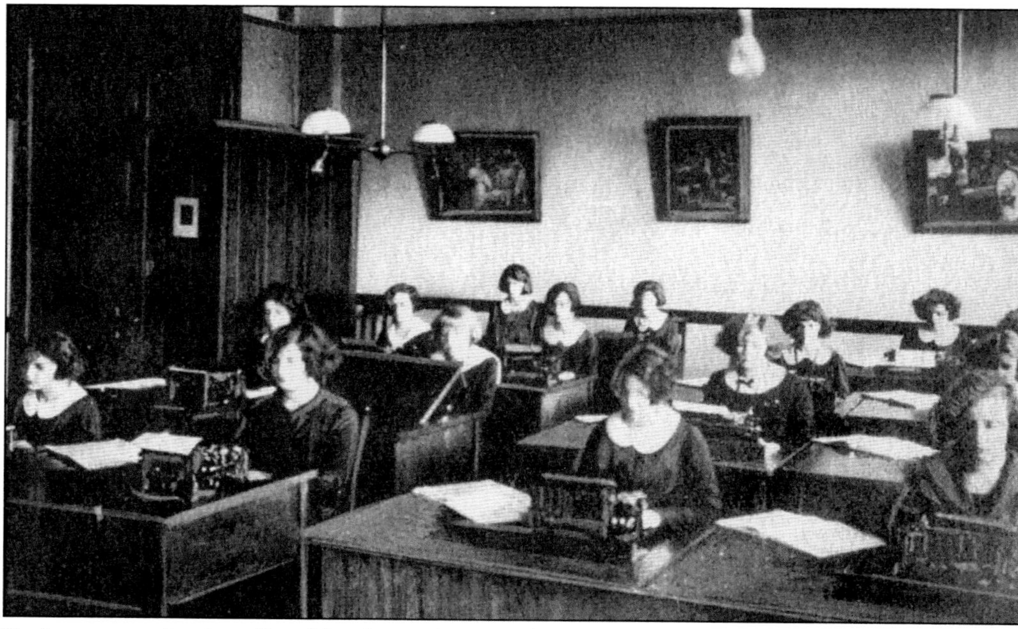

Typing was an elective offered for the students, with classes held in the typing room on the second floor of the academy. In 1901, a cooking school was established, with a small gas burner and shelf of cooking utensils for each student. The class shared a stove and sink. A three-year domestic science course was offered, consisting of practical cookery, food values, table setting, sewing, and dressmaking. In summer 1918, Sr. Marie de Sales, in preparation for a formalized home economics course, traveled to Boston to Miss Farmer's School of Cookery for a course in food study.

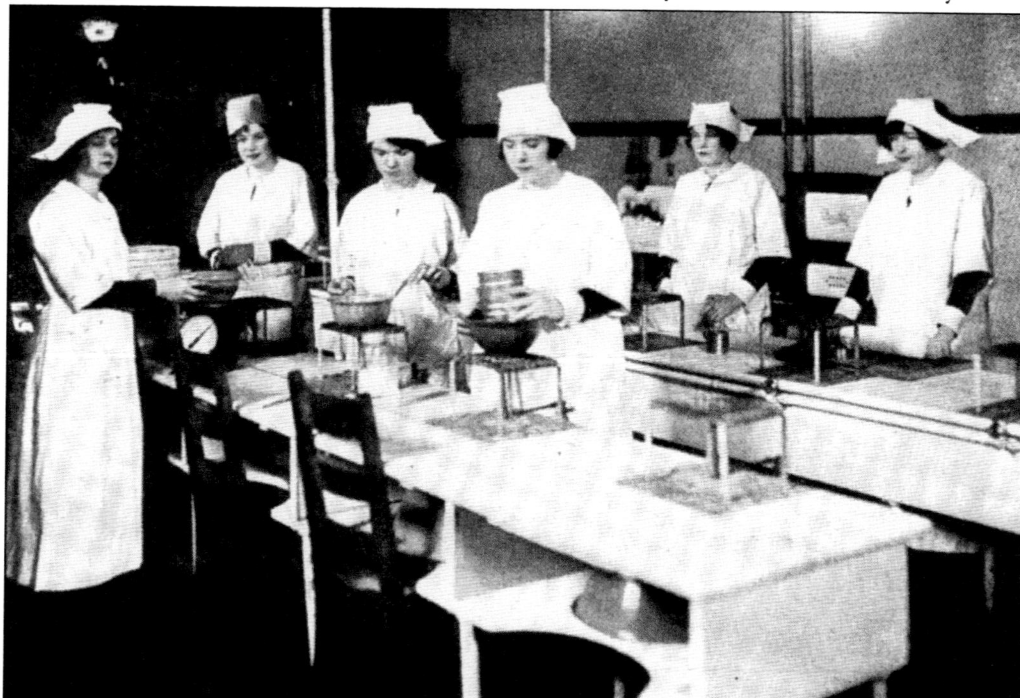

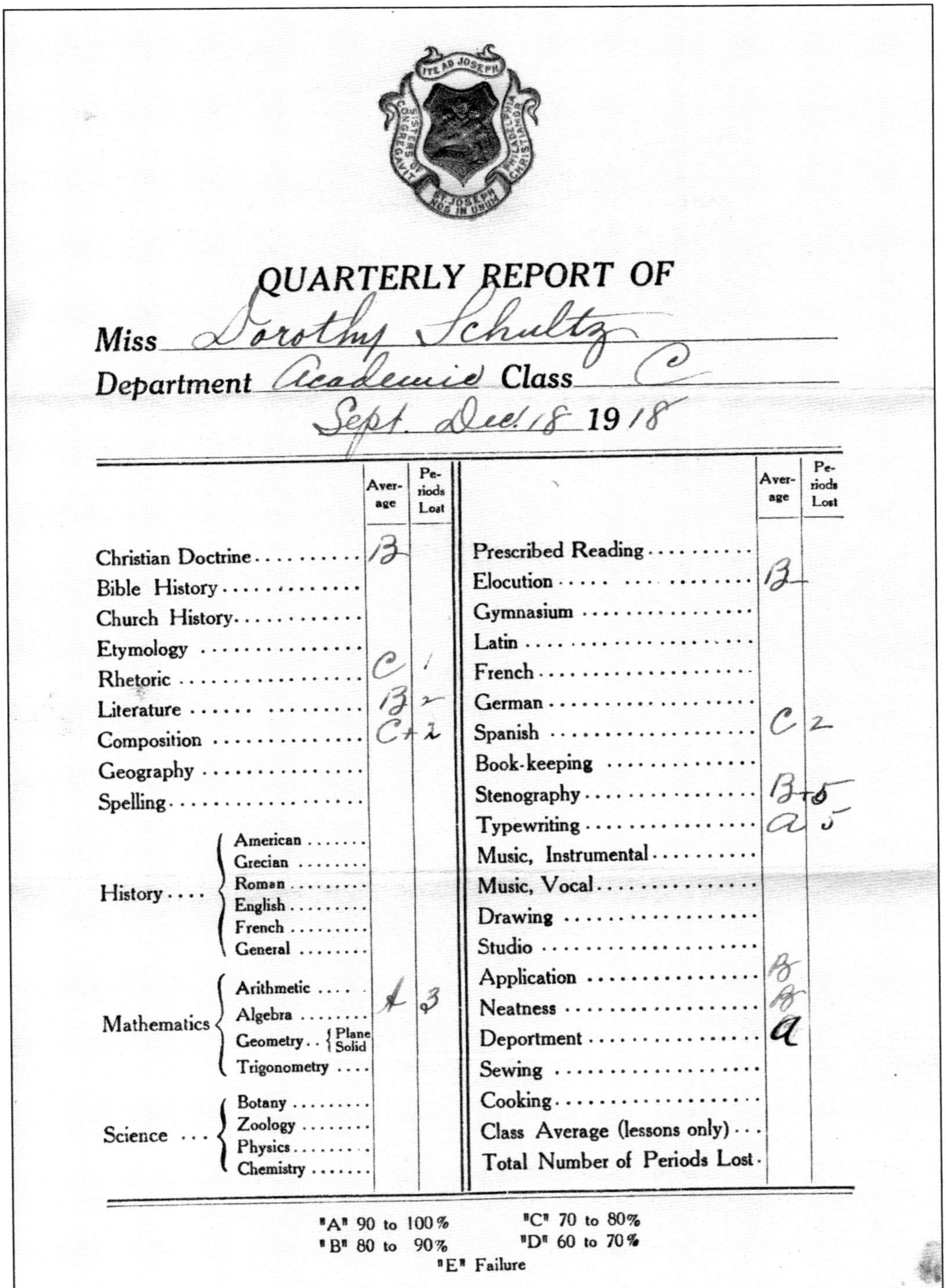

QUARTERLY REPORT OF

Miss Dorothy Schultz

Department Academic Class C

Sept. Dec. 18 1918

	Average	Periods Lost
Christian Doctrine	B	
Bible History		
Church History		
Etymology		
Rhetoric	C	1
Literature	B	2
Composition	C+	2
Geography		
Spelling		
History — American		
History — Grecian		
History — Roman		
History — English		
History — French		
History — General		
Mathematics — Arithmetic		
Mathematics — Algebra	A	3
Mathematics — Geometry (Plane / Solid)		
Mathematics — Trigonometry		
Science — Botany		
Science — Zoology		
Science — Physics		
Science — Chemistry		

	Average	Periods Lost
Prescribed Reading		
Elocution	B	
Gymnasium		
Latin		
French		
German		
Spanish	C	2
Book-keeping		
Stenography	B+	5
Typewriting	A	5
Music, Instrumental		
Music, Vocal		
Drawing		
Studio		
Application	B	
Neatness	B	
Deportment	A	
Sewing		
Cooking		
Class Average (lessons only)		
Total Number of Periods Lost		

"A" 90 to 100% "C" 70 to 80%
"B" 80 to 90% "D" 60 to 70%
"E" Failure

Report cards were issued to the families of students on a quarterly basis. The August report cards were considered an invitation to return for the next semester, as well as a gentle reminder to the parents to pay tuition.

CATALOGUE

OF

Mt. St. Joseph-on-the-Wissahickon

CHESTNUT HILL

PHILADELPHIA, PENNSYLVANIA

Spes Messis in Semine

PHILADELPHIA:
E. A. WRIGHT, ENGRAVER AND PRINTER
1108 Chestnut Street

In an early catalog, the title "Mt. St. Joseph-on-the-Wissahickon" was used to describe the school without mentioning its educational status as a college or academy. With the establishment of Chestnut Hill College in 1924, the school was no longer referred to as the Collegiate Institute but returned to the use of the title Mount Saint Joseph Academy. The period of 1908–1930 was momentous for the Mount, marking the transformation of the traditional convent school with its informal method of instruction and emphasis on the classics into a standardized and accredited modern secondary school. In 1928, the Mount became the first Catholic school in the area to be accredited by the Middle States Association of Colleges and Secondary Schools.

ACADEMIC DEPARTMENT

Motto: "Acquire not only learning, but the habit of learning."

Section D.

CHRISTIAN DOCTRINE: (De Harbe, No. 1, Part II)—Commandments of God and the Church.—Sin in General.—Virtue and Christian Perfection.—Sacrament of Penance.

BIBLE HISTORY: (Sadlier's)—History of the New Testament.—Birth and Infancy of Jesus.—His Miracles.—Jesus Sends His Seventy-two Disciples.—Jesus the Good Shepherd.—The Parable of Jesus.—The Lord's Prayer.

DICTATION:—One period daily.

UNITED STATES HISTORY: (Lawler's Essentials)—The Great Navigators.—Great Explorers.—The Early Missionaries.—The Indians.—Colonial Settlements.—French and English Wars.—The Colonies in 1763.

GEOGRAPHY: (Appleton's, No. 1)—Mathematical, Physical and Political. Geography. Hemispheres. North America. United States generally.

GRAMMAR: (Hart's Revised Grammar)—Orthography; Letters generally, Words and Syllables; Rules for Spelling.

ETYMOLOGY:—Classification of Words.—Attributes of Nouns.—Adjectives.—Character.—Pronouns.—Classification.

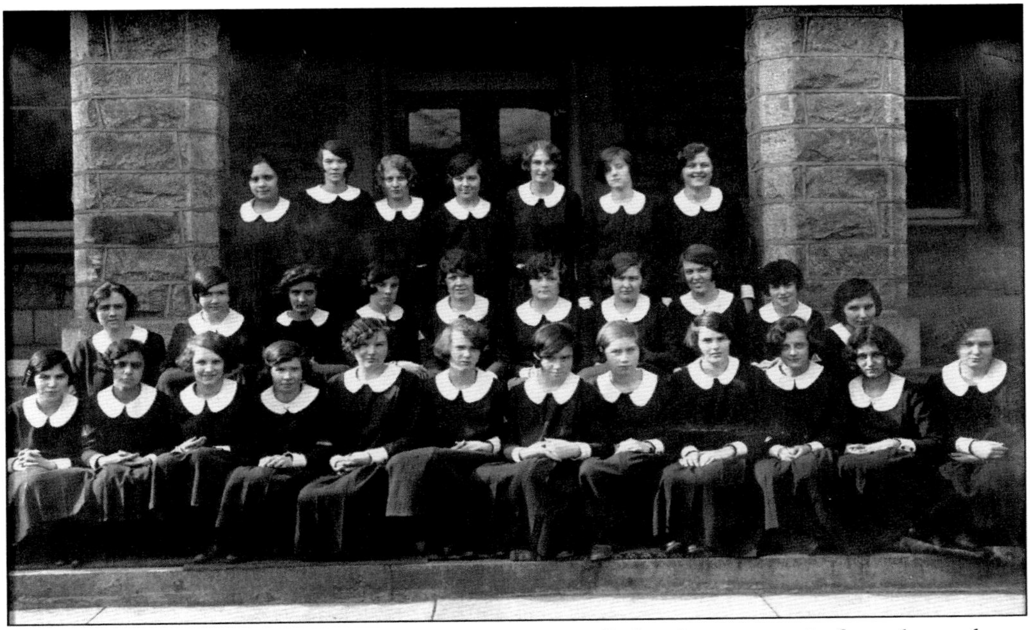

From the beginning, many Sisters of Saint Joseph were called to the community from the academy. In every decade for the first half-century, two or more girls entered the novitiate at Mount Saint Joseph and eventually came back to the school to teach. Pictured here in front of the motherhouse novitiate is the class of 1929.

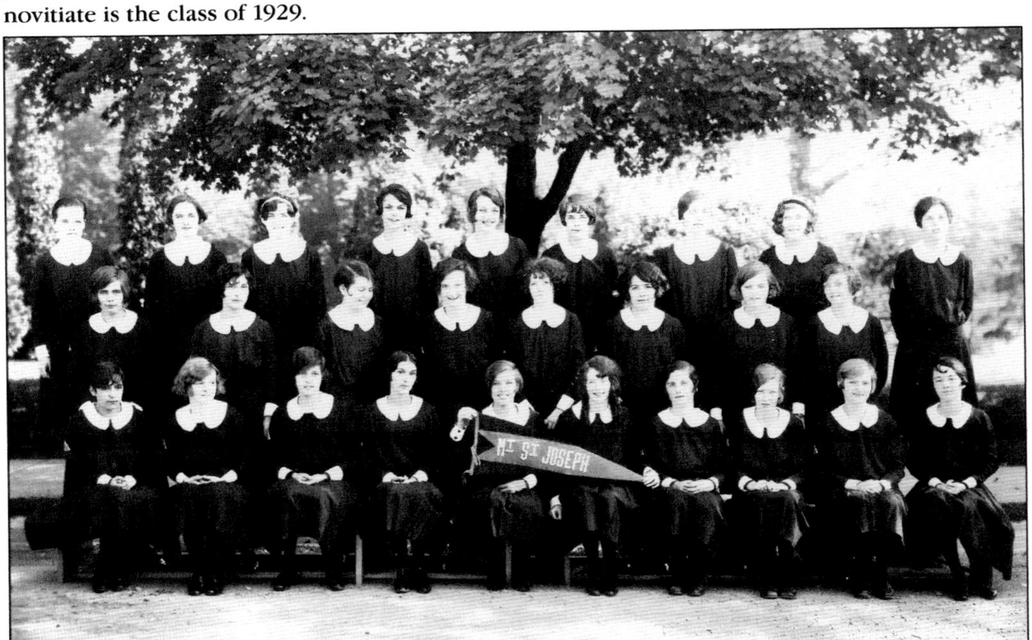

The 1920s to 1930s brought many social changes on campus. Of keen interest to the student body during this era was the debate on the pros and cons of suffrage before and after the adoption of the 19th Amendment in 1919. In the 1920s, two sororities were formed, Sigma Sigma and Sigma Tau. Although the directress of the academy approved the formation, over time, the sororities disbanded.

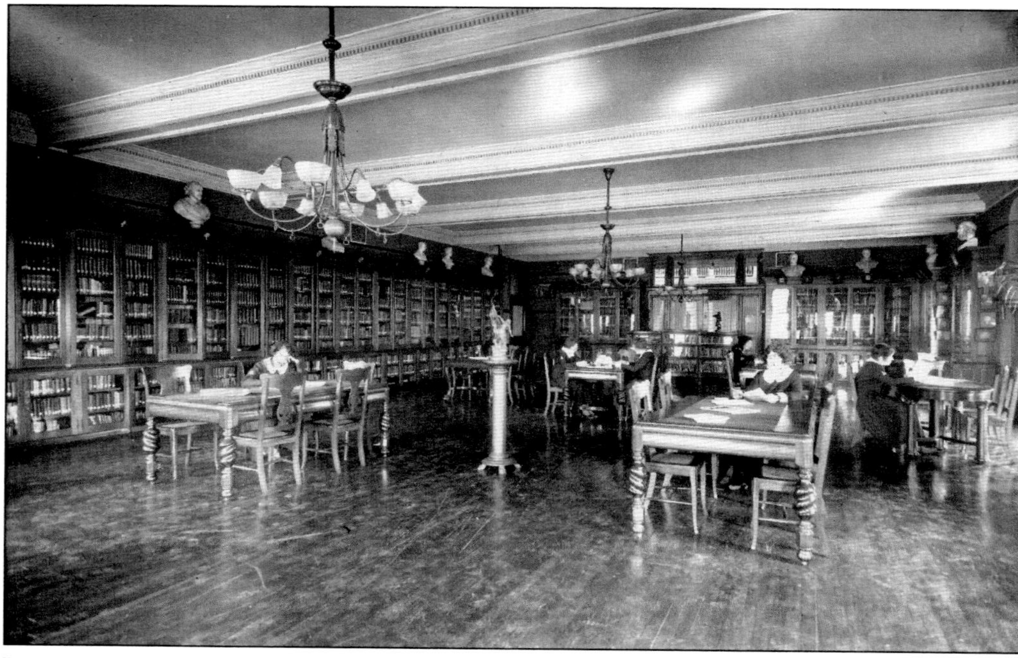

In summer 1930, the development of the library necessitated the removal of study hall from the east wing to the ground floor. The library was comprised of a reading room on the east and a stack room on the west. Two adjoining classrooms were used as a book-repair department. The section of the library above was known as the "Poet's Corner."

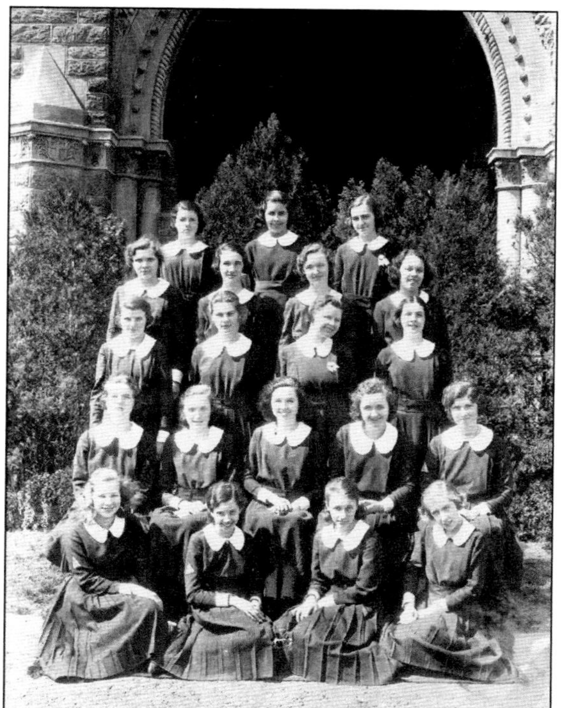

Girls during the 1930s through 1950s wore year-round heavy navy blue wool serge uniforms with knife pleats and heavily starched, buttoned white hemstitched collars and cuffs.

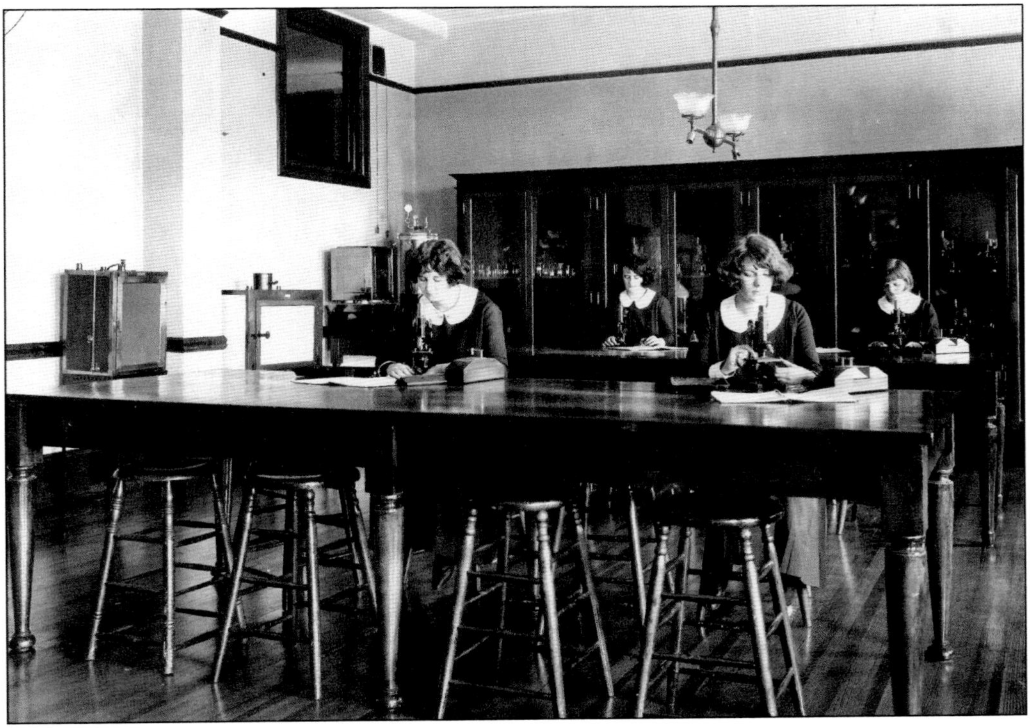

Biology classes during the 1940s consisted of frog dissection and taxidermy.

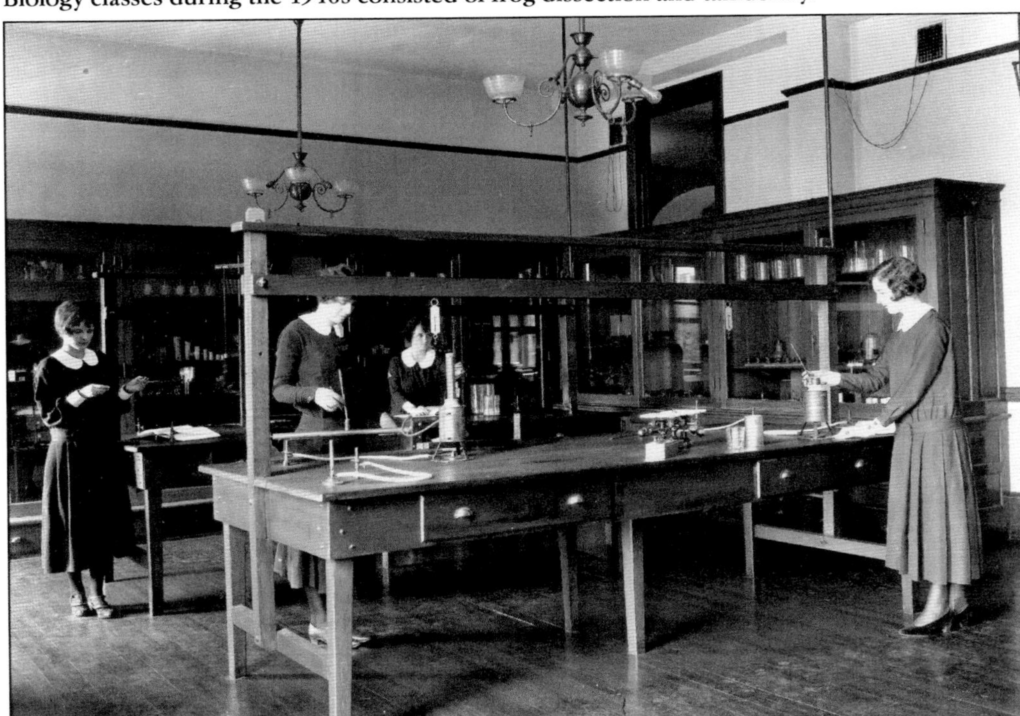

A laboratory course in chemistry was introduced in 1903 at the new building.

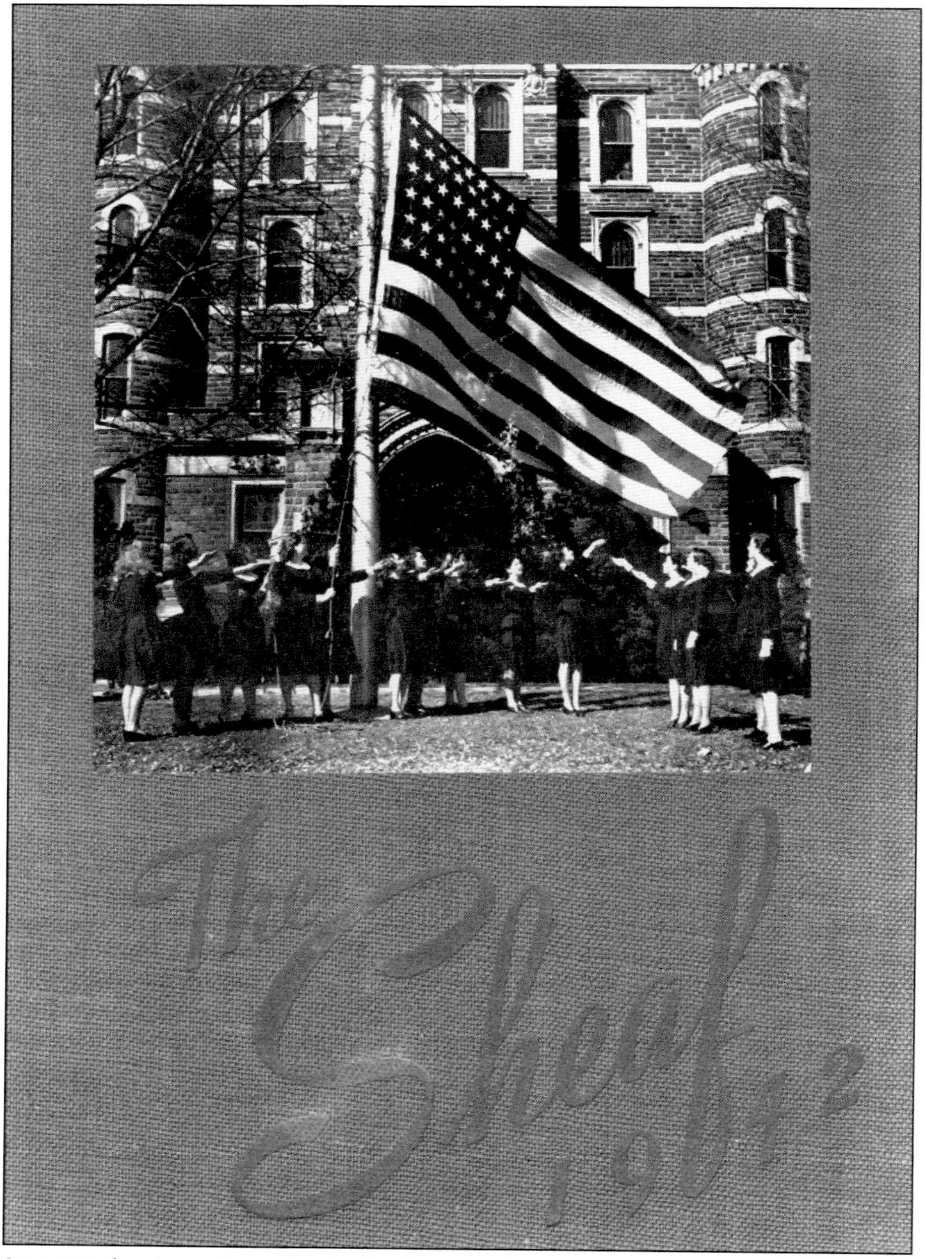

The Mount yearbook was first published in 1918, marking a long-standing tradition for the Mount. Under the direction of Sr. Maria Kostka and with the blessing of Cardinal Dennis Dougherty, the seniors published their school record called the *Sheaf*, a tribute to the motto of the school, Spes messis in semine. In a demonstration of its patriotism, the 1942 *Sheaf* (above) depicts the flag raising in support of the World War II American troops. The flag staff was the gift of Mrs. Clark Thompson of Santa Barbara, California, whose sister and daughter were members of the student body. Maj. R. W. King of the Schuylkill Arsenal and father of another student donated the flag during World War I, which was blessed by the Rev. Dr. John E. Flood, superintendent of Catholic schools in Philadelphia.

At the start of World War II, the students plunged wholeheartedly into the war effort. The school conducted three bond drives in 1943–1944 and raised nearly $3,000 for the Government Relief Fund. Among the acknowledgments by the federal government for the students' support was a decalcomania dedicatory panel in the training planes purchased by the students (right). At the end of the war, Mount Saint Joseph received a citation from the U.S. Treasury Department, commending the school for its service to the War Savings Program through a "Schools at War" campaign that raised $122,648.10 for the purchase of nine jeeps and three parachutes (below).

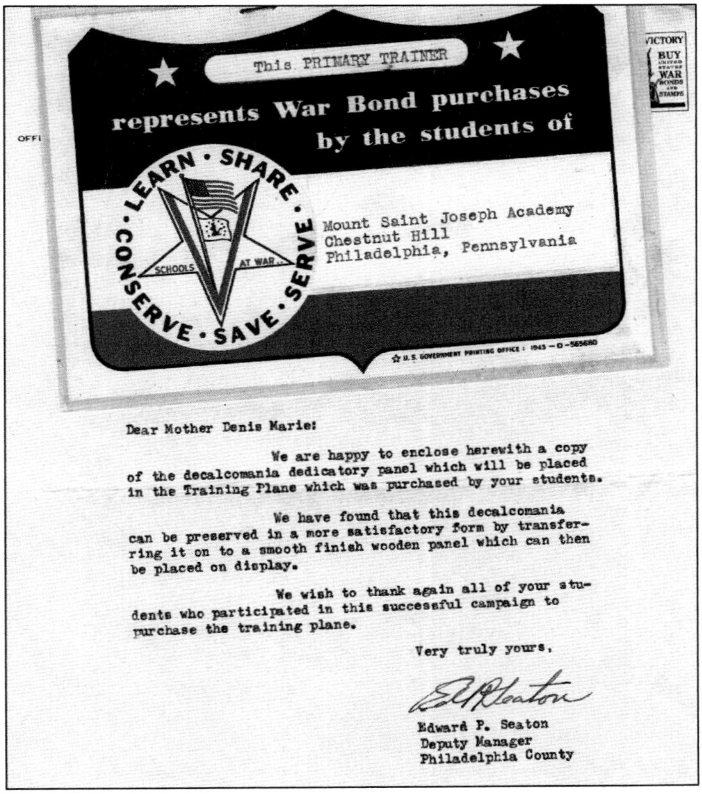

This PRIMARY TRAINER

represents War Bond purchases by the students of

LEARN · SHARE · SERVE · SAVE · CONSERVE · SCHOOLS AT WAR...

Mount Saint Joseph Academy
Chestnut Hill
Philadelphia, Pennsylvania

U.S. GOVERNMENT PRINTING OFFICE : 1943—O—565680

Dear Mother Denis Marie:

We are happy to enclose herewith a copy of the decalcomania dedicatory panel which will be placed in the Training Plane which was purchased by your students.

We have found that this decalcomania can be preserved in a more satisfactory form by transferring it on to a smooth finish wooden panel which can then be placed on display.

We wish to thank again all of your students who participated in this successful campaign to purchase the training plane.

Very truly yours,

Edward P. Seaton
Deputy Manager
Philadelphia County

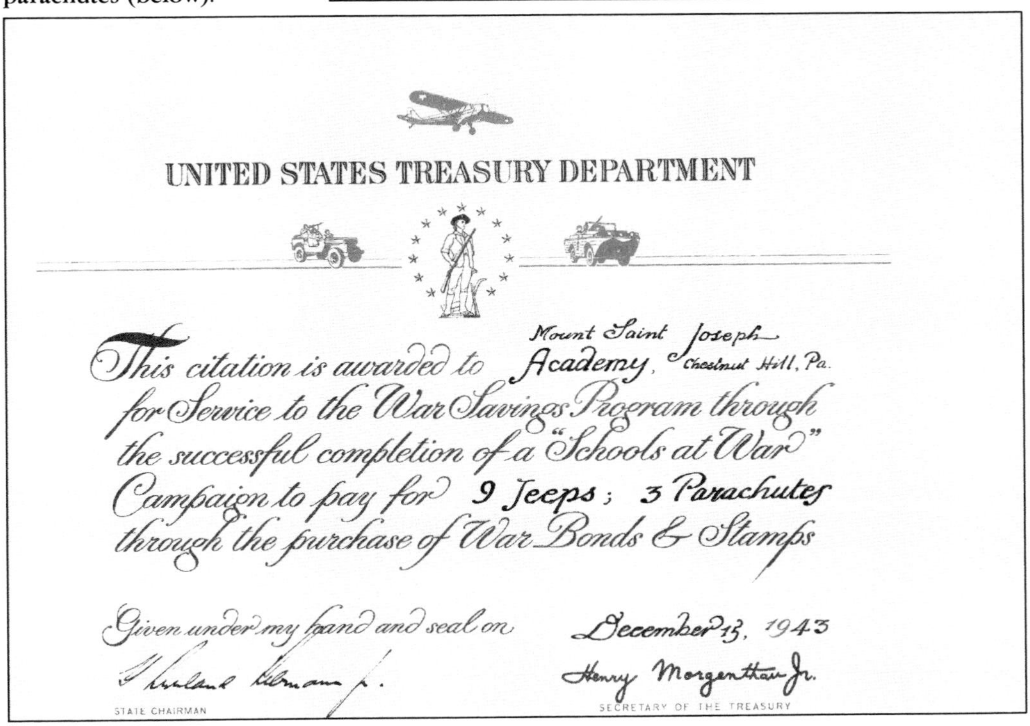

UNITED STATES TREASURY DEPARTMENT

This citation is awarded to Mount Saint Joseph Academy, Chestnut Hill, Pa. for Service to the War Savings Program through the successful completion of a "Schools at War" Campaign to pay for 9 Jeeps; 3 Parachutes through the purchase of War Bonds & Stamps

Given under my hand and seal on December 15, 1943

STATE CHAIRMAN

Henry Morgenthau Jr.
SECRETARY OF THE TREASURY

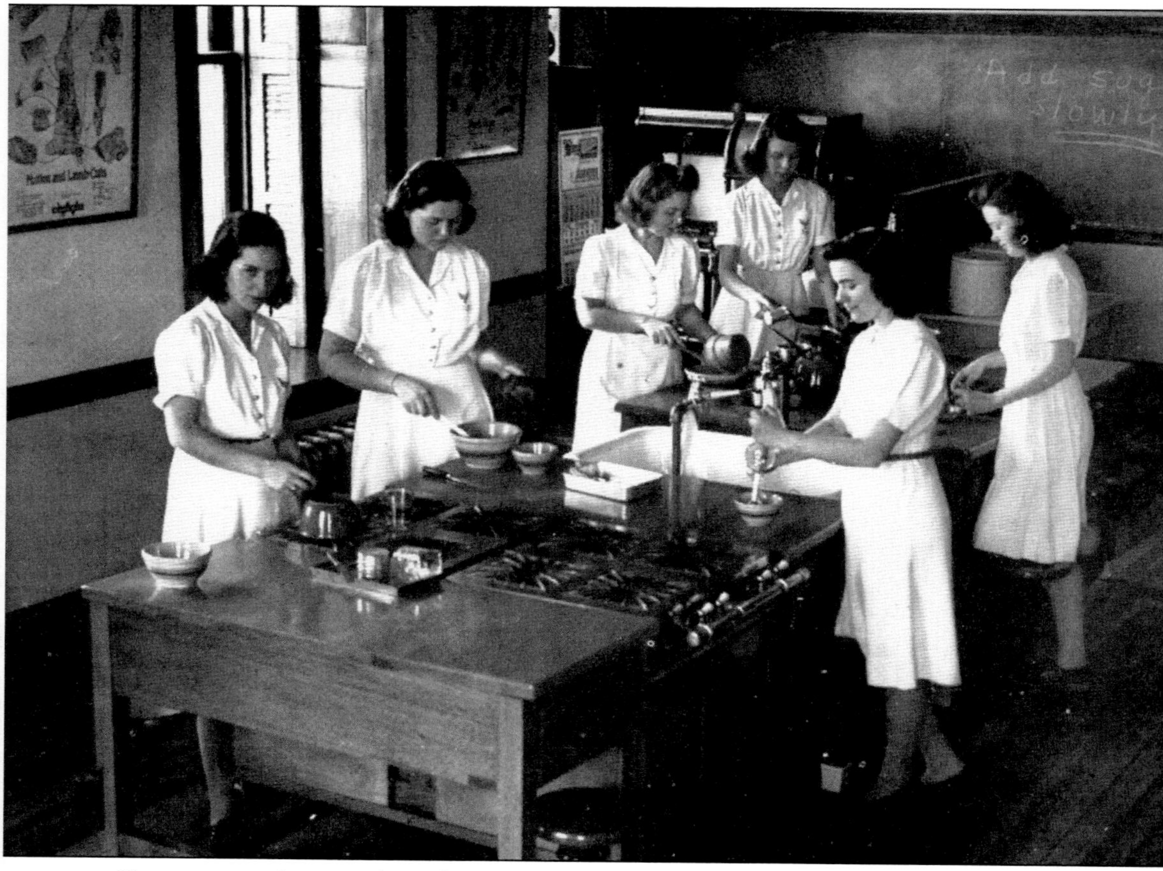

Home economics experienced a renaissance in the 1950s, with the school taking part in the 1954 Betty Crocker Test, a search for the future homemaker of America, an educational program sponsored by General Mills Inc. A "foods teacher" joined the academy faculty in 1955–1956.

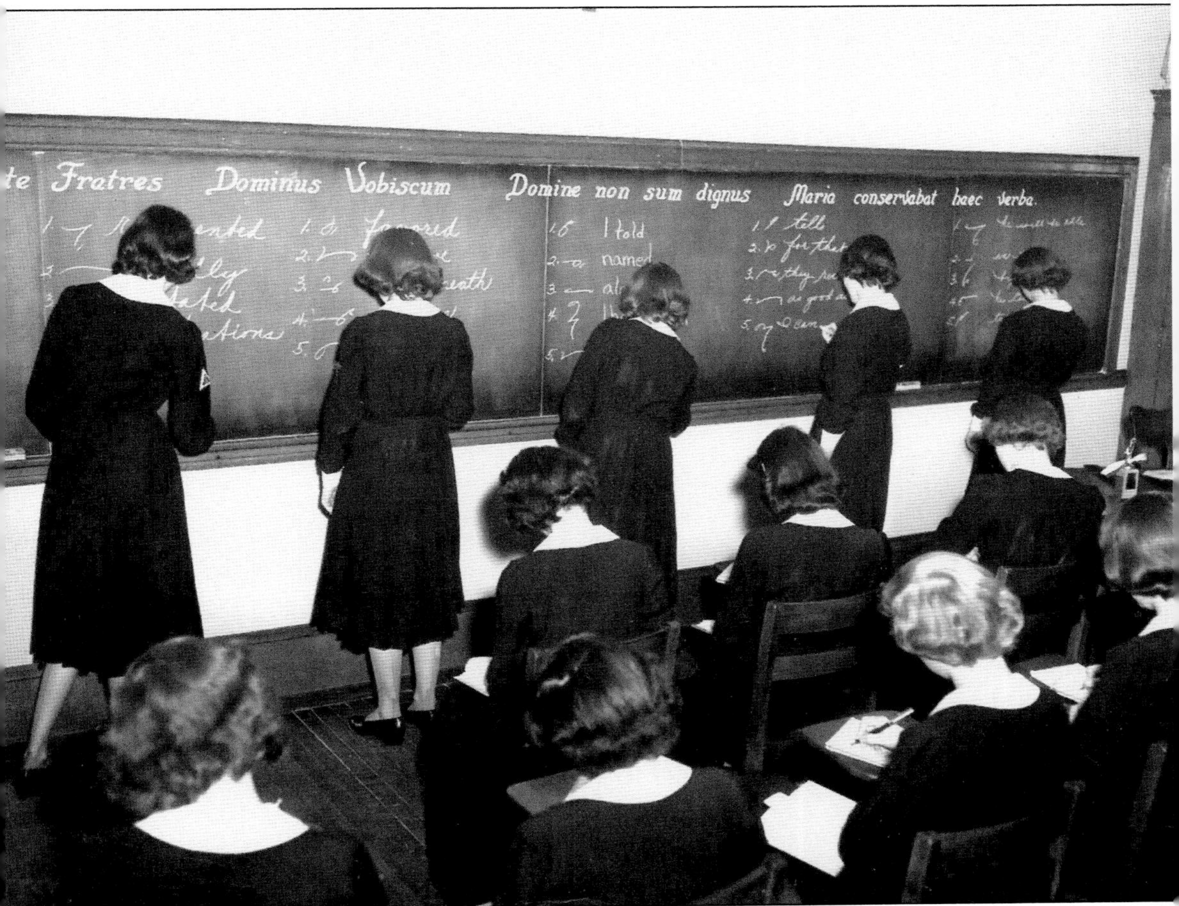

During the 1950s, the Mount offered general or college-preparatory courses, both of which led to graduation and a diploma. All students studied the same subjects in the first two years, with an elective for modern language. At the close of the second year, each student elected for the next two years either the general or the college-preparatory course. The former allowed greater freedom of choice in electives; the latter better prepared the student for entrance into college. In the college-preparatory course, the student chose either a classical program placing emphasis on the study of Latin and modern languages or a program stressing the study of science and mathematics. Classes in stenography (above), typewriting, and home economics were offered. Tuition during this time was $300—about $2,300 in today's dollars.

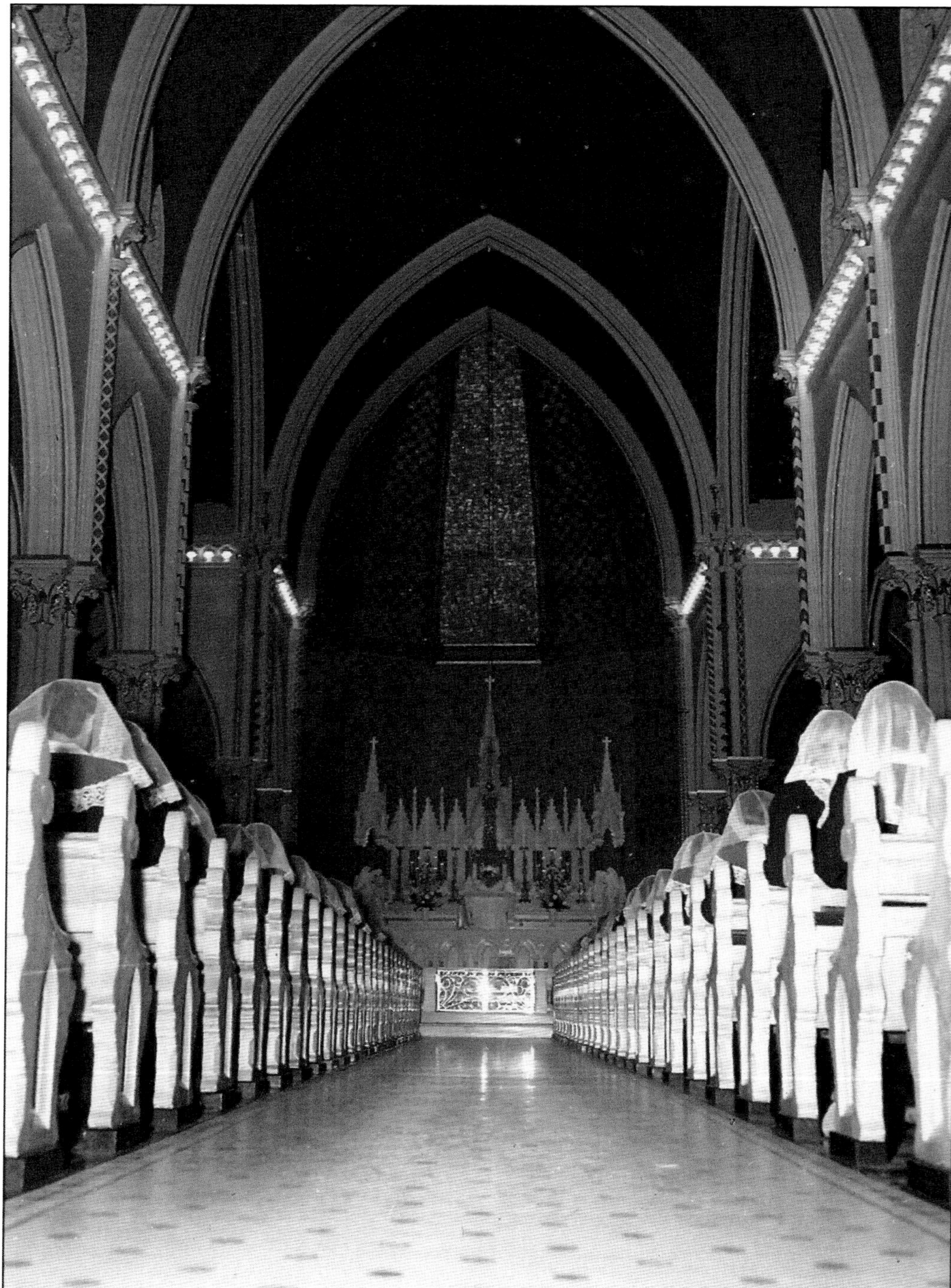

The Motherhouse Convent Chapel was the center of religious activities for the students for more than 58 years. Wearing white veils and Child of Mary medals, students attended weekly sodality prayer services.

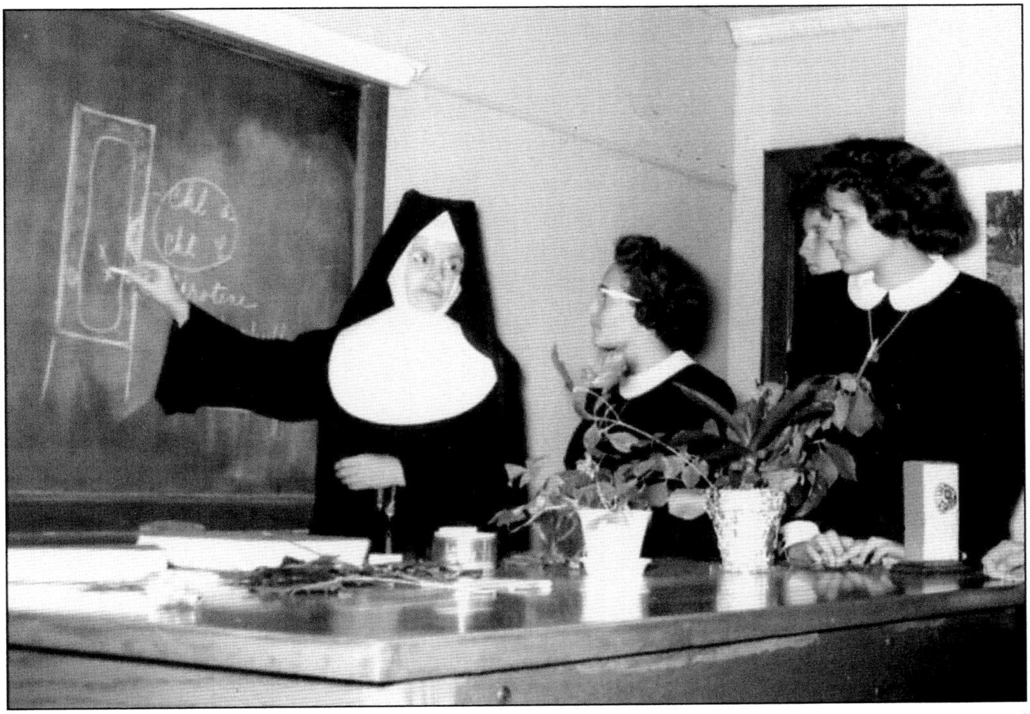

Botany classes were taught at the school as early as 1904. In this photograph, Sr. Paul Daniel instructs students during the 1950s.

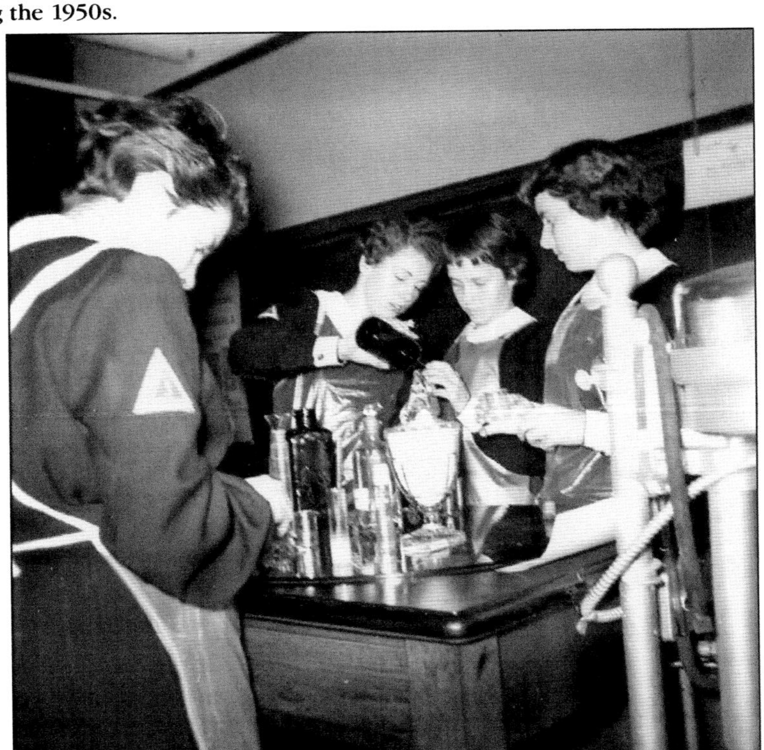

Courses during the 1950s consisted of 45-minute periods of classes, with Sisters of Saint Joseph teaching every subject except speech and gym. Chemistry classes (right) were held in the laboratory on the ground floor.

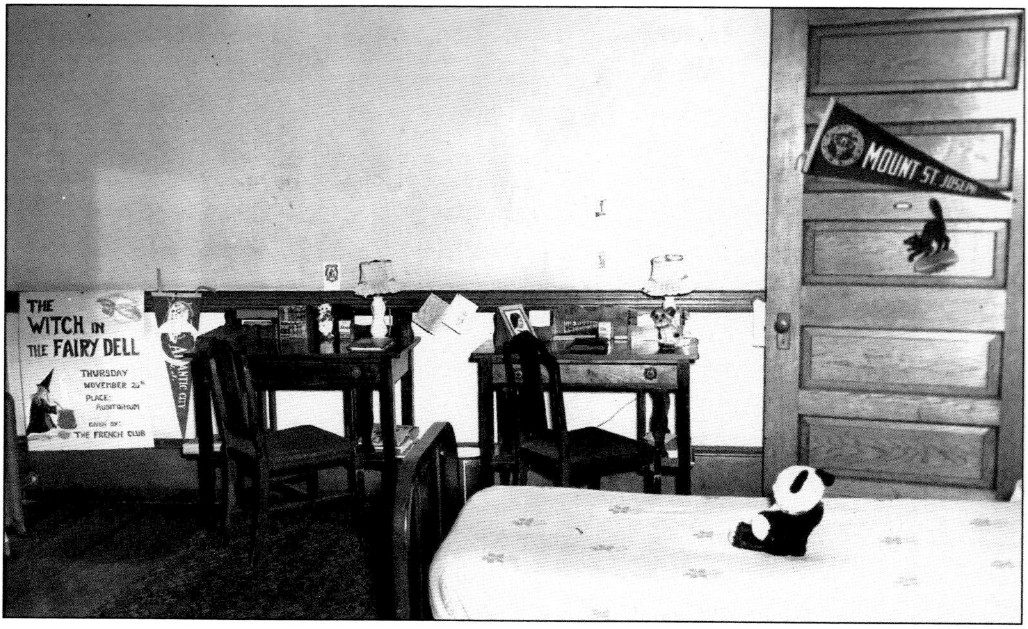

In the early days of the school, regulations regarding silence in the dormitories were as strict as those of convent dormitories. The rule of silence was lifted 50 years later. After World War II, the furnishings were not as austere, and the dormitories became more like a home bedroom. Evening time was referred to as the "sing-song," when students "sipped Cokes and munched pretzels" while singing their favorite melodies.

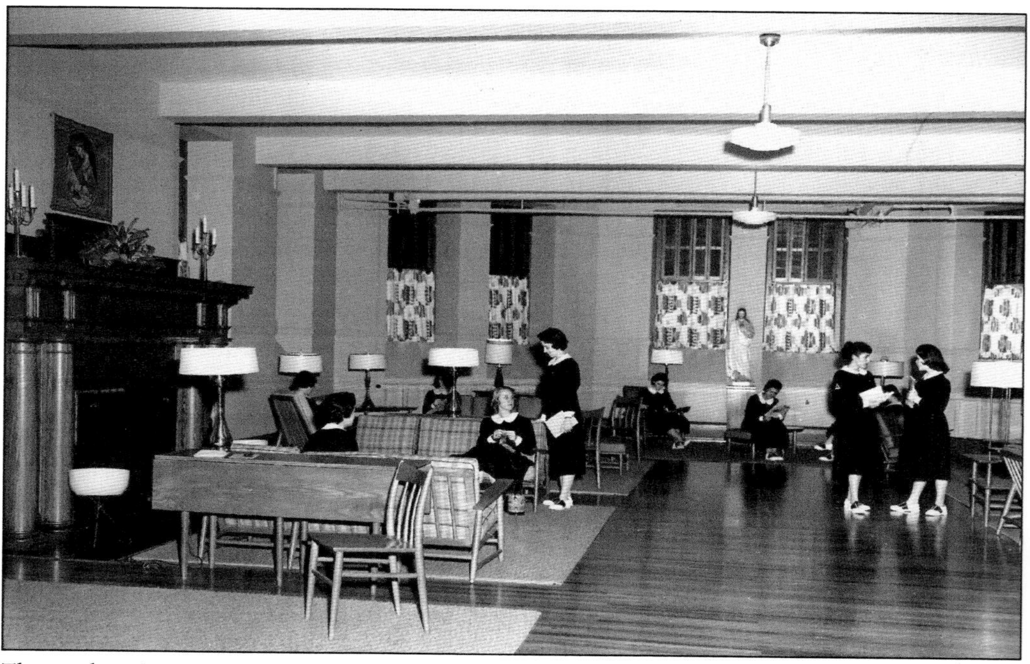

The students' recreation room and study hall, on the ground floor, was dubbed "the Old Rec." Girls assembled in the morning and processed single file, in silence, keeping to the right of the corridor to class.

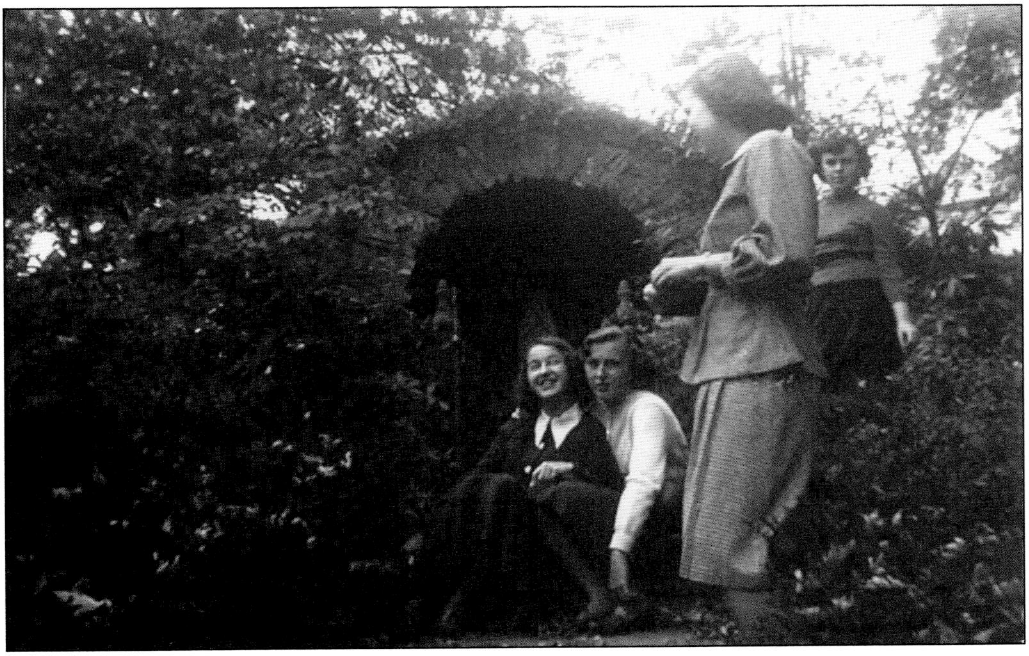

Students from the class of 1950 enjoy a carefree moment in front of the grotto. (Courtesy of Lorraine Sukalski McGlynn '52.)

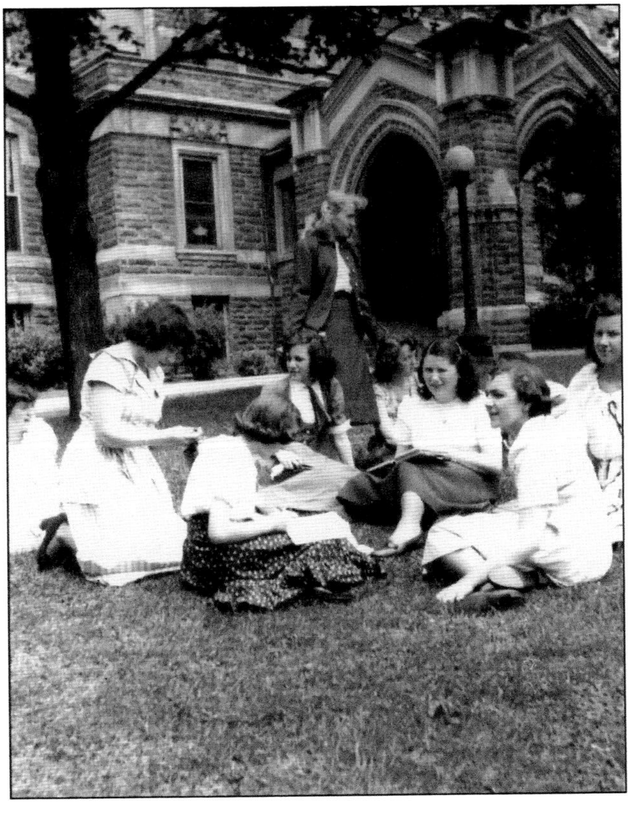

School regulations in 1956 required the girls to engage in "ladylike behavior at all times." Even outside of school hours, sweaters, loafers, jewelry, and socks were not permitted.

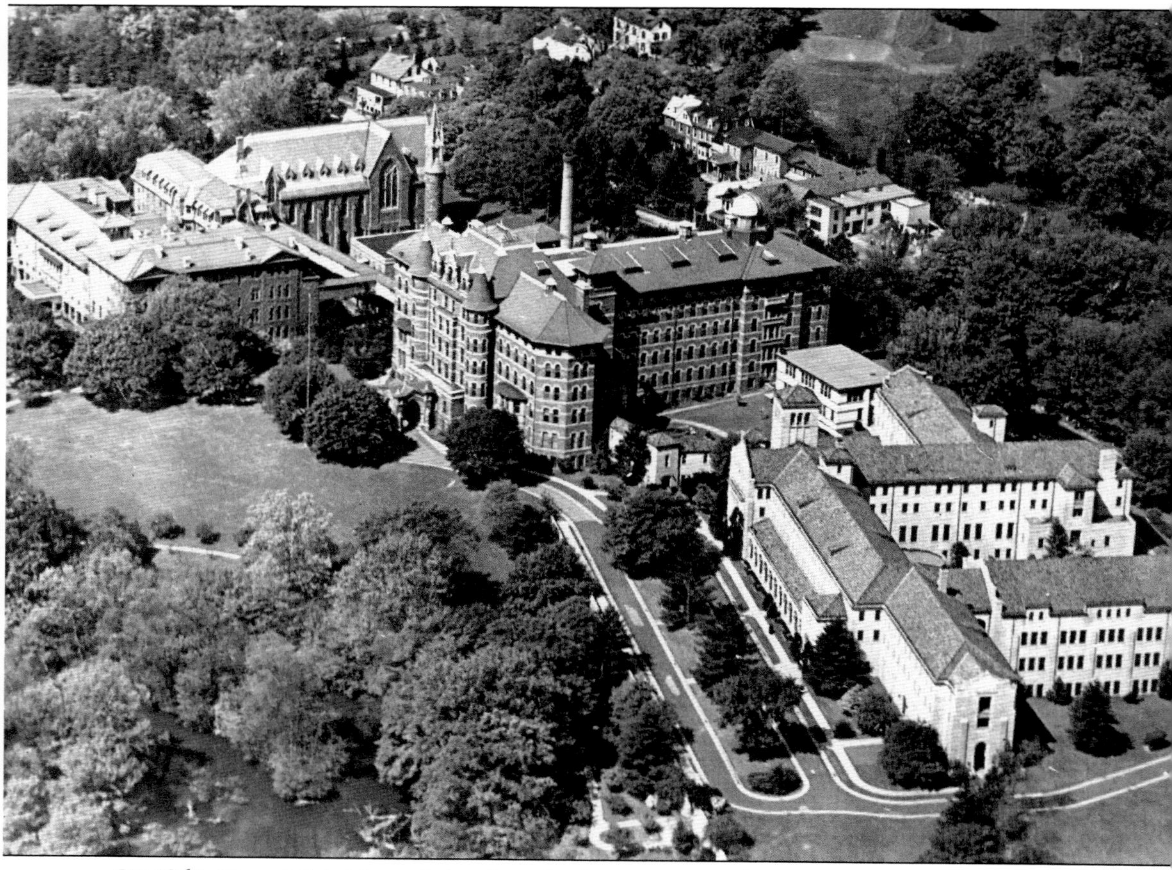

By 1960, Mount Saint Joseph Academy had outgrown its home of more than a century at the Chestnut Hill campus, which by that time housed the growing Chestnut Hill College. Many alumnae fondly remember Saint Joseph's Hall as the "Old Mount."

Three

New Roots in Flourtown

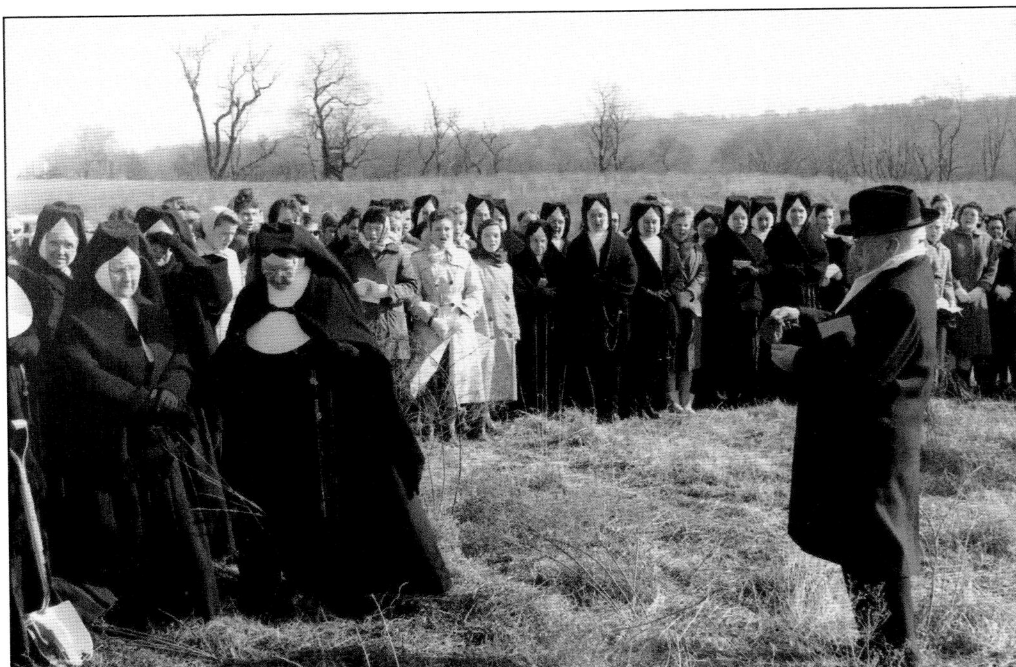

With no room available on the campus in Chestnut Hill, the Sisters of Saint Joseph looked to farmland just northeast of the campus, at the intersection of Wissahickon and Stenton Avenues in Flourtown. Ground was broken for a new school in fall 1960. On the day of the groundbreaking, the student body processed down Northwestern and Wissahickon Avenues to the new campus.

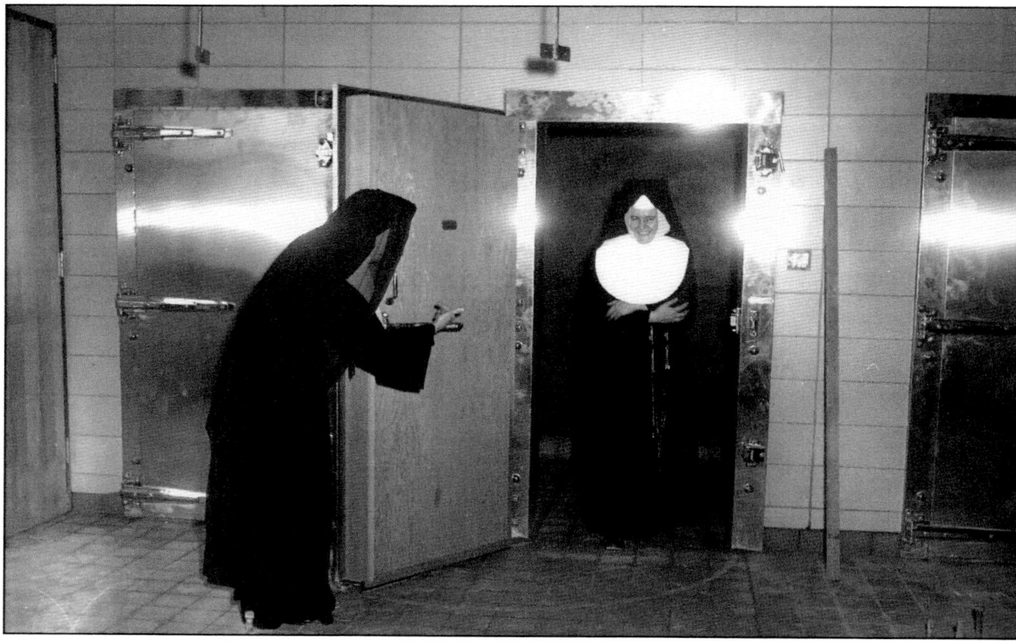

Sisters monitor construction in 1961 from the balcony of the new academy's original library and get a firsthand look at the walk-in freezer in the cafeteria. The farmland at left is today the site of two other sponsored works of the Sisters of Saint Joseph, St. Joseph's Villa, which opened in 1968, serves the sick and infirm Sisters of Saint Joseph and, when possible, laypeople and members of other congregations. Bethlehem Village, which opened in 1984, provides housing to seniors on a limited income. To the right of the sisters, across the driveway and fields, is Bethlehem Pike.

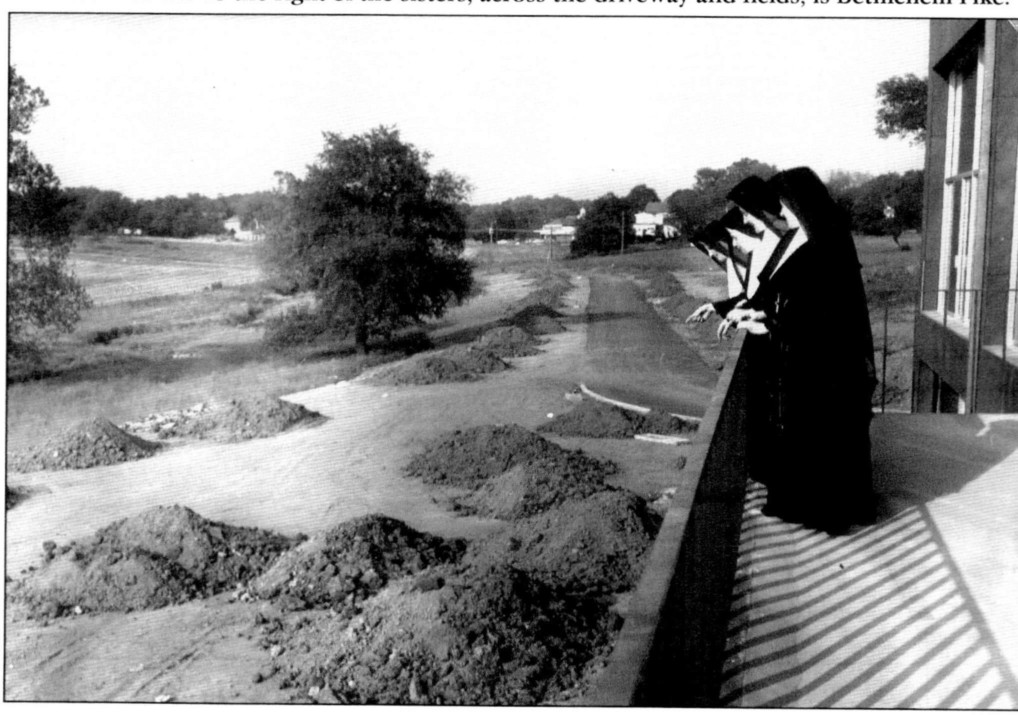

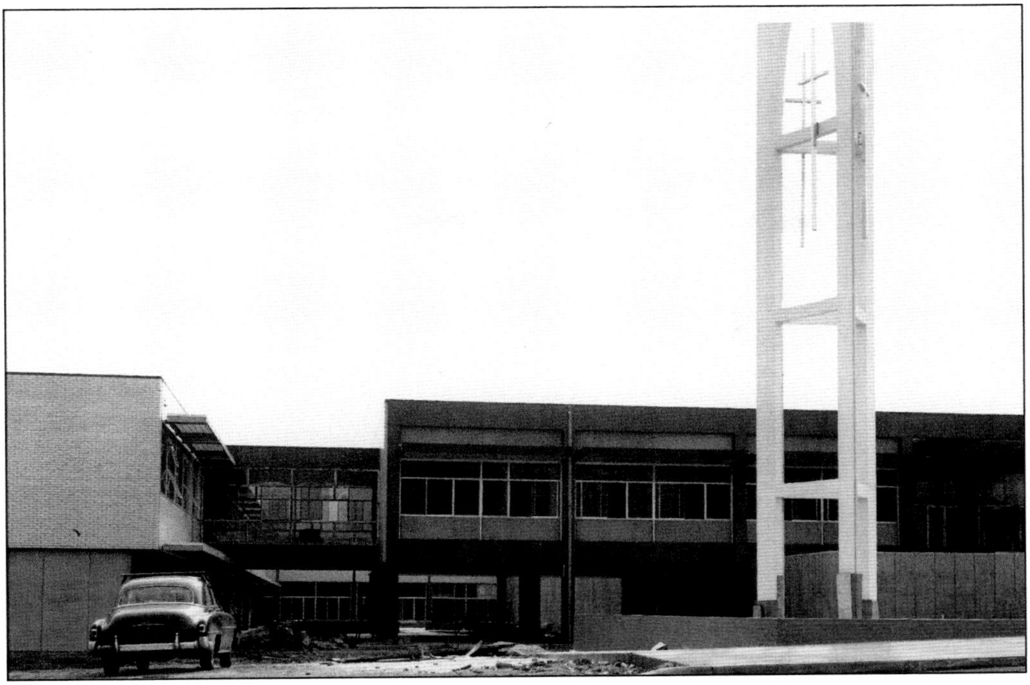

When the new academy opened in 1961, it contained 12 classrooms, 9 special rooms, an auditorium, a library, a student chapel, music rooms, an infirmary, and a cafeteria. Among the special rooms were science laboratories and a modern-language laboratory. The new Mount also included a hockey field and tennis courts. At the opening, it was possible to look from the front of the school into the interior courtyard. A 1970s classroom addition, Sylvester Center, later obscured the view.

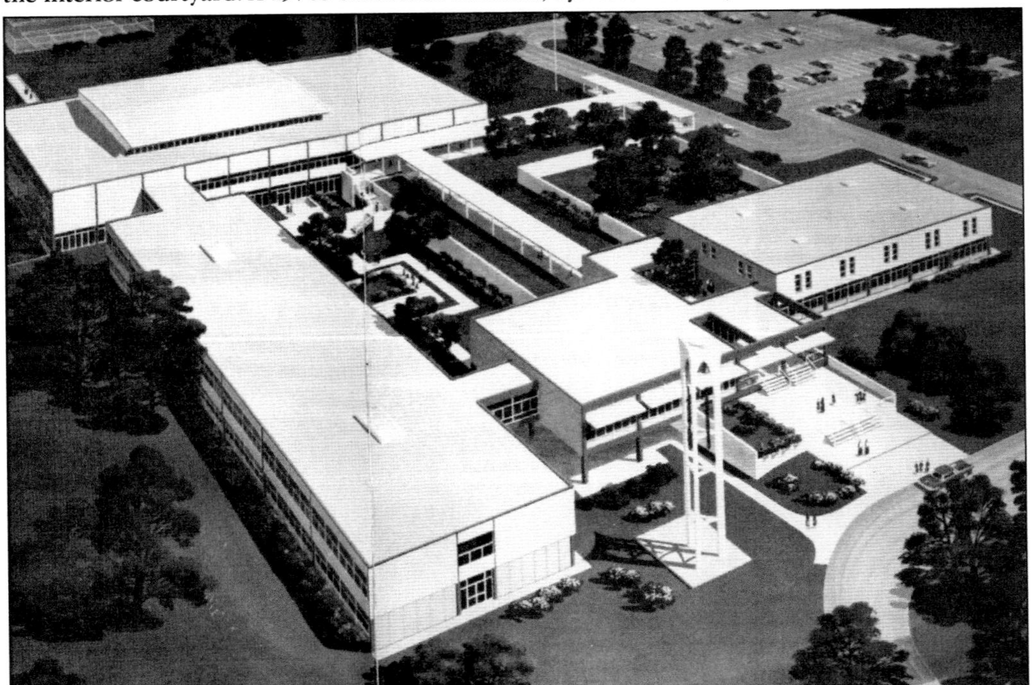

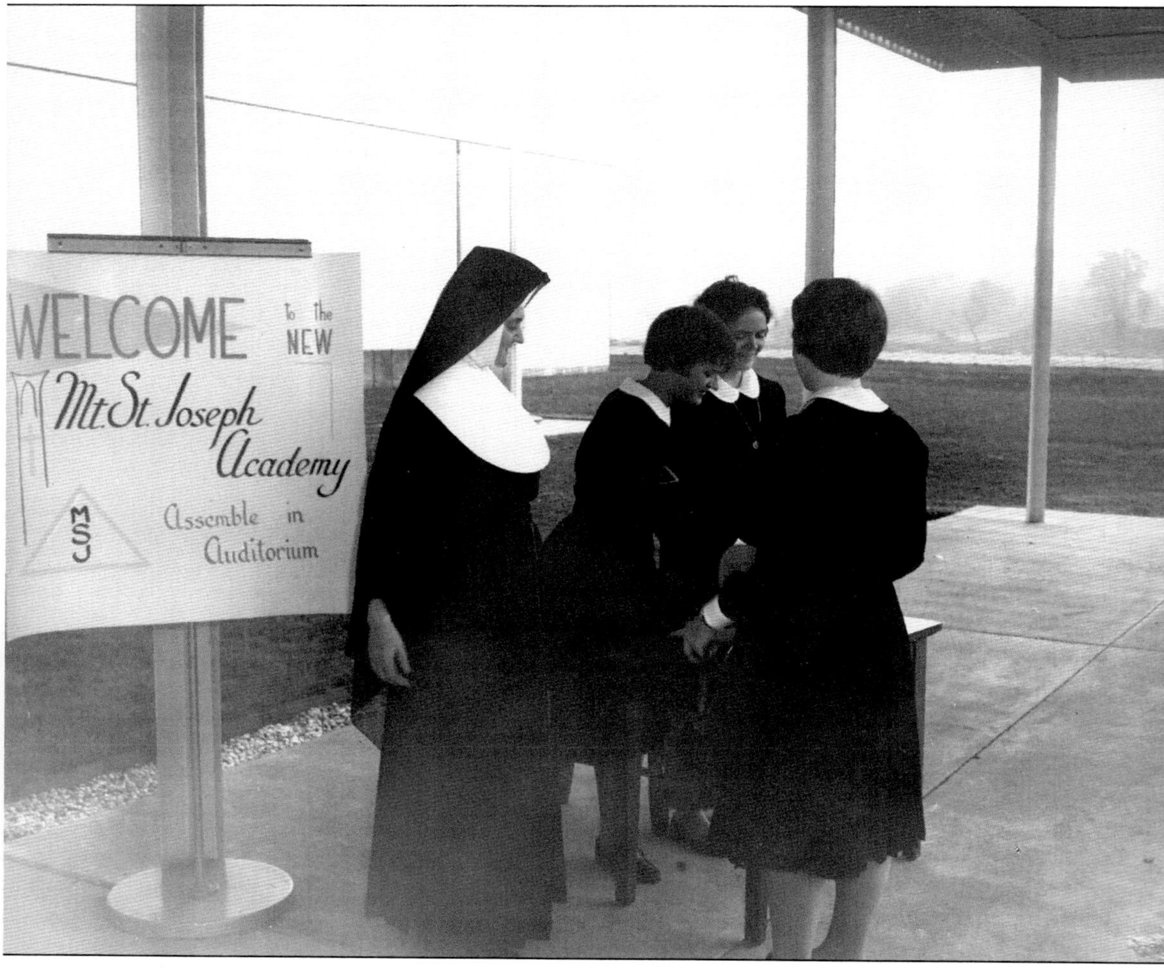

Mother M. Sylvester led the new Mount at its opening in September 1961 and remained principal until the end of the 1966–1967 school year. The student body numbered approximately 300 students from almost 60 parishes in the Philadelphia area, and the faculty included 13 Sisters of Saint Joseph and three laywomen. On the first day of classes, the president and vice president of the student council, Martina Walsh and Suzanne Foster, raised the American flag for the first time over the Mount's new campus.

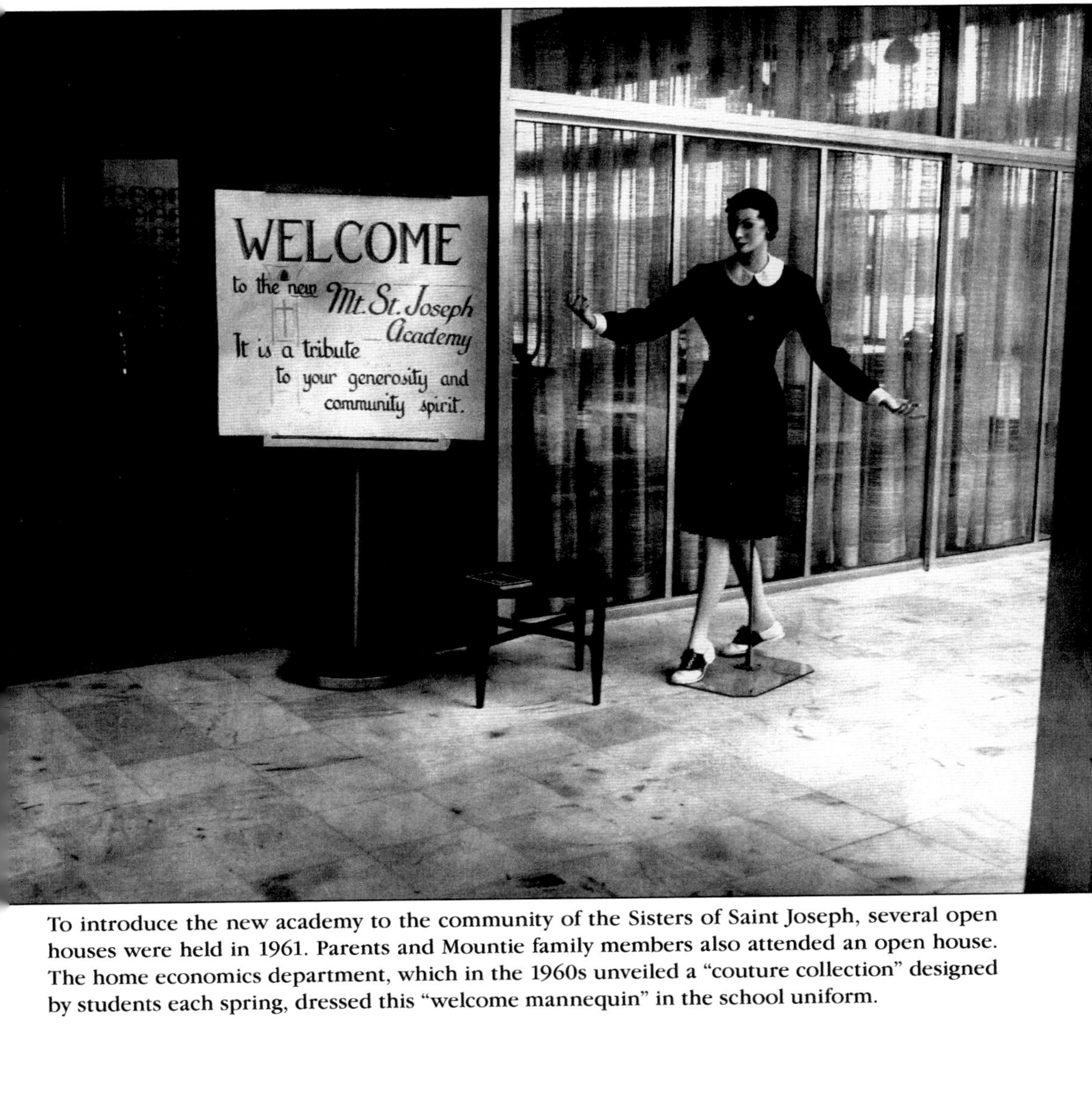

To introduce the new academy to the community of the Sisters of Saint Joseph, several open houses were held in 1961. Parents and Mountie family members also attended an open house. The home economics department, which in the 1960s unveiled a "couture collection" designed by students each spring, dressed this "welcome mannequin" in the school uniform.

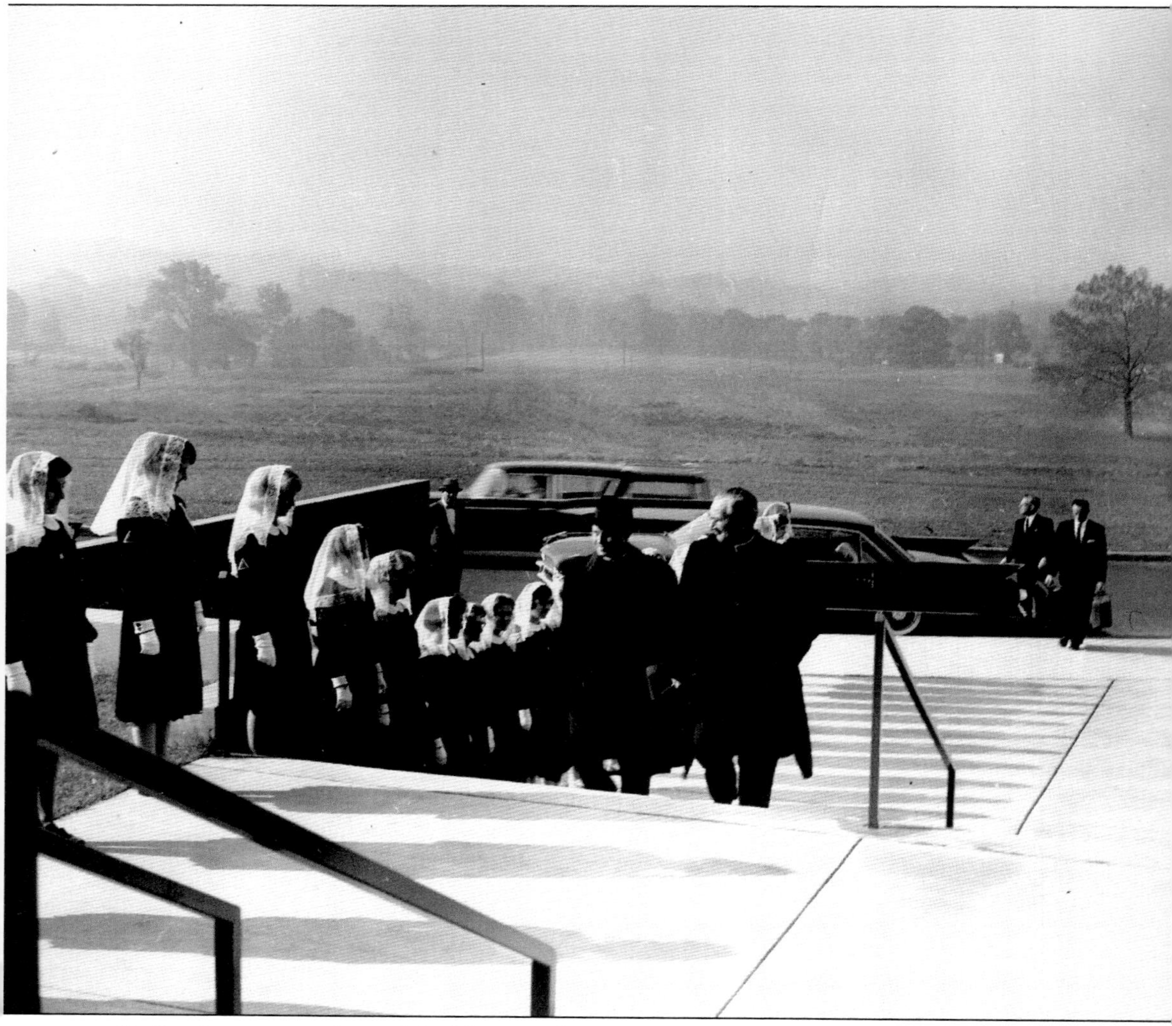

Dedication ceremonies and the blessing of the academy were held on Saturday, October 28, 1961, at 11:00 a.m. The Most Rev. John J. Krol, D.D., J.C.D., officiated, and the Right Rev. Msgr. John J. Graham, D.D., delivered the dedication address. Mount students, wearing pre–Vatican II white veils, lined the front stairway and hallways of the school in a show of welcome for Archbishop Krol and Monsignor Graham.

Nolen and Swinburne, a Philadelphia architecture firm from 1953 to 1974, designed the new academy and won an architectural award for the use of slate in the design, most visible at the front entrance of the school. The firm was well known for designing commercial buildings. Other work included the Housing and Urban Development Building in Washington, D.C., and the state office building in Philadelphia.

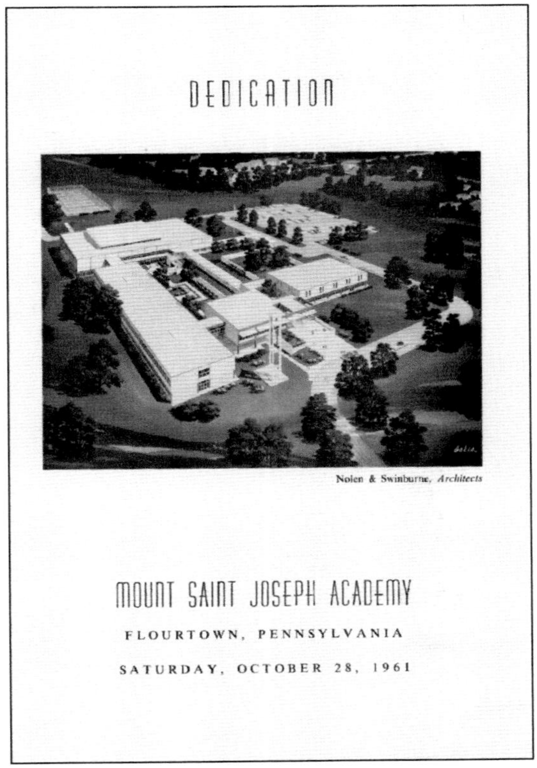

DEDICATION

Nolen & Swinburne, *Architects*

MOUNT SAINT JOSEPH ACADEMY

FLOURTOWN, PENNSYLVANIA

SATURDAY, OCTOBER 28, 1961

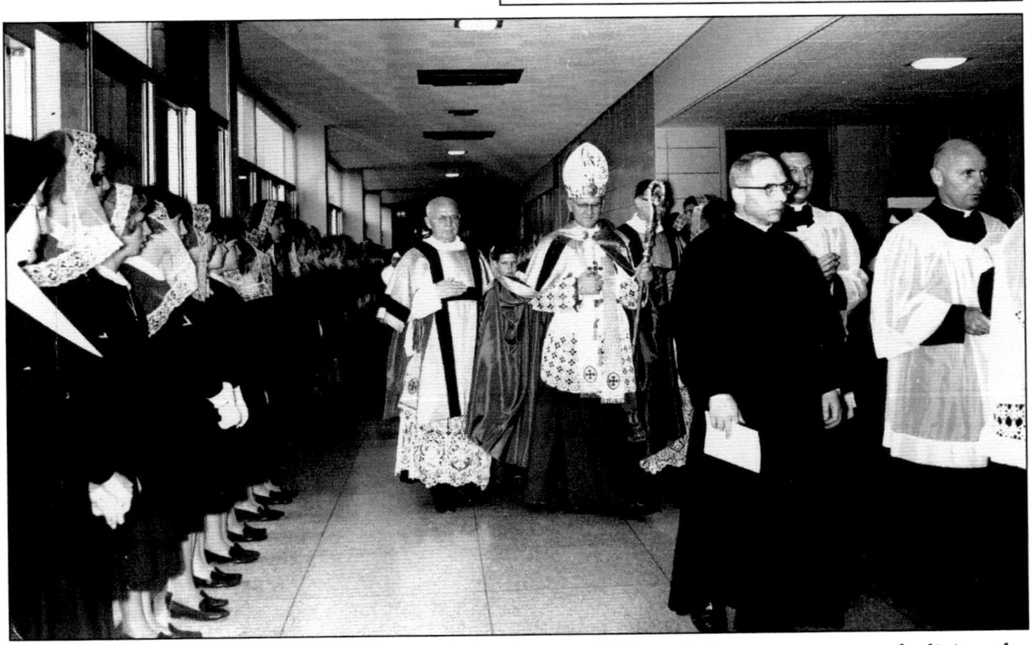

As part of the dedication ceremonies, Archbishop Krol blessed the art room, symbolizing the blessing of the entire school. At the time, the art room was in the main classroom section of the school, on the second floor. Archbishop Krol had been named to head the Archdiocese of Philadelphia earlier that year. The future cardinal also blessed the academy's cornerstone.

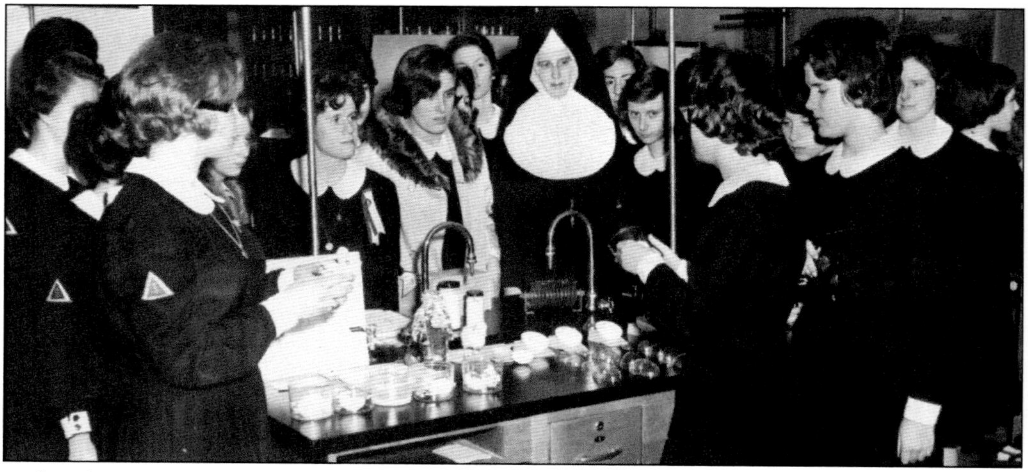

At the Chestnut Hill campus, upperclassmen gave tours of the school to freshmen at the beginning of the school year. In fall 1961, all students, organized by homeroom, were given tours of the new school on the first day of classes, with the Sisters of Saint Joseph serving as tour guides. The new school afforded new activities. The *Mount*, the school literary magazine, was first published in 1962. The *Campanile,* the school newspaper, was first published in 1963.

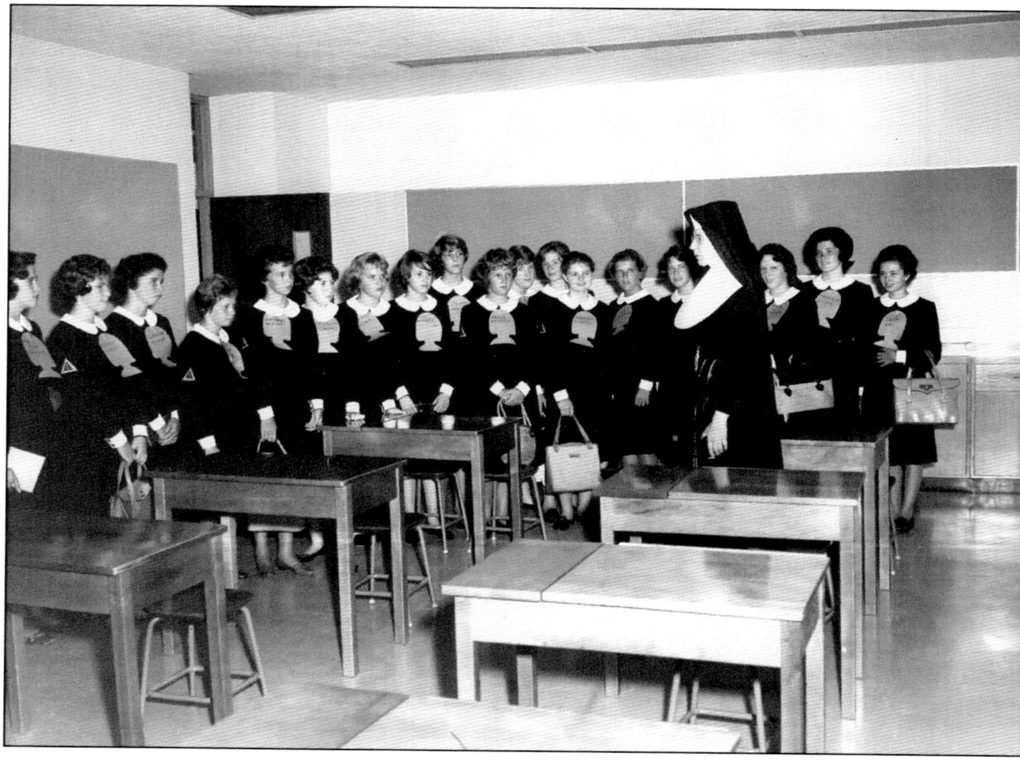

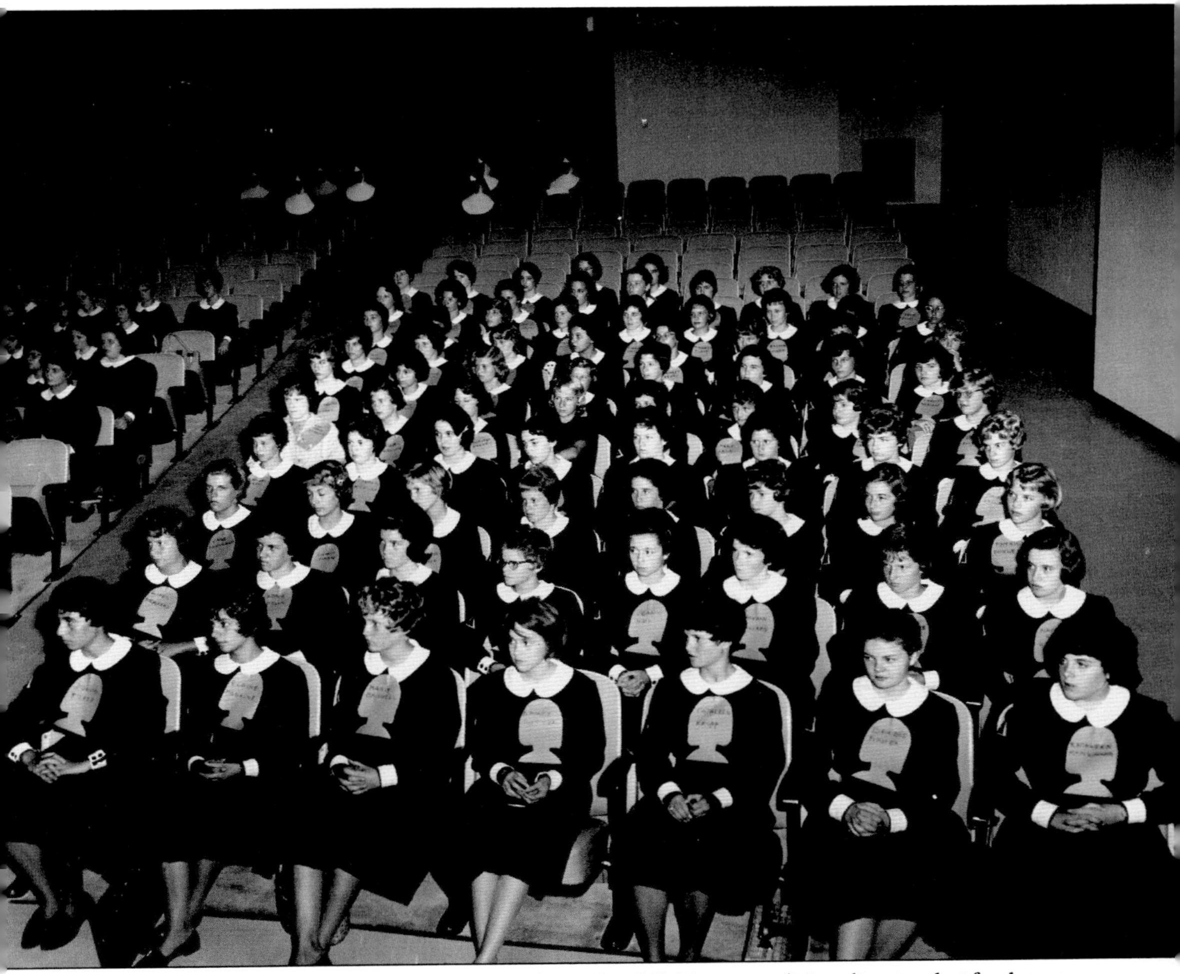

About 80 freshmen began classes at the new academy that fall. Mount tradition dictates that freshmen and sophomores sit in the side sections of Fournier Auditorium, while juniors and seniors sit in the middle, a practice that continues today. Among the first lessons were the procedures for air raid drills—signaled by five short rings of the bell. Students were to move quickly and in silence to their assigned shelter areas. They could return to class when the "all clear" was sounded.

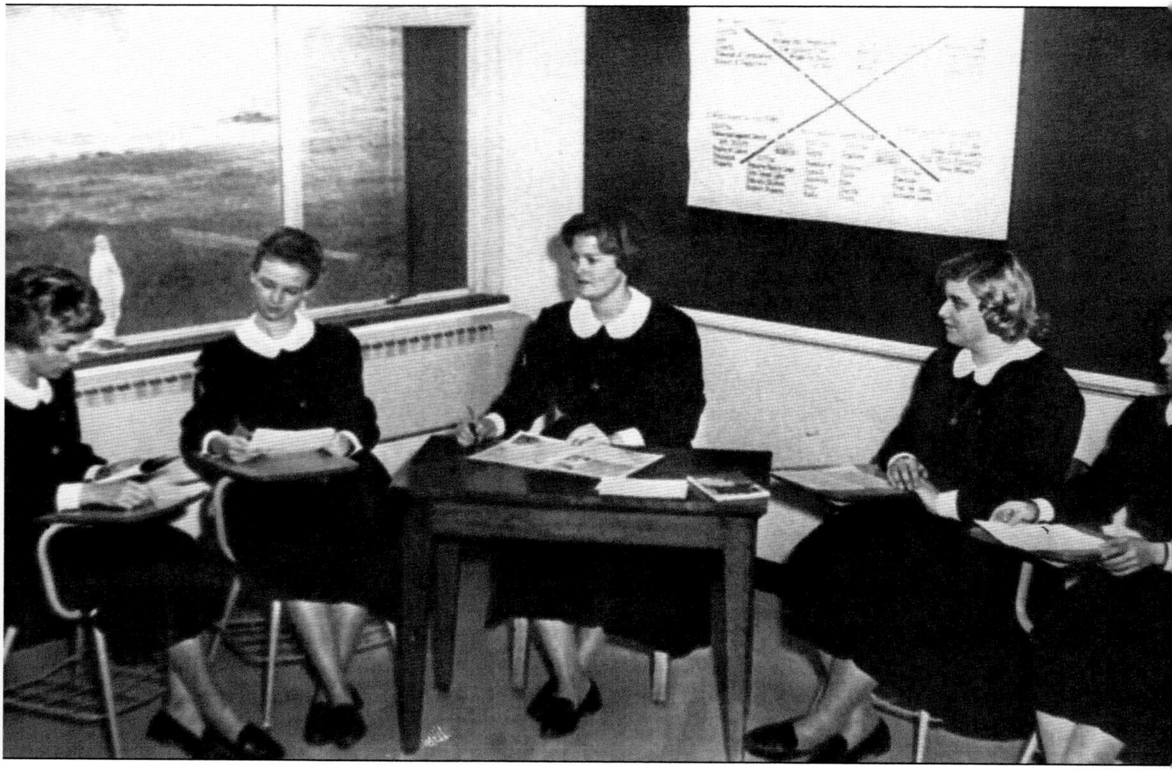

The program of study included a range of courses, including advanced-placement English and mathematics, home economics, and stenography. Students who received 90 percent or more in religion and four major subjects on their report cards received first honors. Those who received 85 percent or more in religion and four major subjects received second honors. The *Campanile* published the names of the students who earned first honors. The March 1967 *Campanile* reported that 23 students achieved first honors and that juniors led the other classes in honors earned. In March 1969, the *Campanile* reported that 37 students earned first honors, and freshmen and juniors tied for honors earned.

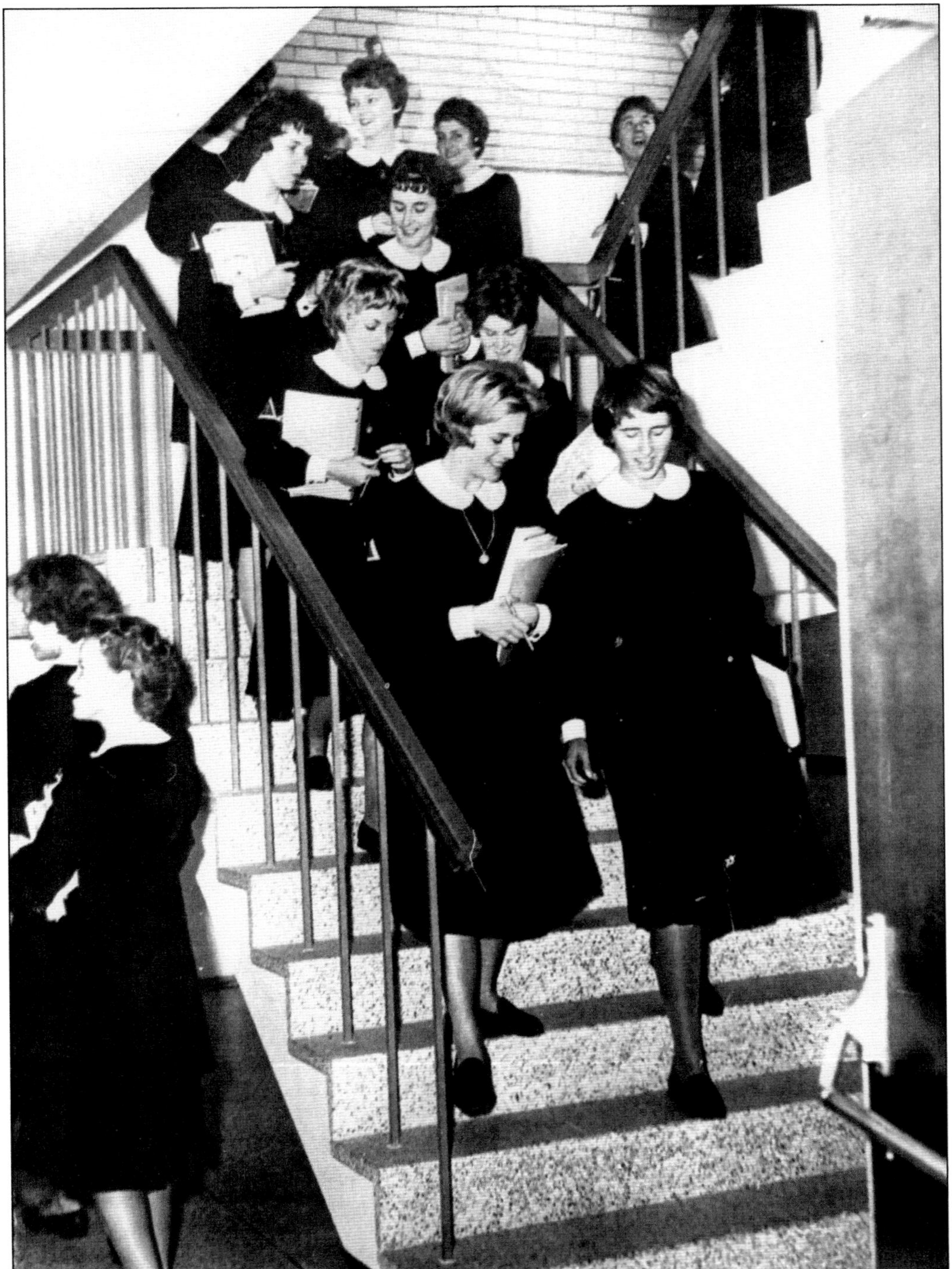

According to the 1964 student handbook, "Cleanliness, neatness, correct posture, and good taste should mark the appearance of a student of Mount Saint Joseph Academy. The school uniform must be clean and pressed, the collars and cuffs always white and starched. In length, the uniform must reach the middle of the knee. Stockings and uniform shoes must be worn at all times."

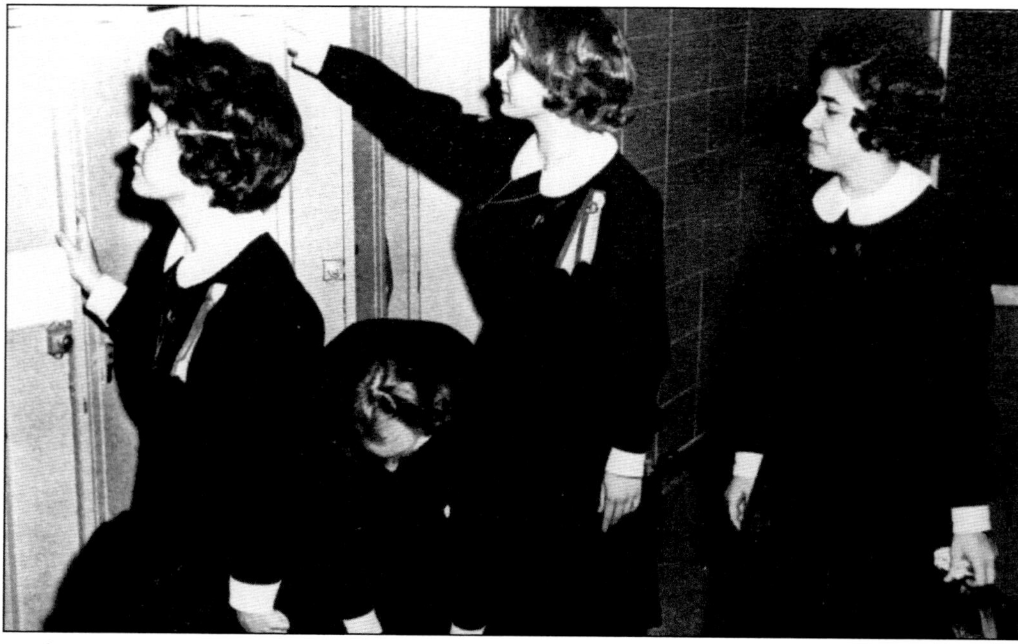

Student council members served a true disciplinary function in the early 1960s. They are pictured here conducting locker inspections in 1962. Student council members also could grant permission to fellow students to make outgoing telephone calls on the school's pay telephone if a faculty member was not present. They also moderated detentions.

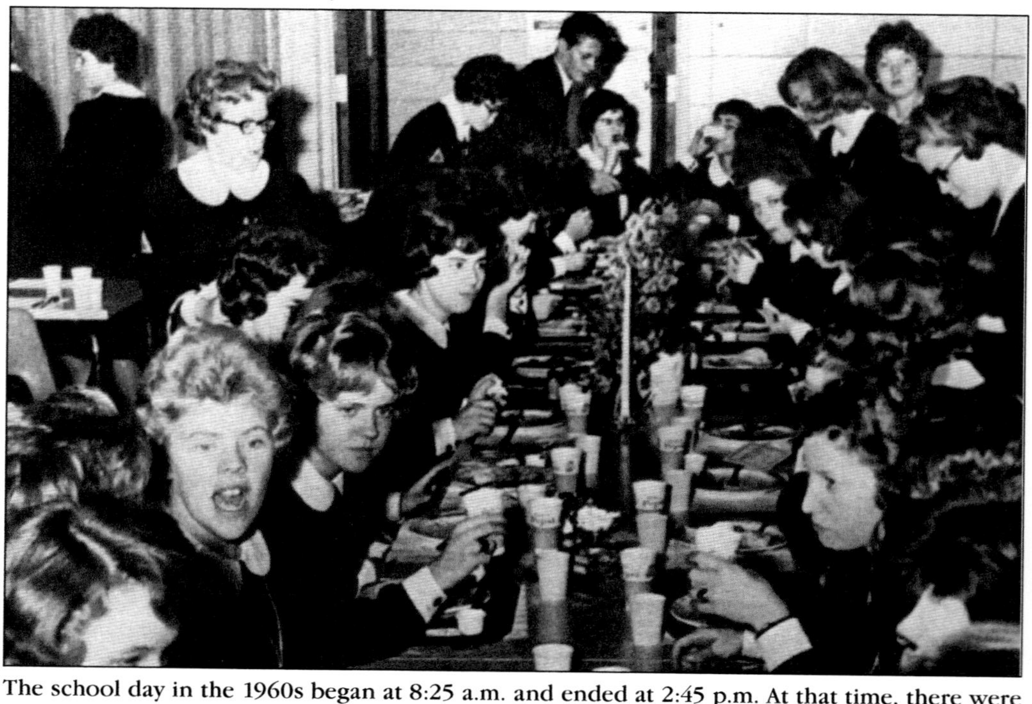

The school day in the 1960s began at 8:25 a.m. and ended at 2:45 p.m. At that time, there were only two lunches at the Mount: during fourth period, which was at 11:00 a.m., and fifth period, which was at 11:45 a.m.

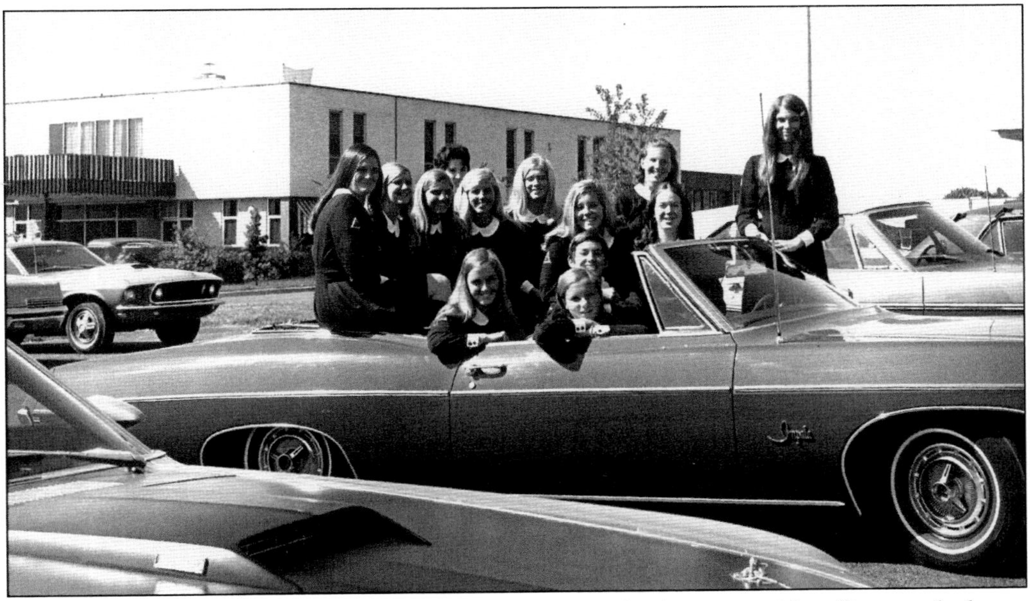

The end of the 1960s and early 1970s was a time of change for the Mount. After 49 years, the heavy serge uniform with starched collars and cuffs was replaced in the 1969–1970 school year by both summer and winter uniforms. In the 1970s, formal study periods were changed to free periods. Girls were even allowed to sign out of the building to use the school grounds.

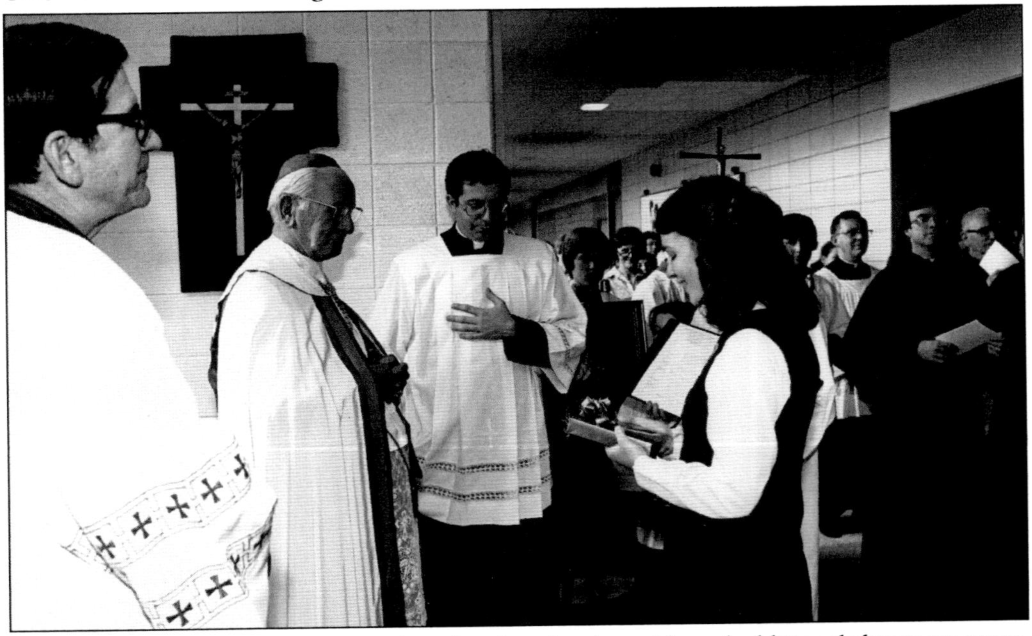

As enrollment increased, it became clear that the school would need additional classroom space. Sr. Maria Teresa, a history teacher, suggested that classrooms could be added under the raised section of the school near the front entrance. Sylvester Center opened during the 1973–1974 school year. In the late 1970s, the Neumann Addition was built adjacent to the auditorium to create additional space for art and music education. Cardinal Krol returned to the Mount to dedicate the addition on April 22, 1979.

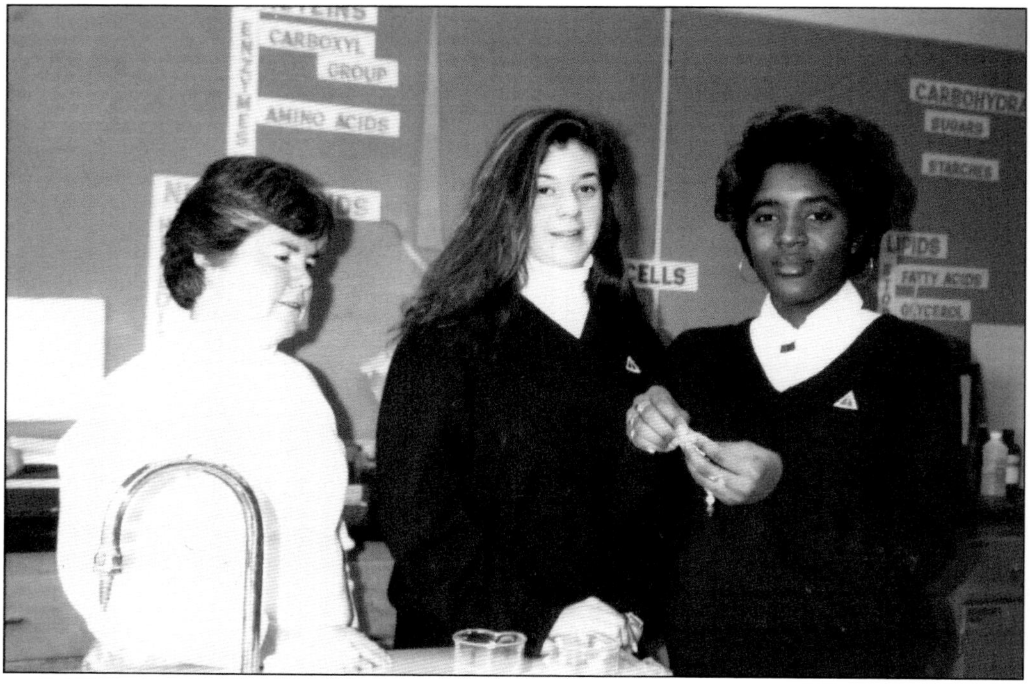

Driven by the mission of the Sisters of Saint Joseph, a stellar faculty (shown below in 1991), and high-achieving students, the academic reputation of the academy continued to advance throughout the 1980s and 1990s. In 1992–1993 and again in 1997–1998, the U.S. Department of Education named the Mount a Blue Ribbon School of Excellence. This distinction is reserved for the top schools in the country.

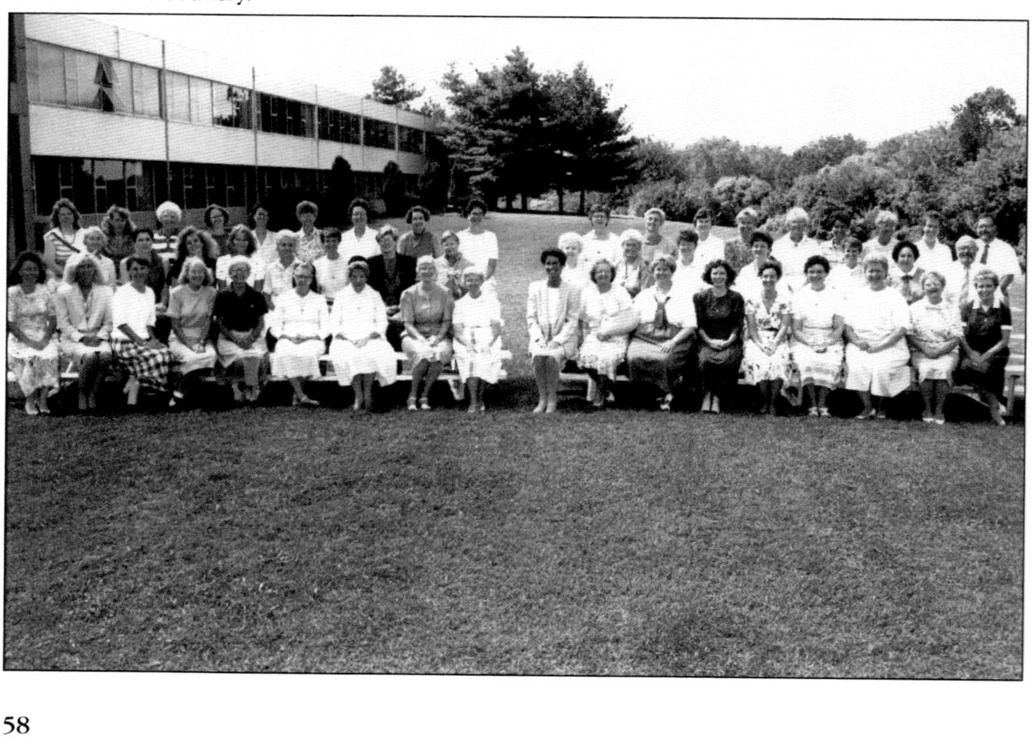

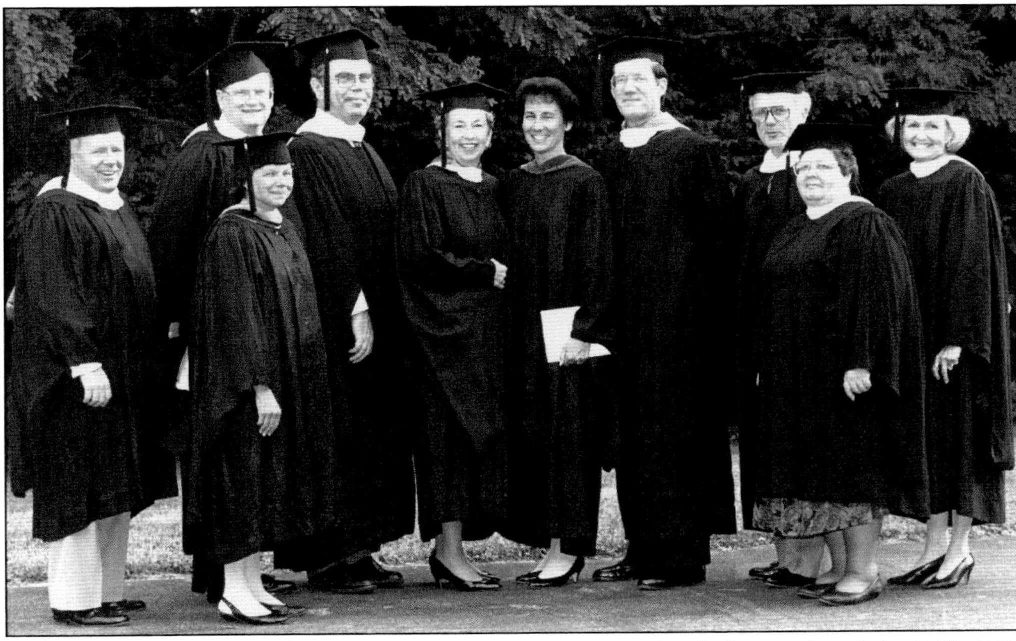

Under the leadership of Sr. Mary Dacey, who became principal at the beginning of the 1988–1989 school year, the academy developed its first strategic plan during the 1989–1990 school year. The plan recommended the establishment of a board of directors, and the first one convened in 1991–1992. In fall 1994, the Mount adopted the president-principal model of school leadership. Sr. Mary Dacey became the Mount's first president. Sr. Karen Dietrich became principal. The new model of leadership allows the president to focus on institutional advancement issues, while the principal handles academics and day-to-day operations.

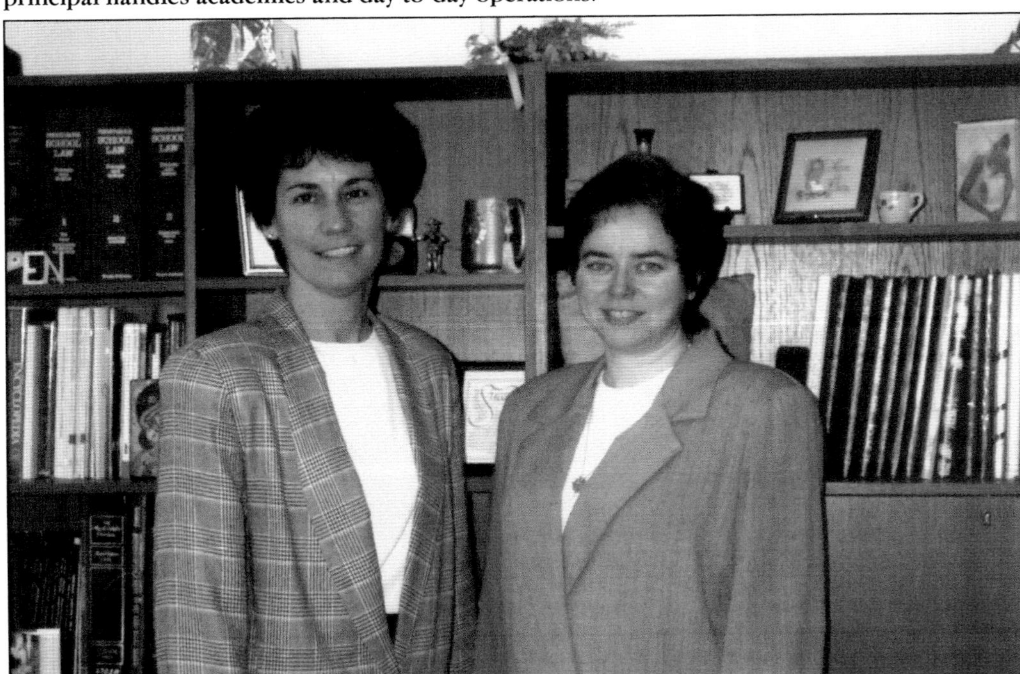

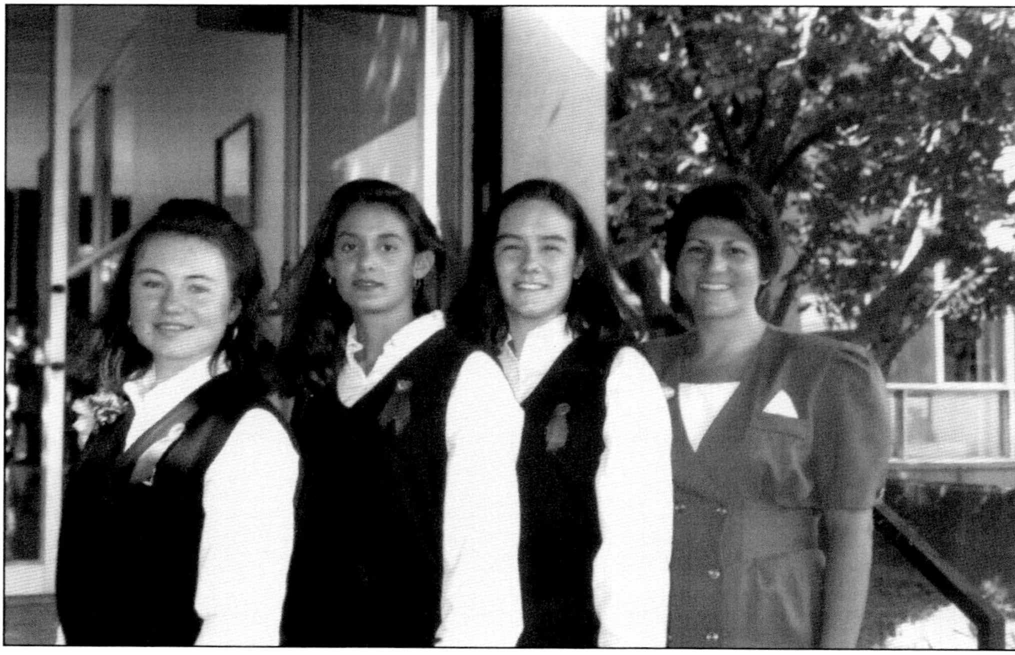

In addition to sponsoring events such as the father-daughter dance and mother-daughter fashion show, the Mount Saint Joseph Academy Student Council introduced an open forum event in the mid-1990s. Concerns and suggestions were collected at the homeroom level, and selected issues were presented to the administration at an all-school assembly.

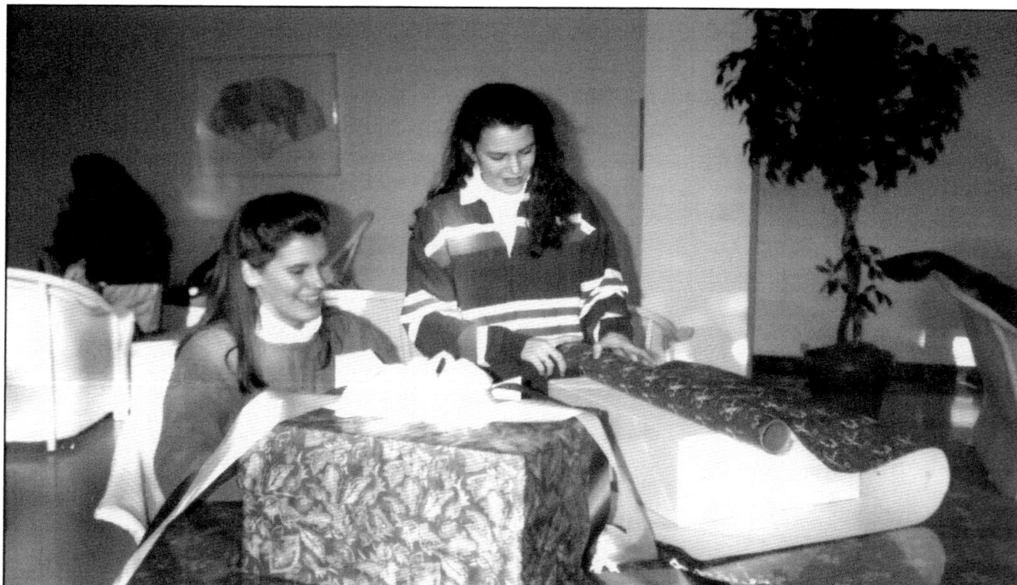

Community Service Corps (CSC) was an integral part of Mount life during the 1990s. CSC had been revived during the 1981–1982 school year after a 10-year hiatus. One of the most important CSC-sponsored events throughout the year was Operation Santa Claus. Each homeroom adopted an area family and purchased and wrapped Christmas gifts, which teams of students delivered on Christmas Eve. The tradition of Operation Santa Claus continues today.

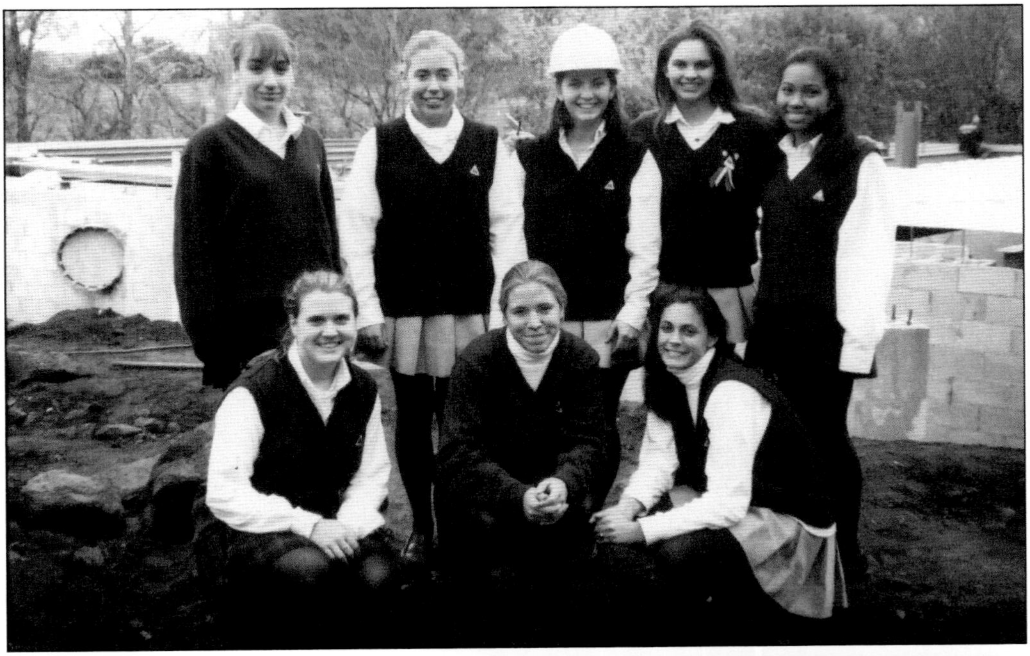

In the mid-1990s, the Mount began a $5 million capital campaign for the addition of new space as well as the establishment of an endowment. Countless members of the Mount community contributed, and a substantial gift from the Connelly Foundation helped the Mount to exceed the goal. At the time, the foundation's donation was the largest it had made to a girls' school. Groundbreaking for the Fournier Wing took place in spring 1996, and the new space opened for the 1997–1998 school year. The Fournier Wing includes a library/media center, six classrooms, computer/writing center, guidance suite with private space for individual counseling and for exploring college and career choices, and faculty work areas.

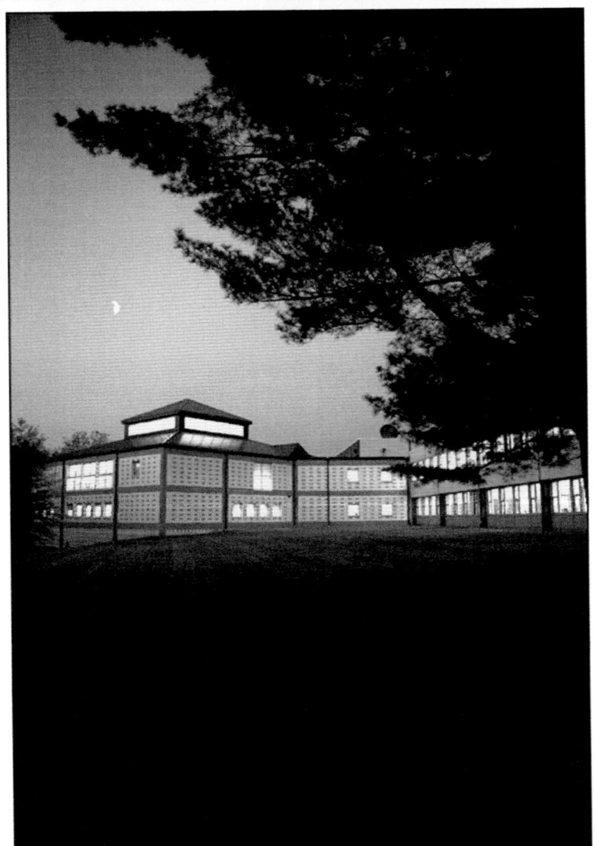

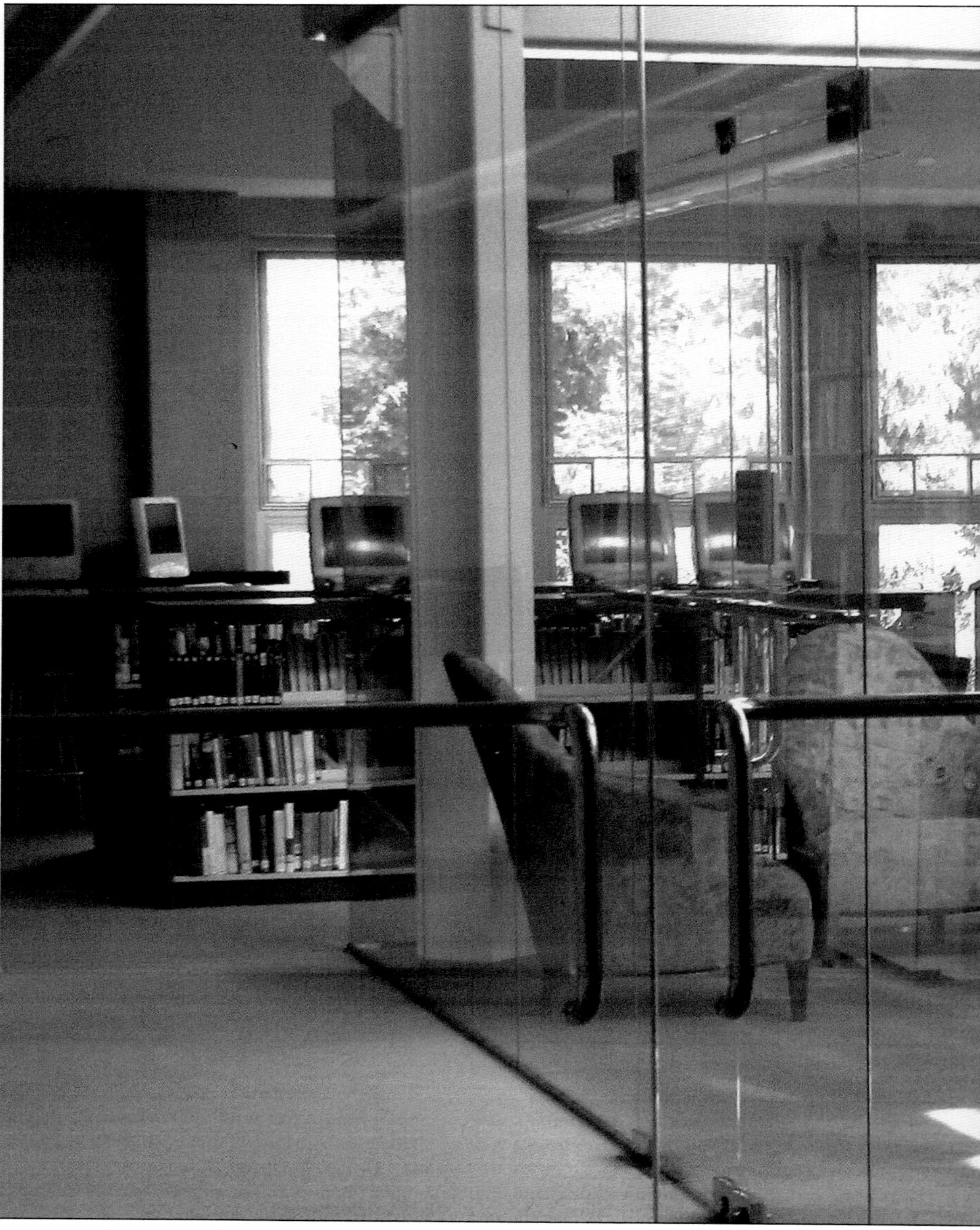

The Fournier Wing's centerpiece is the library, thanks to a donation by the Betz family. The library, a state-of-the-art media center with computer, telecommunication, and video capabilities, has at

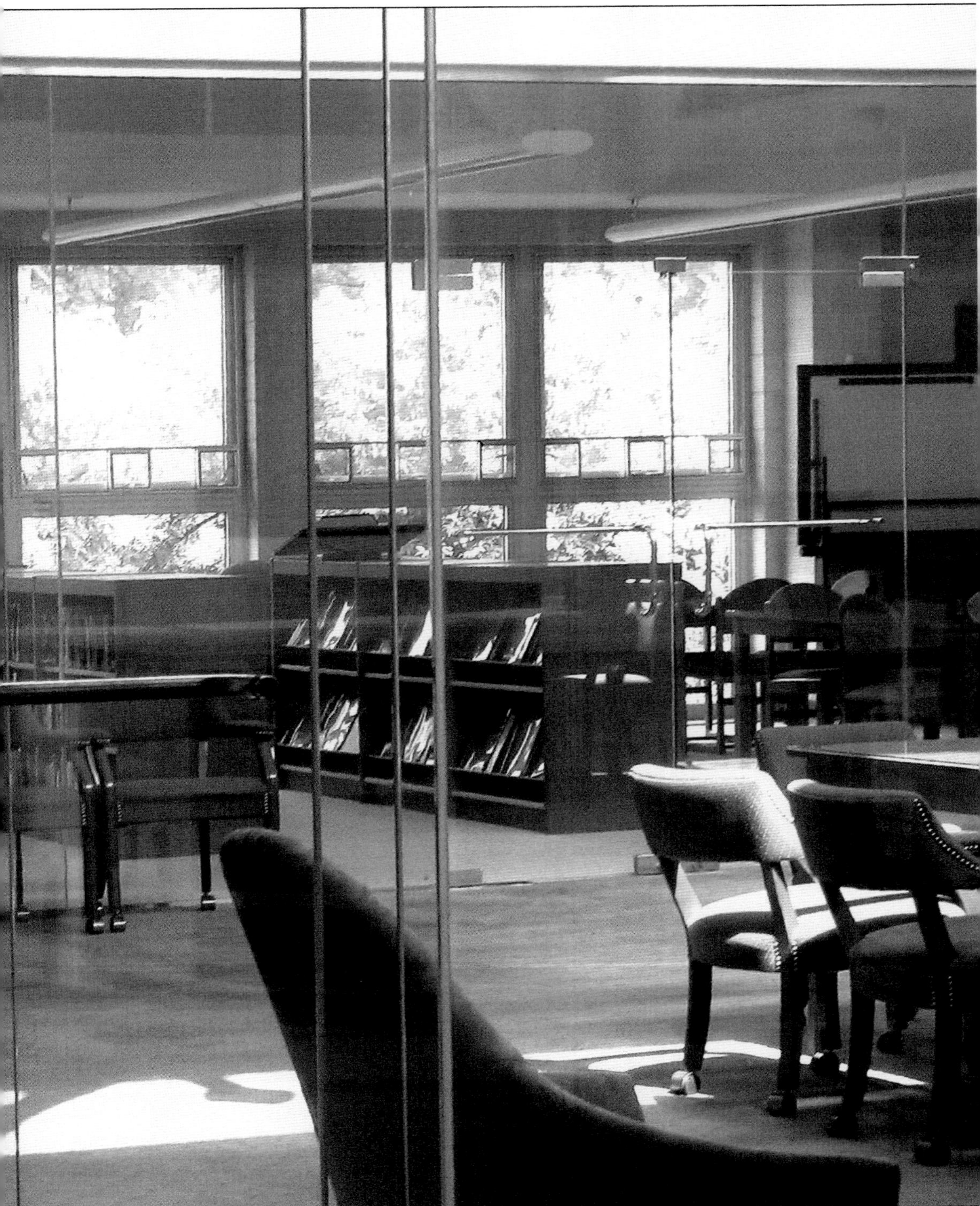

its center a glass-enclosed atrium. Affectionately known as "the fishbowl," the atrium was made possible by the Heck family.

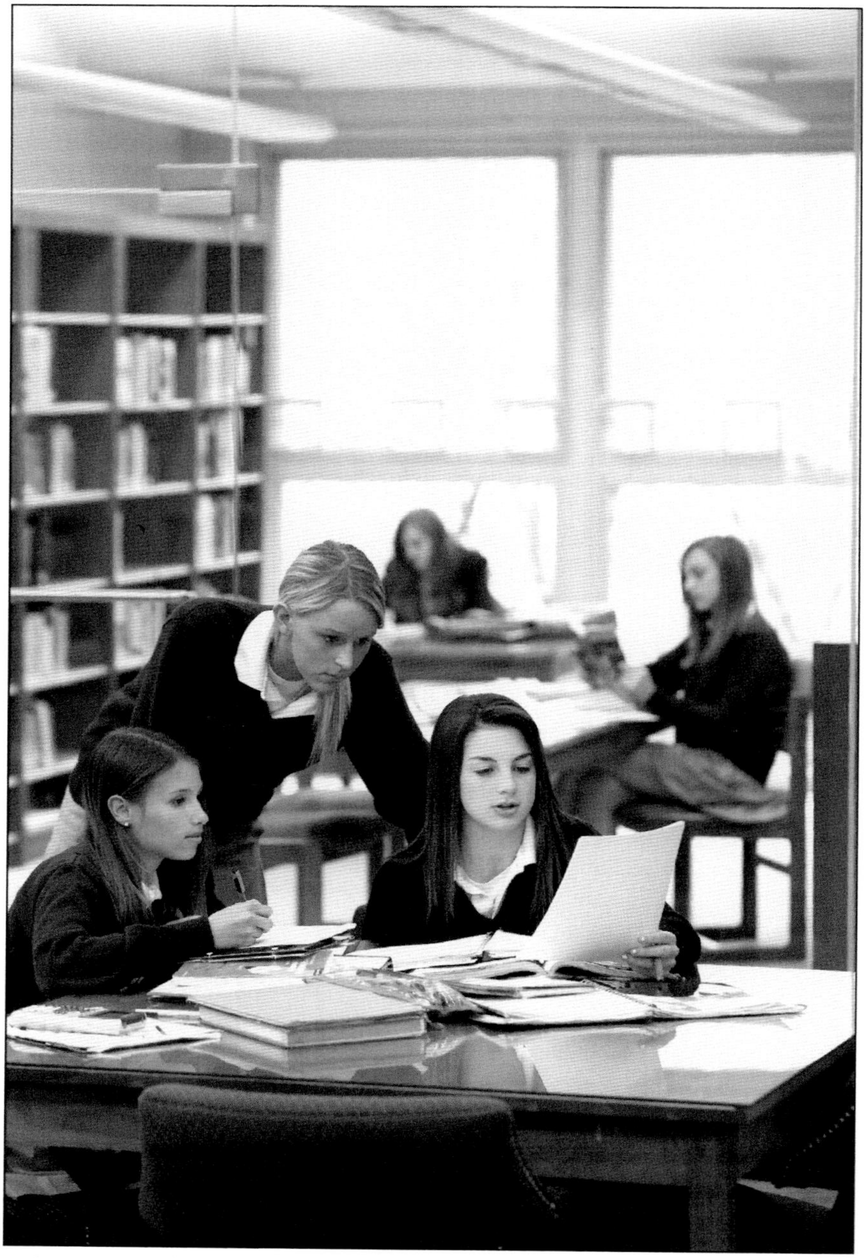

The new wing was not the only big change at the Mount in the late 1990s. The 1997–1998 school year also saw the introduction of block scheduling, for which students take three or four subjects per term, instead of the traditional six or seven, for a total of seven or eight credits per school year. Each class period is 80 minutes long, and most courses last for 16 weeks (September to January or January to June). Advanced-placement courses meet every other day for the entire school year. The late 1990s also saw the Mount's most recent uniform change, and members of the class of 1998 began their freshman year in a new uniform. Blue blazers (worn for formal occasions), green sweaters, and plaid skirts replaced navy blue sweaters and gray skirts, but penny loafers remained the uniform shoe.

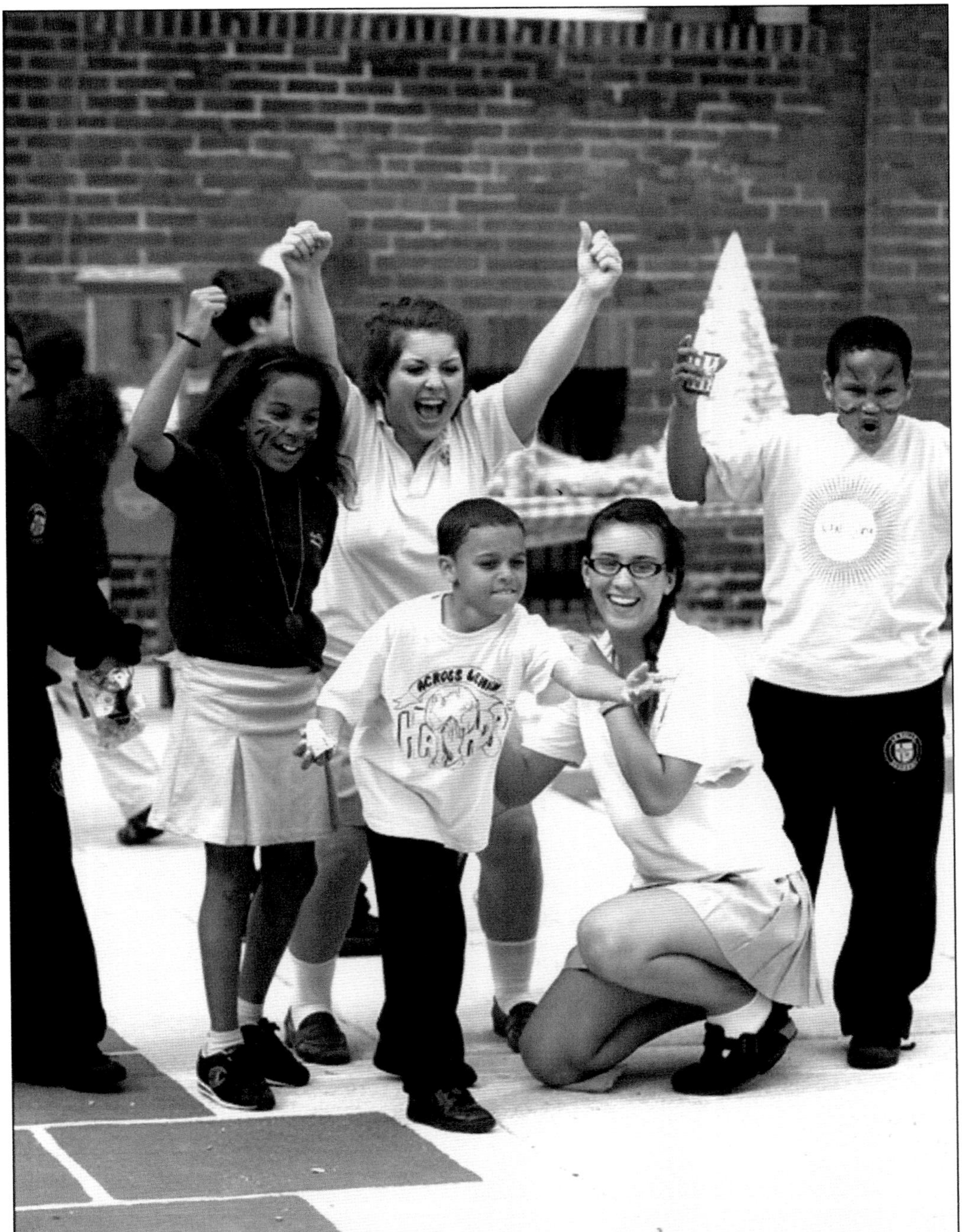

LaSalle Academy in North Philadelphia educates students in grades three through eight whose parents and guardians desire but cannot afford a quality Catholic education. The Mount began a partnership with LaSalle Academy in 2003 and sponsors many programs throughout the year for its students, including tutoring and mentoring programs. The LaSalle Academy carnival is held in May each year to celebrate the friendship enjoyed between the Mount and LaSalle Academy students.

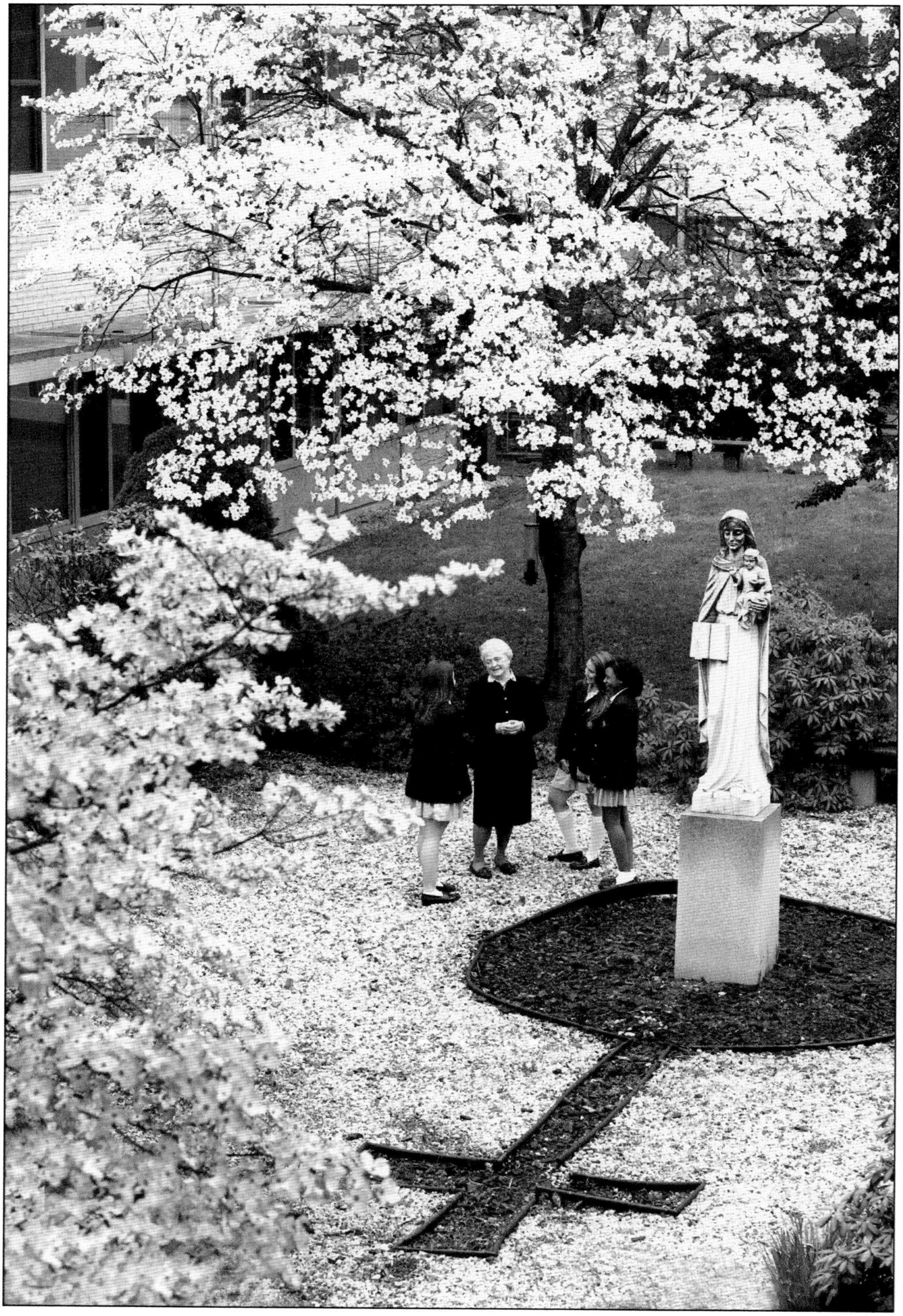

Since the opening of the new Mount, enrollment has more than doubled, the number of full-time faculty has tripled, and the number of course offerings has quadrupled.

Four

On the Field, Court, and River

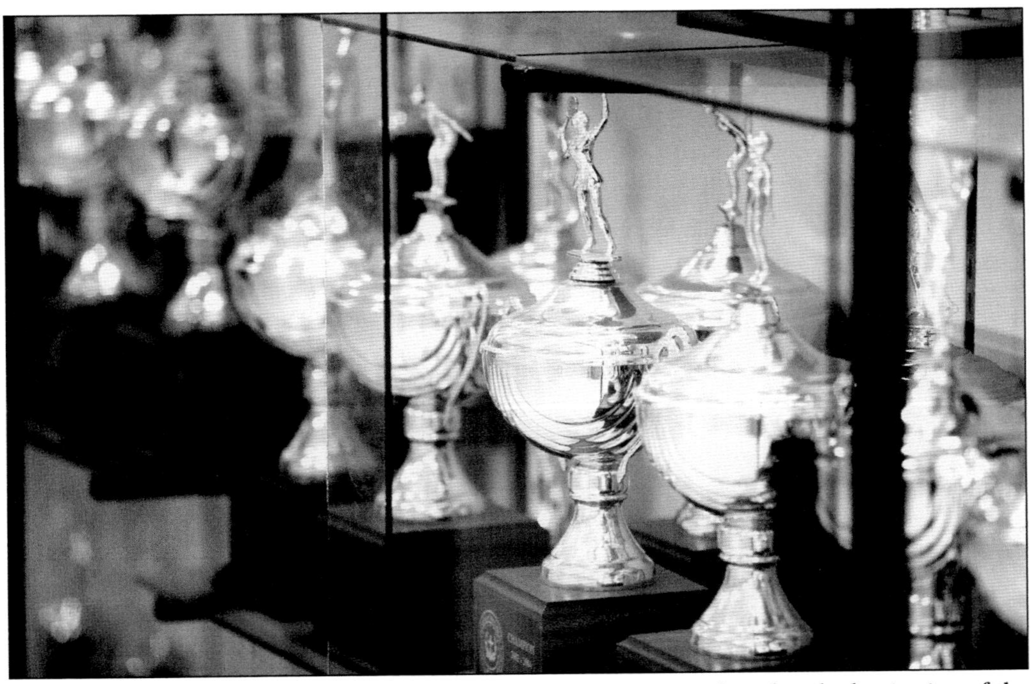

Sports became an important part of Mount life as they were introduced at the beginning of the 20th century. Mounties have accomplished a variety of athletic achievements through the decades, as evidenced by the trophy case in the hallway.

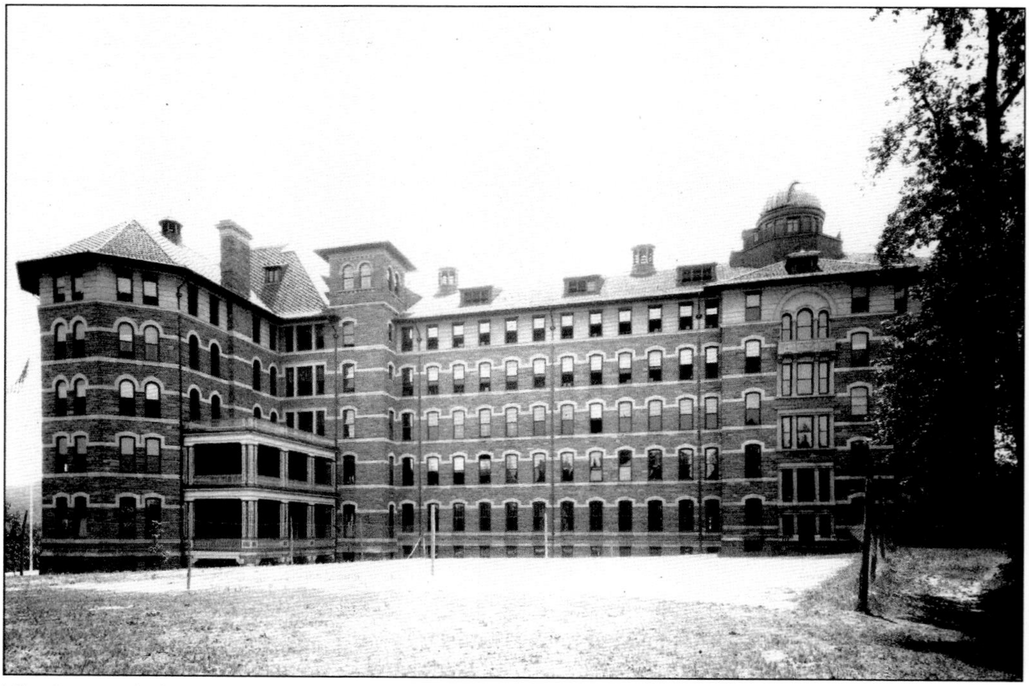

The first male lay teacher and permanent staff member was a "gymnasium teacher" hired at the Chestnut Hill building's opening in 1903. In May 1906, the school held its first Sports Day, in which girls demonstrated fencing and other athletic pursuits. Blue, red, and white ribbons were awarded, and Catherine Sommers, who received the most, also was given a silver loving cup inscribed with "Mount St. Joseph." Mary Ellen Ruffner won the fencing class prize—a pair of foils. In spring 1916, a tennis court opened and girls played in their gym bloomers. By that fall, it was as popular as basketball. The fifth floor of the building to the right, behind the players, is the Mount's gymnasium.

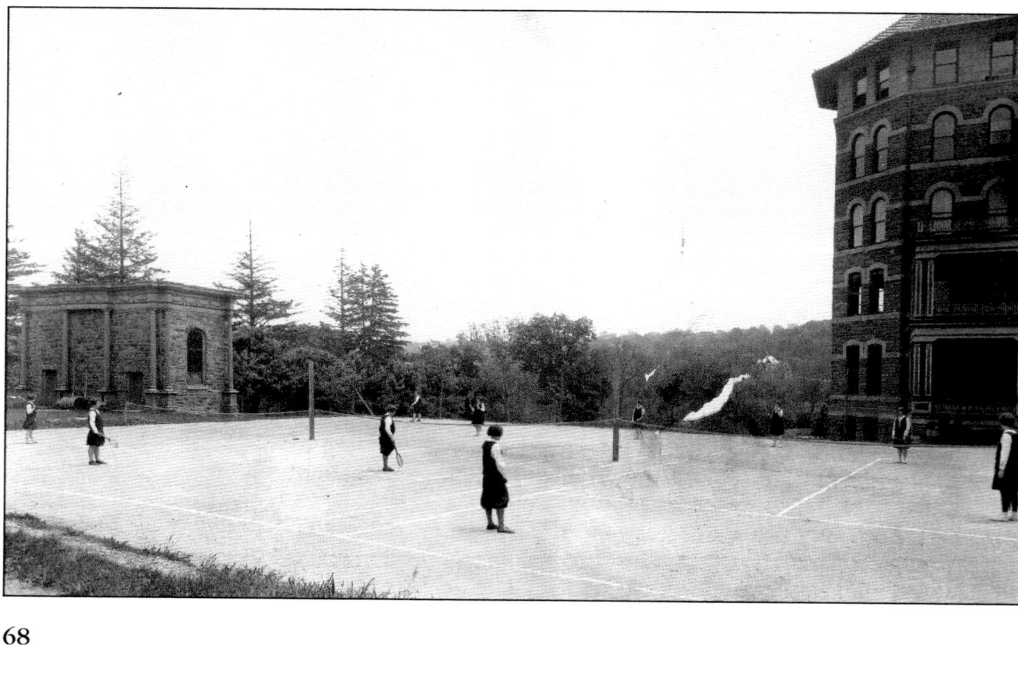

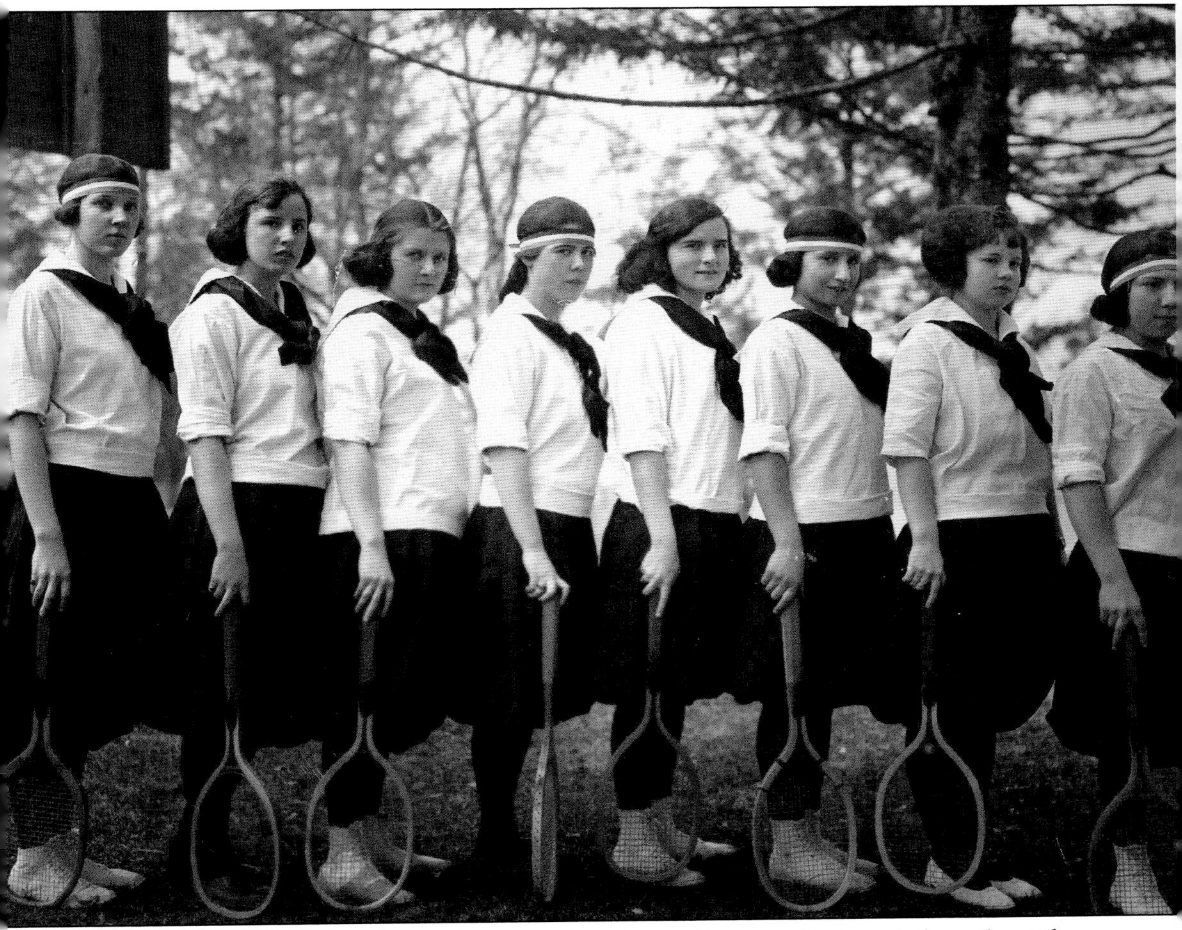

Although tennis was one of the first sports introduced at the Mount—this team is from the early 1920s—it was only a club sport until 1974, when it became a varsity sport. The early gym uniform hardly lent itself to freedom of movement. The coarse black serge bloomers reached below the knee, accompanied by a long-sleeve attached top. Either a yellow or red silk tie designated interclass teams.

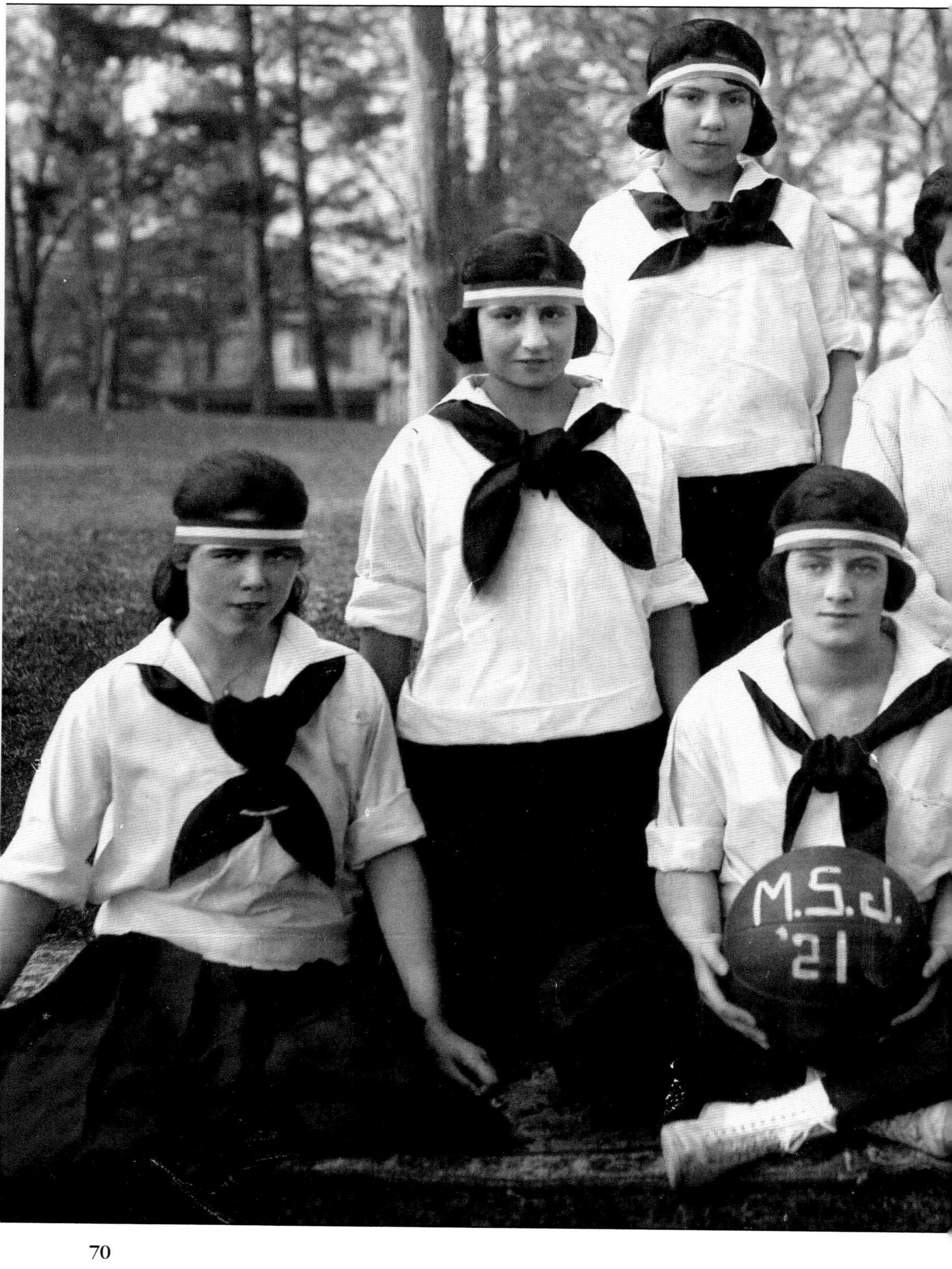
M.S.J.
'21

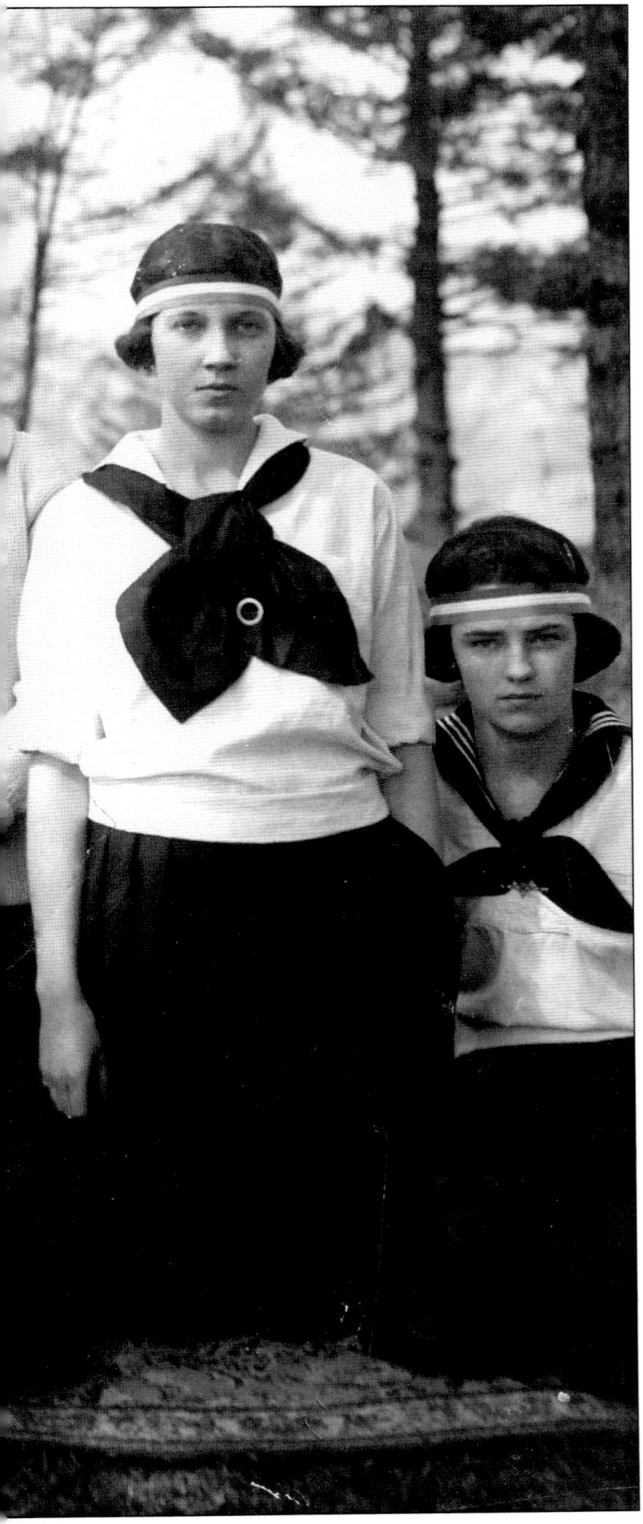

Basketball was introduced in 1903, but it was limited to intramural contests. By 1916, games against other schools were organized. The Mount's most famous rivalry was with the Amazon team from the Catholic Girls High School. The 1921 basketball team, shown here, challenged the Amazons to a game at the Mount and won. In March 1932, the Mount girls defeated the Chestnut Hill College freshmen girls, 38-30.

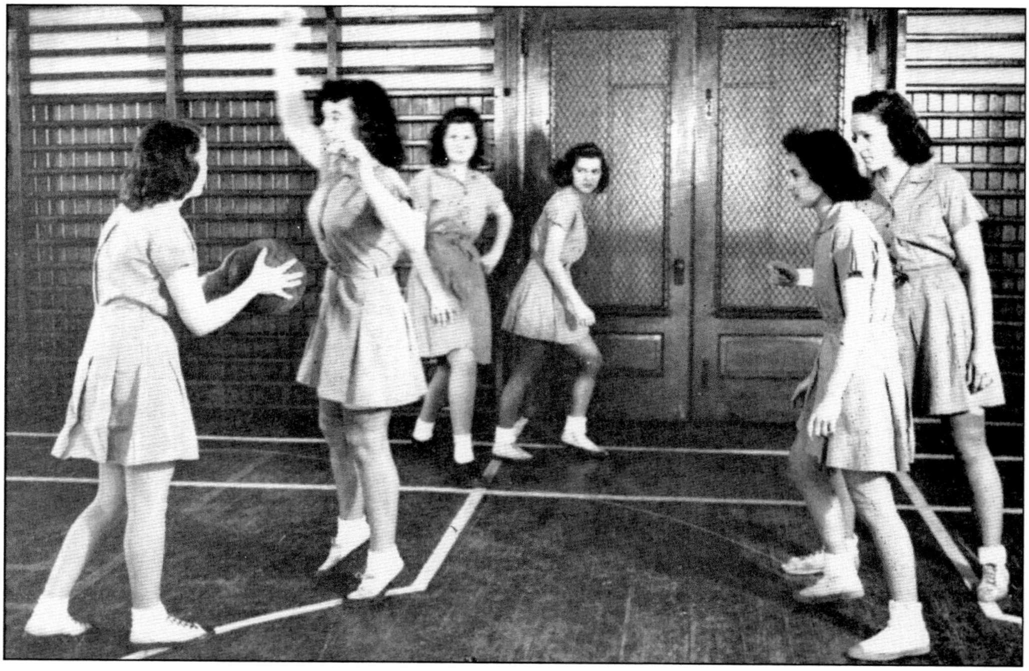

The fifth-floor gymnasium, alas, had a low ceiling. During a game, any ball that hit the ceiling was considered out of bounds. The basketball games were popular to watch, and the gymnasium was surrounded by windows for natural light and fresh air.

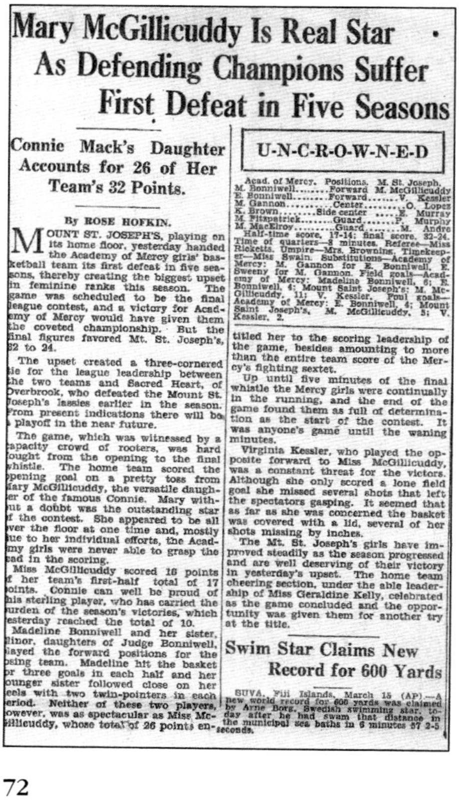

Mary McGillicuddy Is Real Star As Defending Champions Suffer First Defeat in Five Seasons

Connie Mack's Daughter Accounts for 26 of Her Team's 32 Points.

By ROSE HOFKIN.

MOUNT ST. JOSEPH'S, playing on its home floor, yesterday handed the Academy of Mercy girls' basketball team its first defeat in five seasons, thereby creating the biggest upset in feminine ranks this season. The game was scheduled to be the final league contest, and a victory for Academy of Mercy would have given them the coveted championship. But the final figures favored Mt. St. Joseph's, 32 to 24.

The upset created a three-cornered tie for the league leadership between the two teams and Sacred Heart, of Overbrook, who defeated the Mount St. Joseph's lassies earlier in the season. From present indications there will be a playoff in the near future.

The game, which was witnessed by a capacity crowd of rooters, was hard fought from the opening to the final whistle. The home team scored the opening goal on a pretty toss from Mary McGillicuddy, the versatile daughter of the famous Connie. Mary without a doubt was the outstanding star of the contest. She appeared to be all over the floor at one time and, mostly due to her individual efforts, the Academy girls were never able to grasp the lead in the scoring.

Miss McGillicuddy scored 16 points of her team's first-half total of 17 points. Connie can well be proud of this sterling player, who has carried the burden of the season's victories, which yesterday reached the total of 10.

Madeline Bonniwell and her sister, Elinor, daughters of Judge Bonniwell, played the forward positions for the losing team. Madeline hit the basket for three goals in each half and her younger sister followed close on her heels with two twin-pointers in each period. Neither of these two players, however, was as spectacular as Miss McGillicuddy, whose total of 26 points entitled her to the scoring leadership of the game, besides amounting to more than the entire team score of the Mercy's fighting sextet.

Up until five minutes of the final whistle the Mercy girls were continually in the running, and the end of the game found them as full of determination as the start of the contest. It was anyone's game until the waning minutes.

Virginia Kessler, who played the opposite forward to Miss McGillicuddy, was a constant threat for the victors. Although she only scored a lone field goal she missed several shots that left the spectators gasping. It seemed that as far as she was concerned the basket was covered with a lid, several of her shots missing by inches.

The Mt. St. Joseph's girls have improved steadily as the season progressed and are well deserving of their victory in yesterday's upset. The home team cheering section, under the able leadership of Miss Geraldine Kelly, celebrated as the game concluded and the opportunity was given them for another try at the title.

U-N-C-R-O-W-N-E-D

Acad. of Mercy.	Positions.	M. St. Joseph.
M. Bonniwell	Forward	M. McGillicuddy
E. Bonniwell	Forward	V. Kessler
M. Gannon	Center	O. Lopez
K. Brown	Side center	E. Murray
M. Fitzpatrick	Guard	P. Murphy
M. MacElroy	Guard	M. Andre

Half-time score, 17-14; final score, 32-24. Time of quarters—8 minutes. Referee—Miss Ricketts. Umpire—Mrs. Browning. Timekeeper—Miss Swain. Substitutions—Academy of Mercy: M. Gannon for E. Bonniwell, E. Sweeny for M. Gannon. Field goals—Academy of Mercy: Madeline Bonniwell, 6; E. Bonniwell, 4; Mount Saint Joseph's: M. McGillicuddy, 11; V. Kessler. Foul goals—Academy of Mercy: E. Bonniwell, 4; Mount Saint Joseph's, M. McGillicuddy, 5; V. Kessler, 2.

Swim Star Claims New Record for 600 Yards

SUVA, Fiji Islands, March 15 (AP).—A new world record for 600 yards was claimed by Arne Borg, Swedish swimming star, today after he had swam that distance in the municipal sea baths in 6 minutes 57 2-5 seconds.

Mary McGillicuddy, daughter of famed Philadelphia Athletics manager Connie Mack, was the star forward and high scorer on the Mount's basketball team in the late 1920s. At the time that "Mary Mack" played, there were six players on the court: two forwards, two guards, a center, and a side-center. The guards were not permitted to shoot.

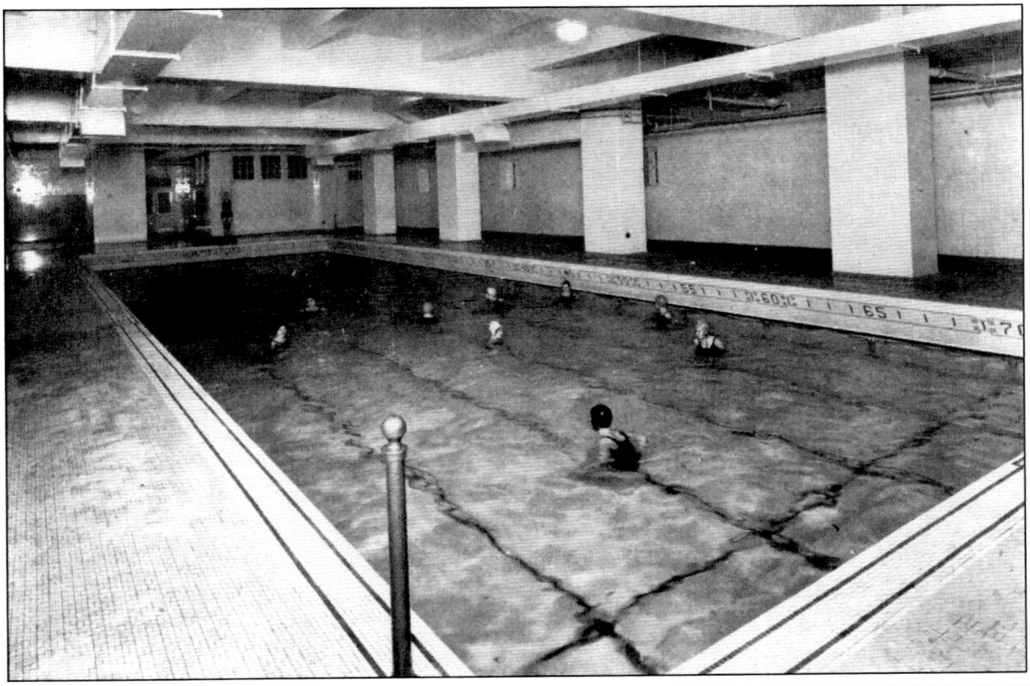

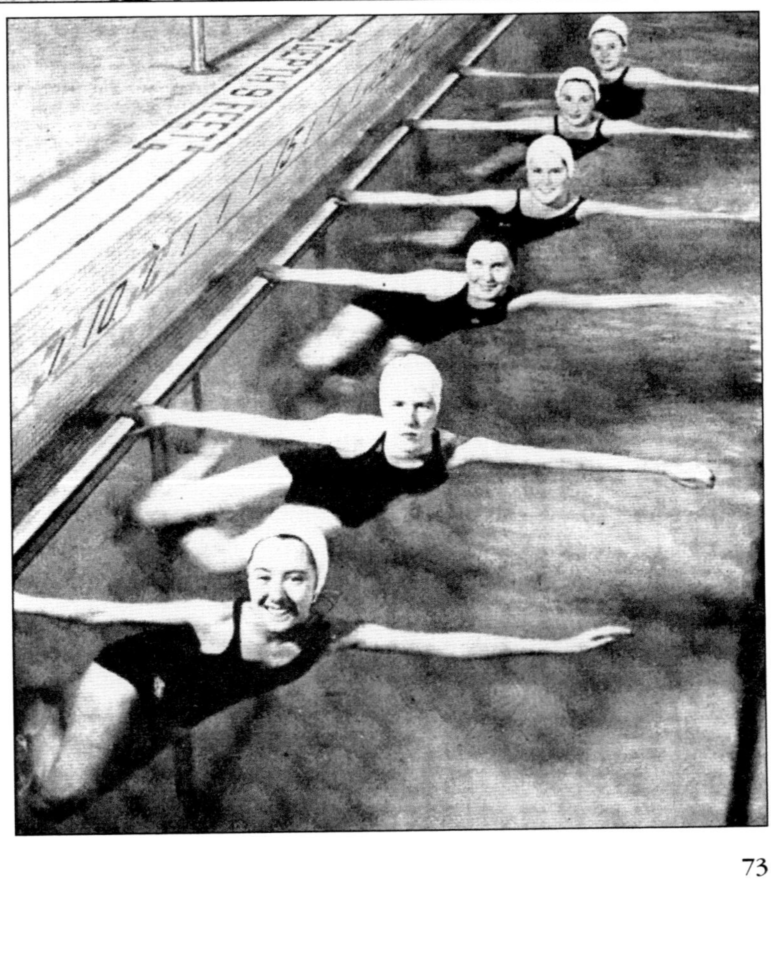

The pool on the Mount's Chestnut Hill campus, shown shortly after its opening in 1928, was a required stop for every student. Even in the water, the uniform rule was applied, and the Sisters of Saint Joseph provided swimsuits. The Mount's current home in Flourtown, though, has no pool. That does not stop upperclassmen from advising unsuspecting freshmen to visit the "pool on the third floor." The Mount swim team now travels to LaSalle College High School and Temple University's Ambler campus for daily practice.

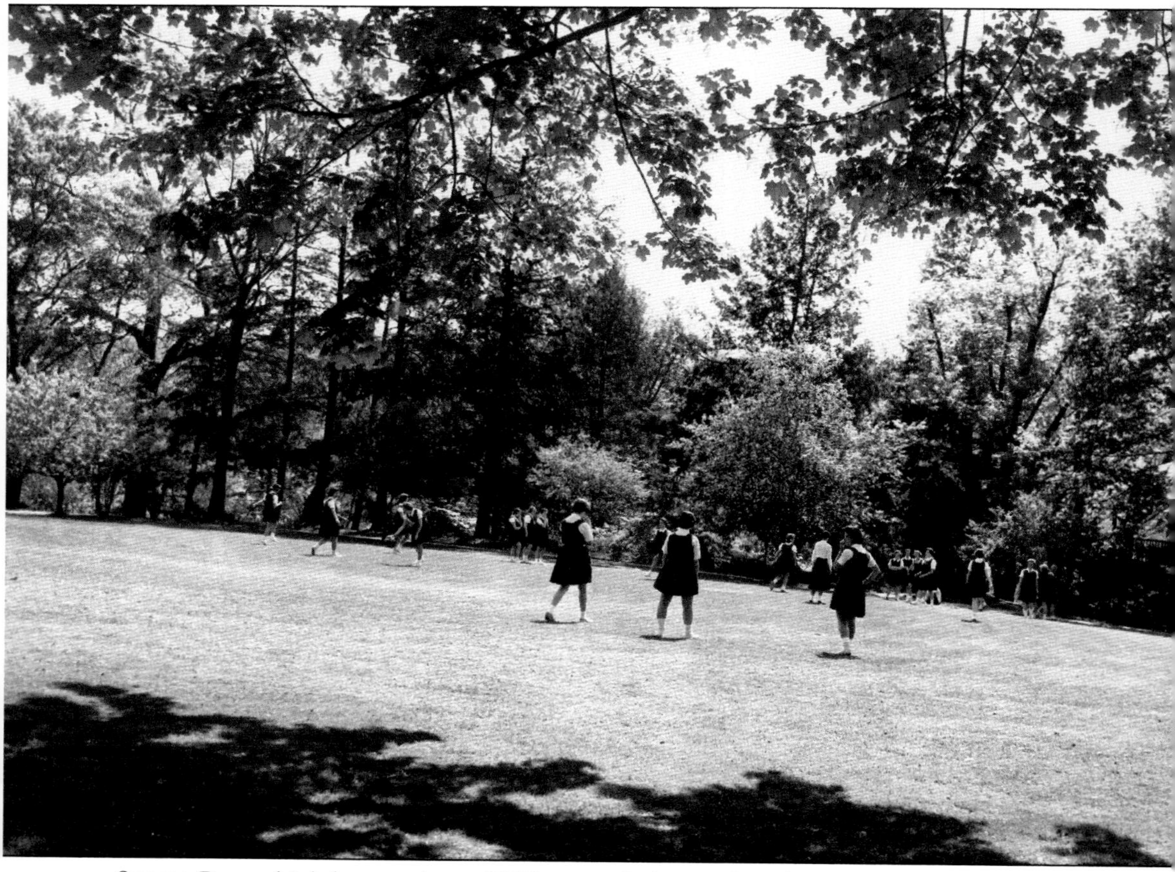

Sports Day, which began about 1906, extended over five days by 1912 and even featured Shakespearean plays. By 1927, the athletic association (AA) sponsored an official field day, known as AA Day, which included hockey, running, jumping, shot put, and javelin. In the 1960s, the events of the day were followed by hoagies and Tastykakes, to the delight of the girls. AA Days took place on Ascension Thursday.

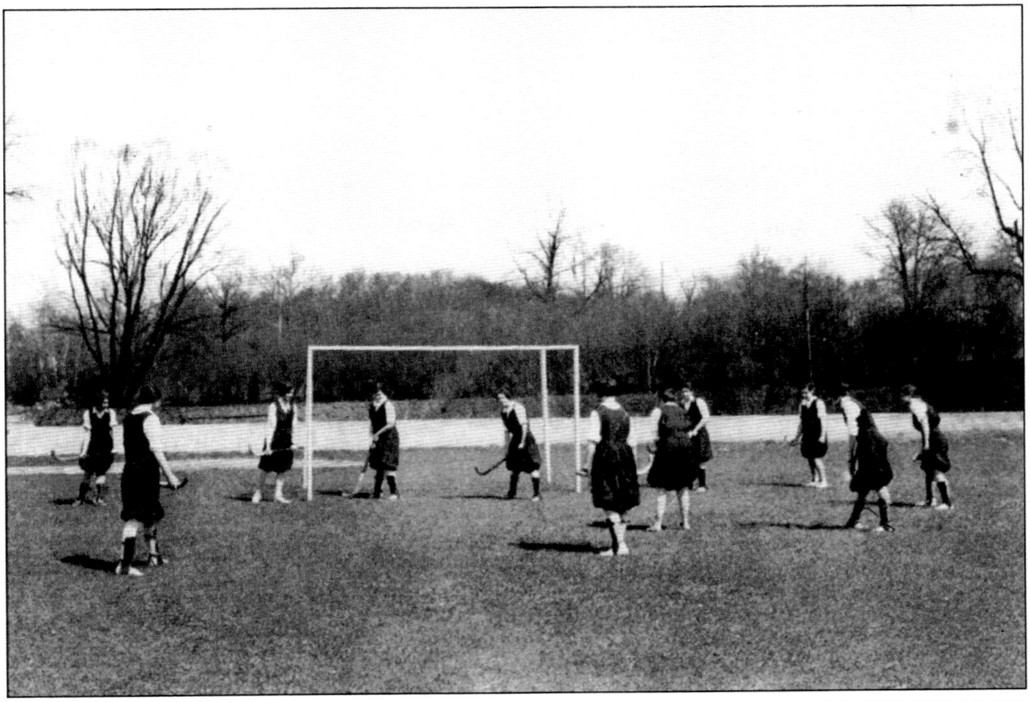

Field hockey began as a sport at the Mount in 1942. The team, shown during an away game, played along the flood bank of the Wissahickon Creek at the Chestnut Hill campus. In the 1930s, the games were followed by hot dog and marshmallow roasts.

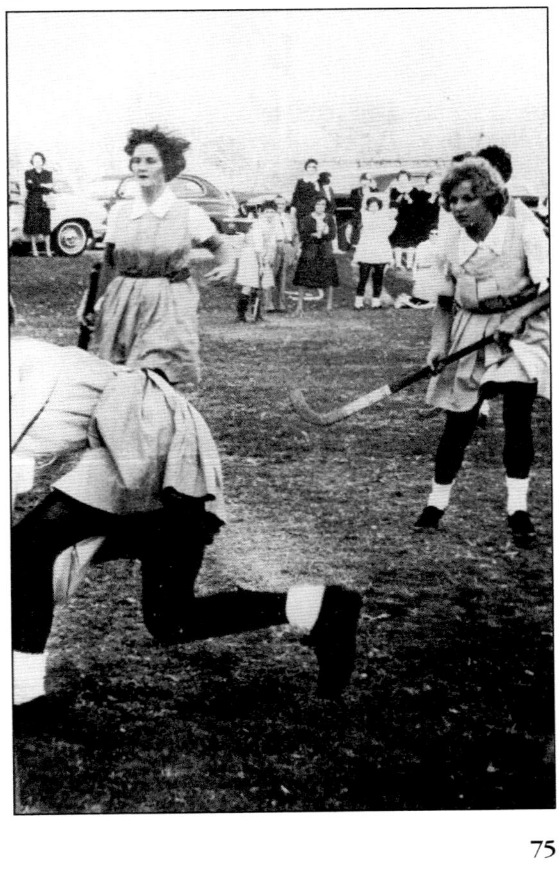

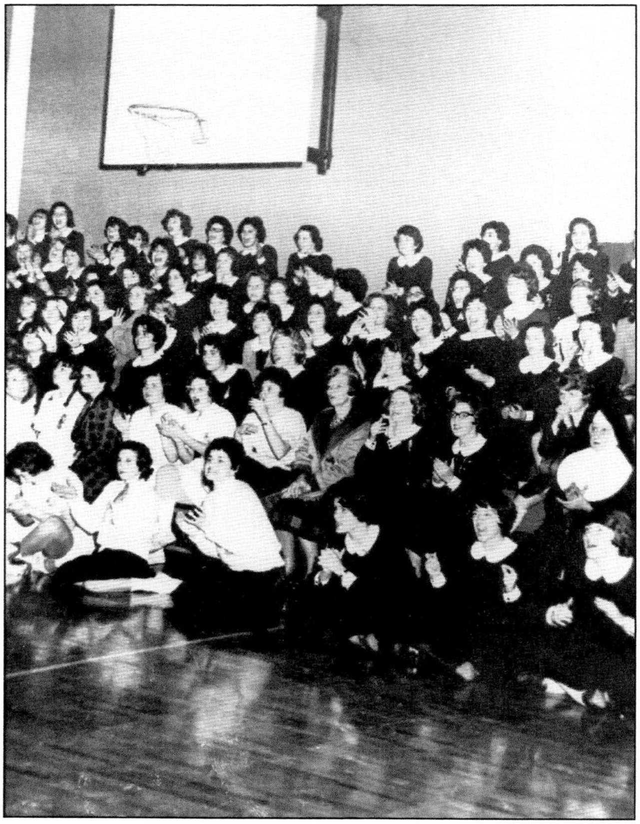

In the 1920s, "school spirit" was the new term on everyone's lips, in reference to an old-fashioned love of the school, interest in its welfare, pride in its achievements, and loyalty to its ideals and traditions. There has been no shortage of Mount spirit through the years. In the photograph of a pep rally (left), Mother Sylvester (far right) shows her spirit in the bleachers. The photograph below shows a pep rally in the mid-1990s. These rallies are favorites of the students, as the Mounties and school community gather in the gymnasium. Teams perform a skit or cheer to rev up the crowd.

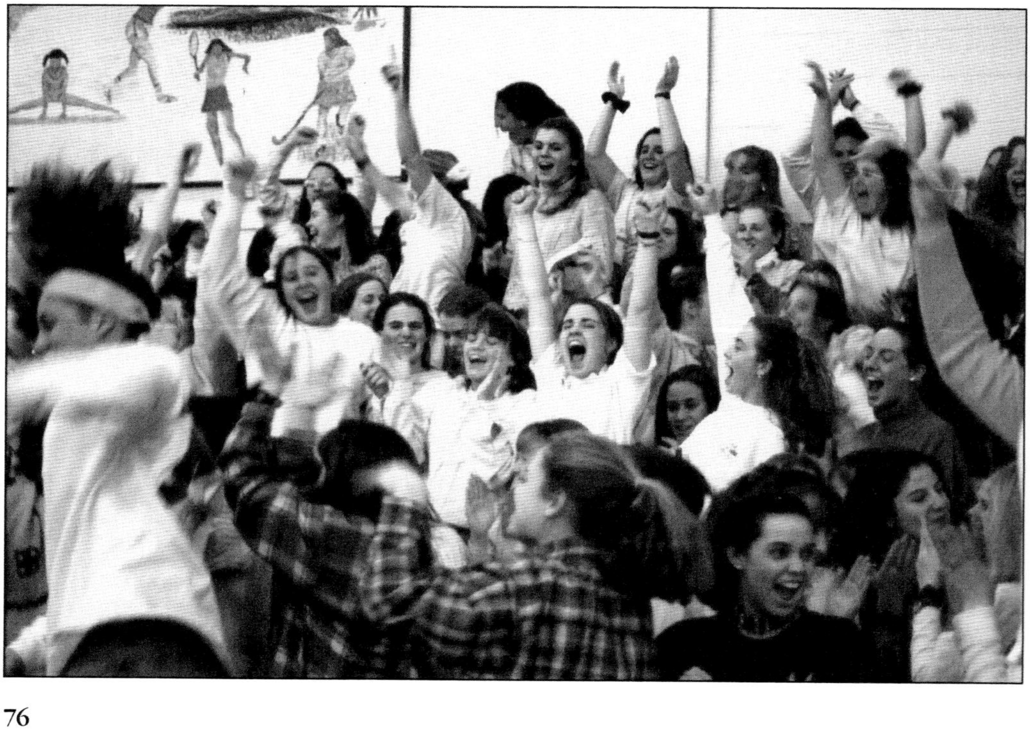

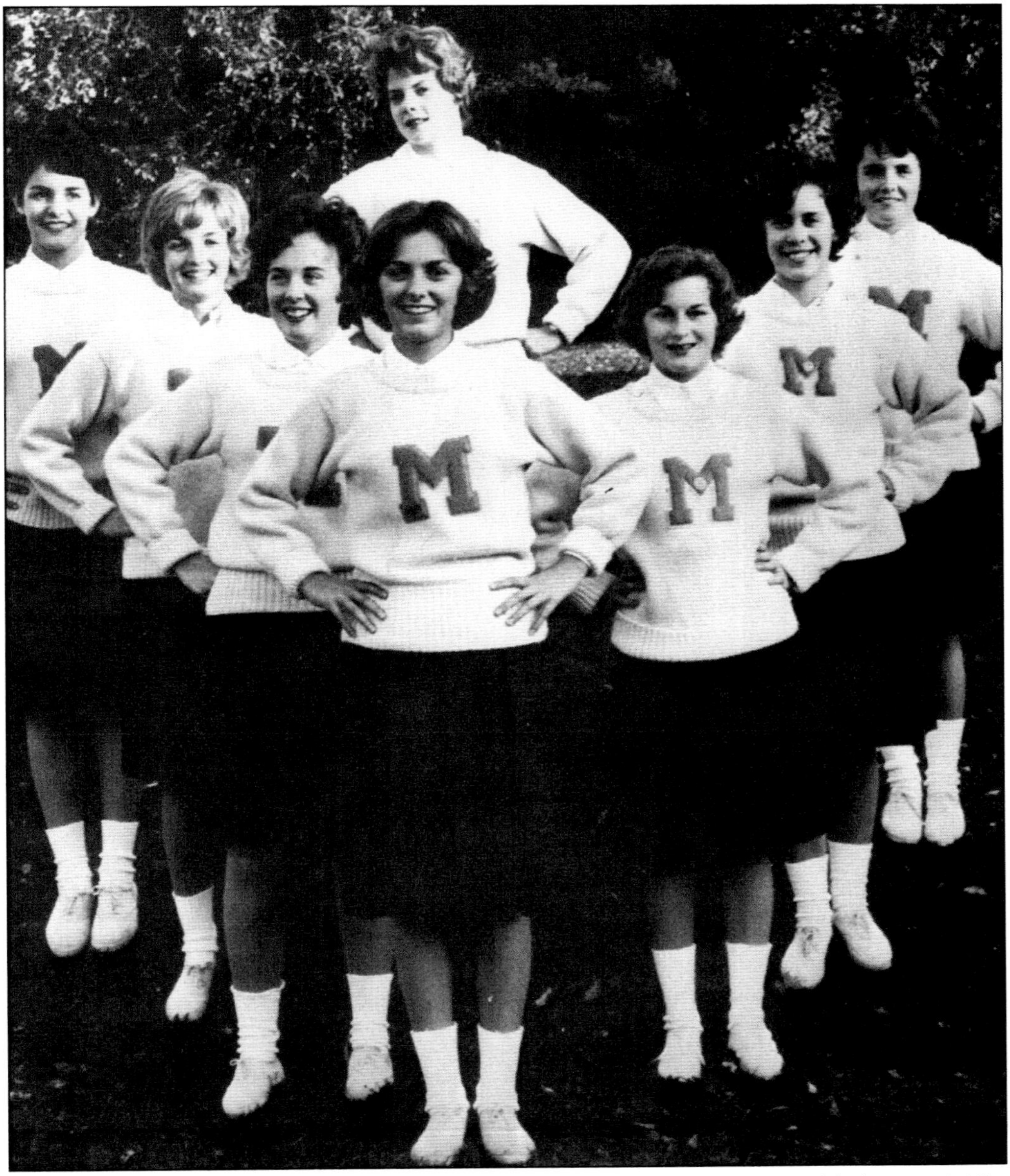

Cheerleading began at the Mount in 1962, and a junior varsity squad was added in 1972. The cheerleaders spread the spirit of the purple, white, and gold throughout the school community. Today the girls cheer for the basketball team and other sports and participate in competitions.

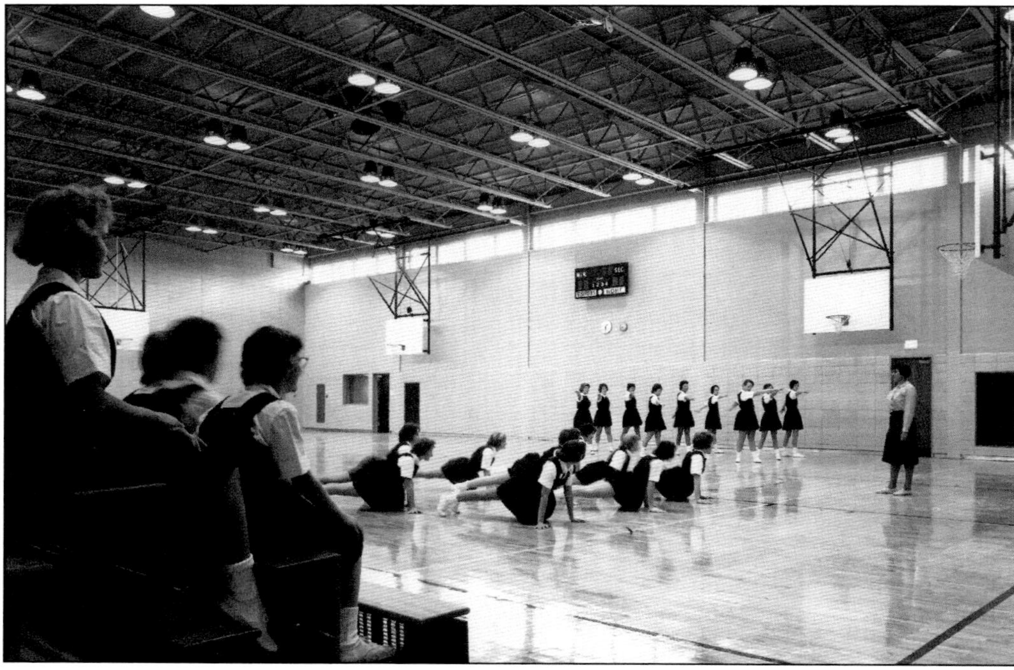

When the Mount moved to Flourtown in 1961, the students were thrilled to have a gymnasium complete with high ceilings. In addition to the home of physical education, the gymnasium also hosts pep rallies, Celebrauction, mixers, the Soph Hop, and Charity Day. Before 2000, the Mount nickname was the Chiefs, and the Chief mascot attended pep rallies and sporting events to boost school spirit. The Chief gave way to the Magic, a wizard adorned with purple and gold, who encourages fans to "believe in magic."

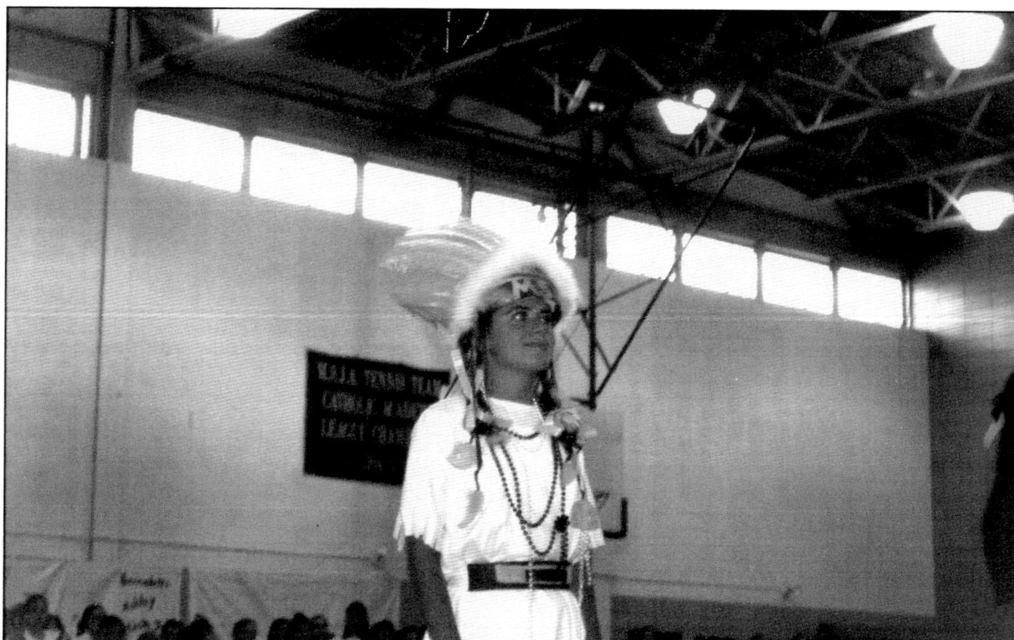

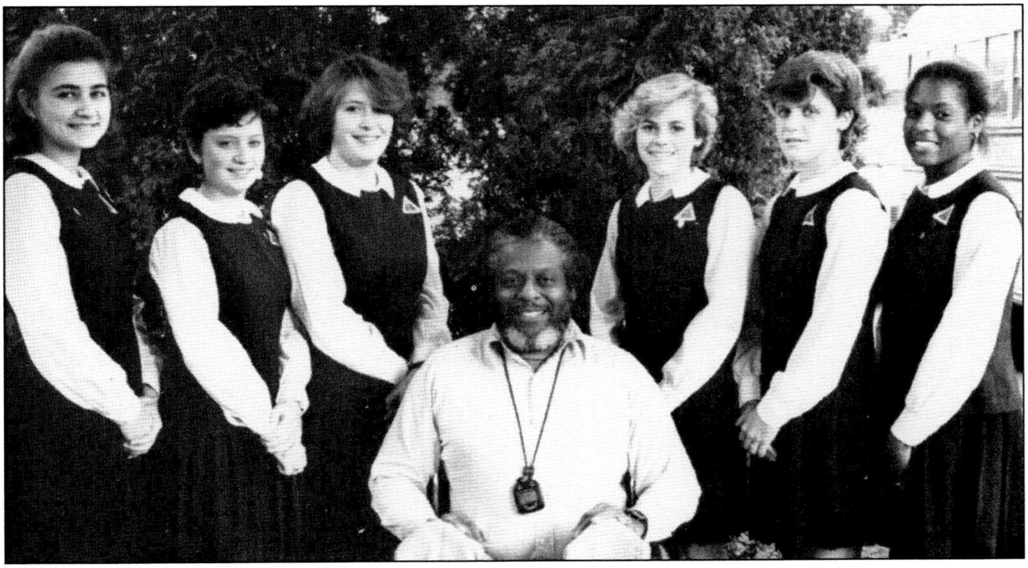

The Mount's track team in its inaugural 1985–1986 season was coached by Bill Guy. Father of Lisa Guy '86, a senior on the team, coach Guy embodied sportsmanship and success by leading the 21-member team to qualify for state championship meets in its first indoor season. Along with his daily regimen of sprints on the Valley Green trail and three laps around the infamous "Mount Mile," he is fondly remembered for encouraging each of his runners to beat her personal best.

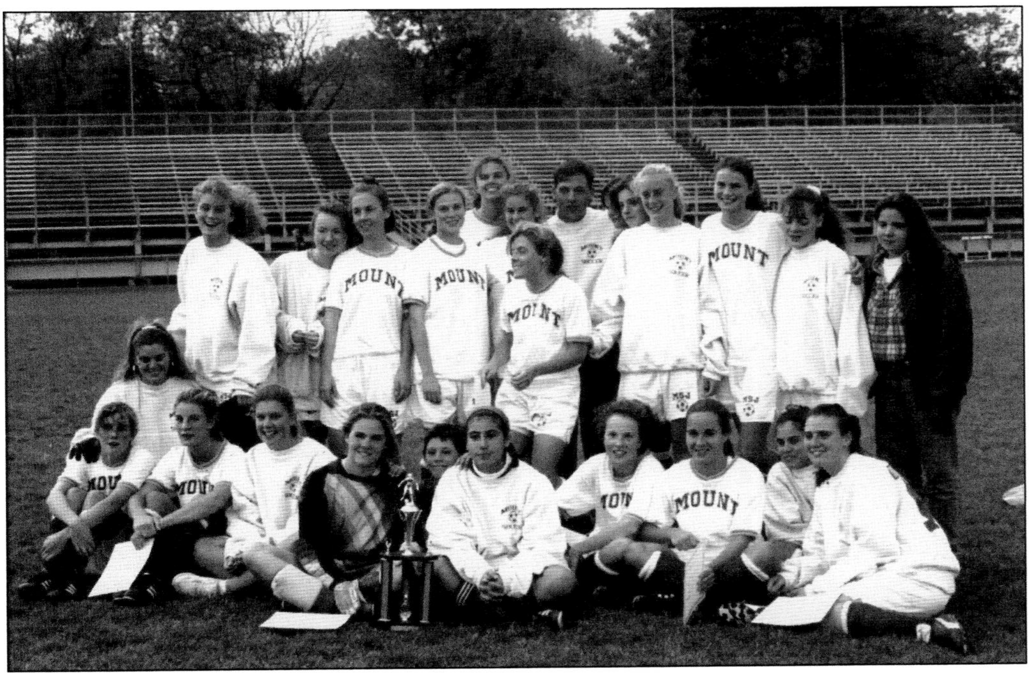

The Mount competes at both varsity and junior varsity levels in soccer. The 1993 Mount soccer team made it to the Pennsylvania Interscholastic Athletic Association (PIAA) District I girls championship game but was defeated by Catholic Academy league rival Villa Joseph Marie at the United German Hungarian Club.

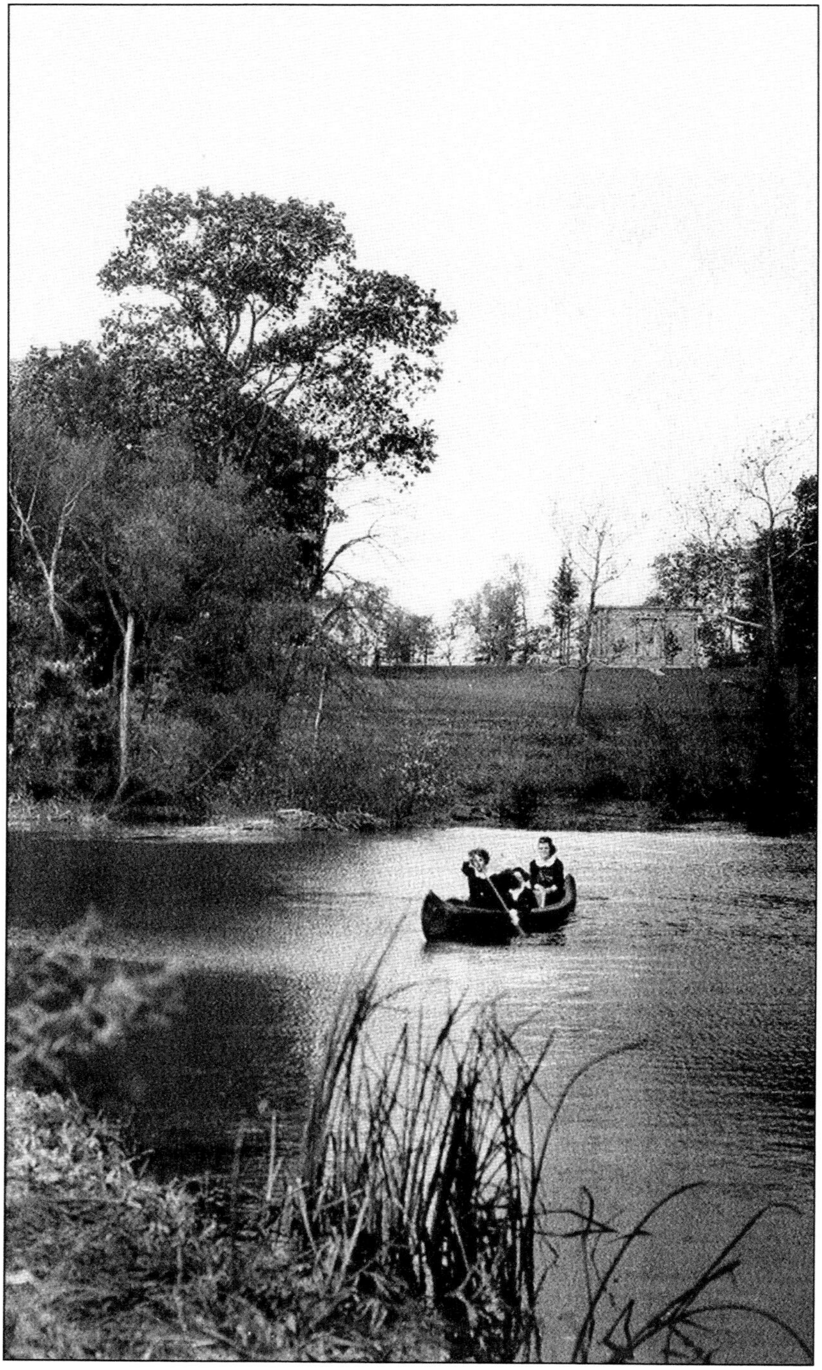

Before 1900, Mounties could be seen on the Wissahickon Creek in two boats they called *May Queen* and *St. John*. Mount crew had its early roots in the 1920s along the Wissahickon, where the school had built a boathouse that housed canoes. The girls took the boats out during their recreation time. After Chestnut Hill College opened, the girls occasionally put canoes in the swimming pool.

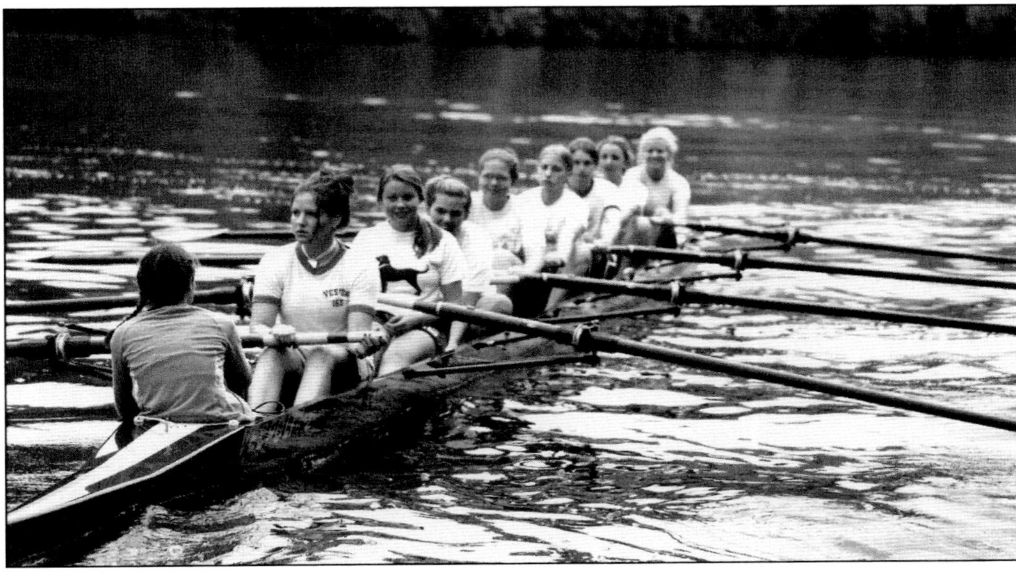

Since its revival in 2000, crew has become one of the most popular Mount sports. Girls can be found on the water in fall and winter, but prime season is spring. Regattas are held on Sundays from mid-March to June, and many supporters line the banks of the Schuylkill River to cheer on the girls.

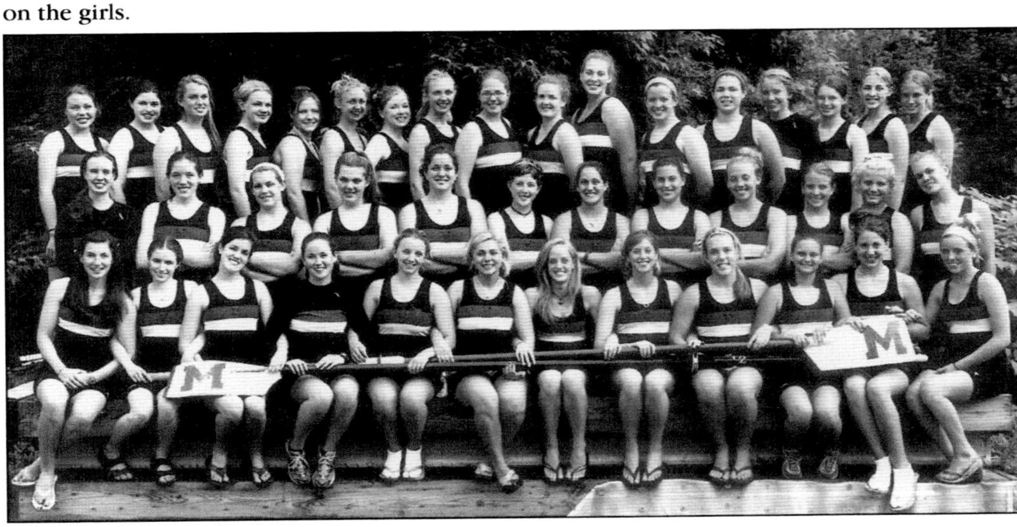

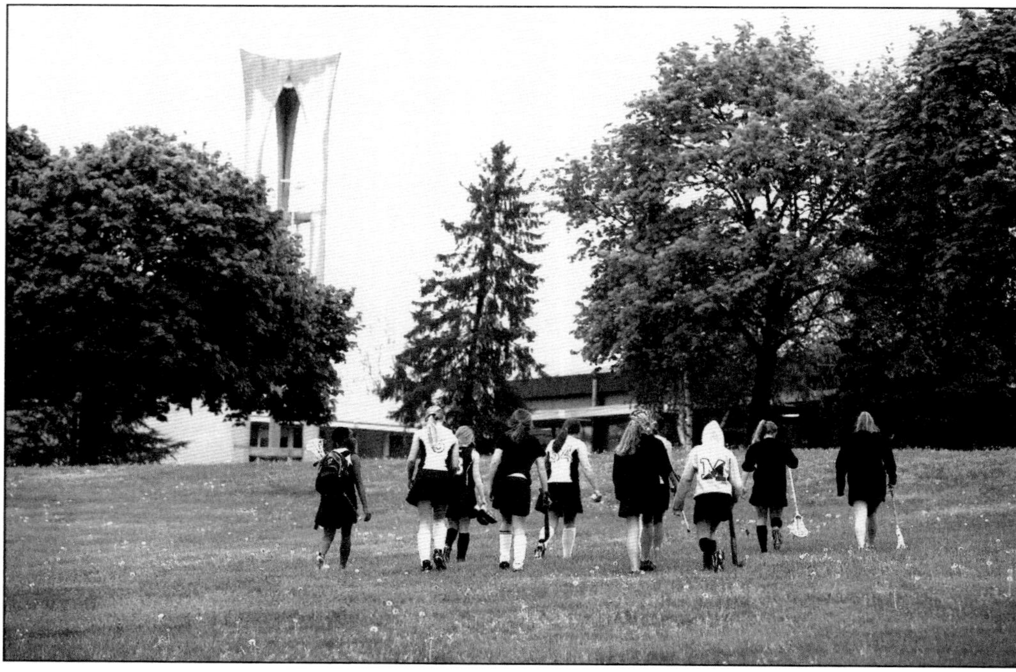

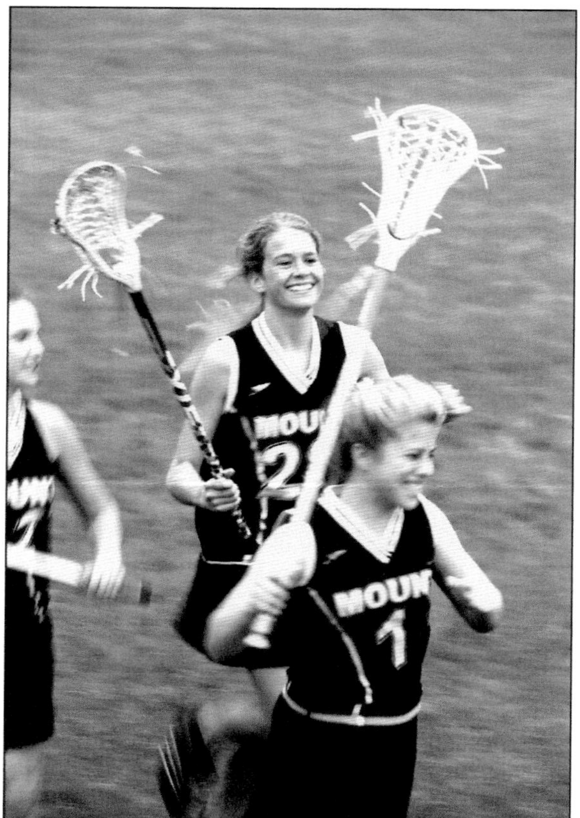

Lacrosse, which has become an increasingly popular sport in the northeastern United States, began as an official Mount sport in 1991. Tryouts are held in March each year, and the season extends through May.

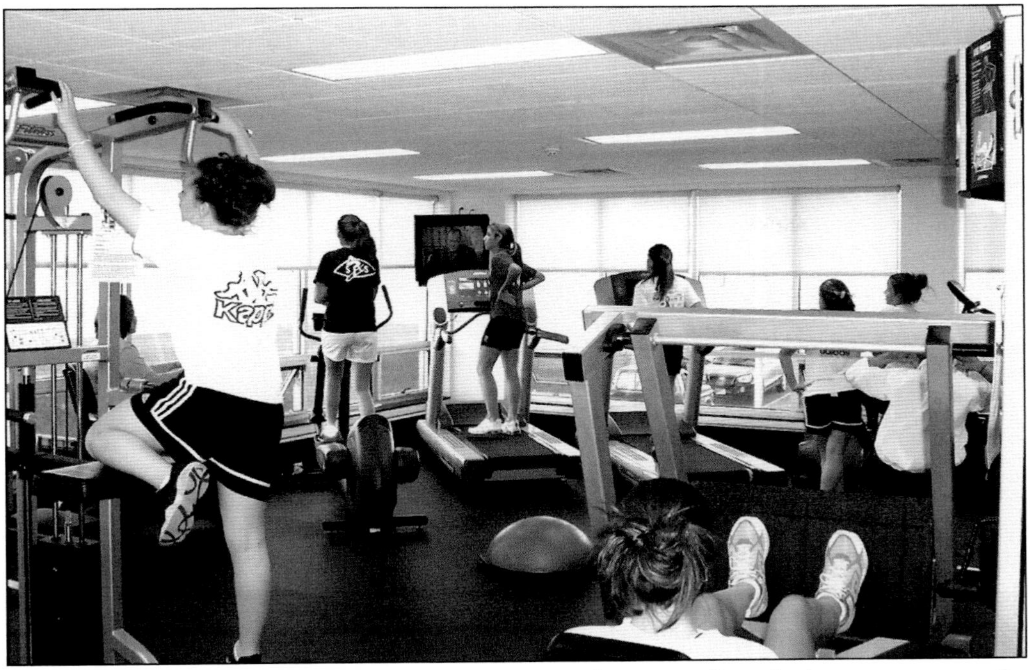

Strong minds, strong bodies. The Sisters of Saint Joseph continually make improvements to the school's athletic fields and resources. In 2003, the gymnasium area was renovated to include a new locker room, a health-class area, and a state-of-the-art fitness center. In fall 2004, a new track surrounding a soccer field was completed, along with two new softball fields.

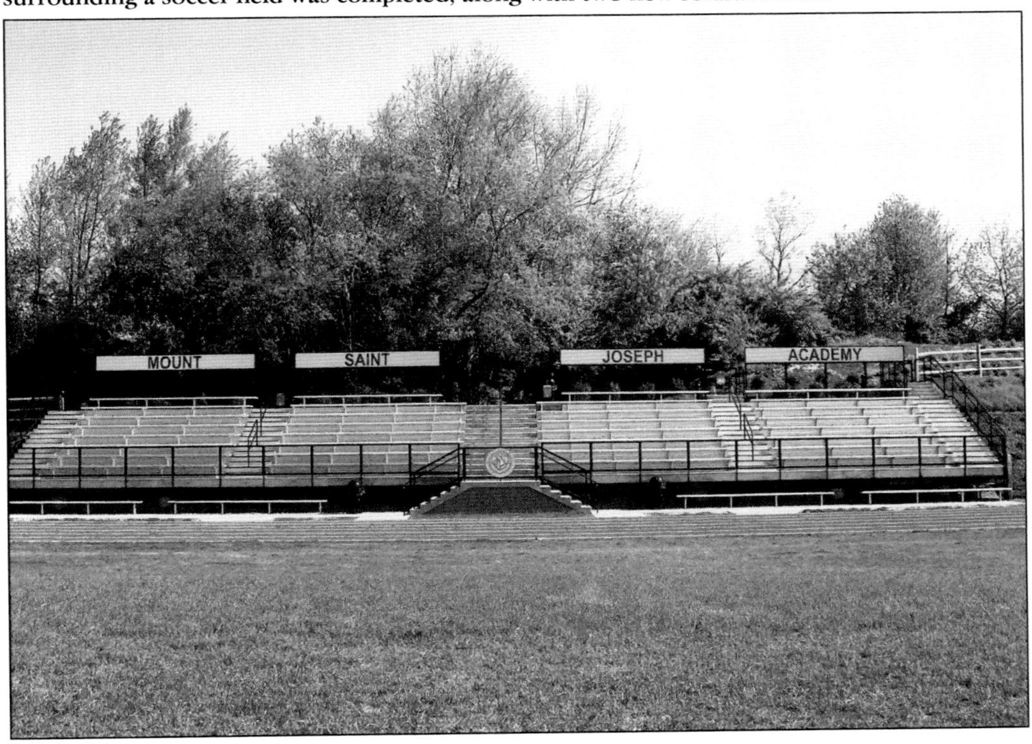

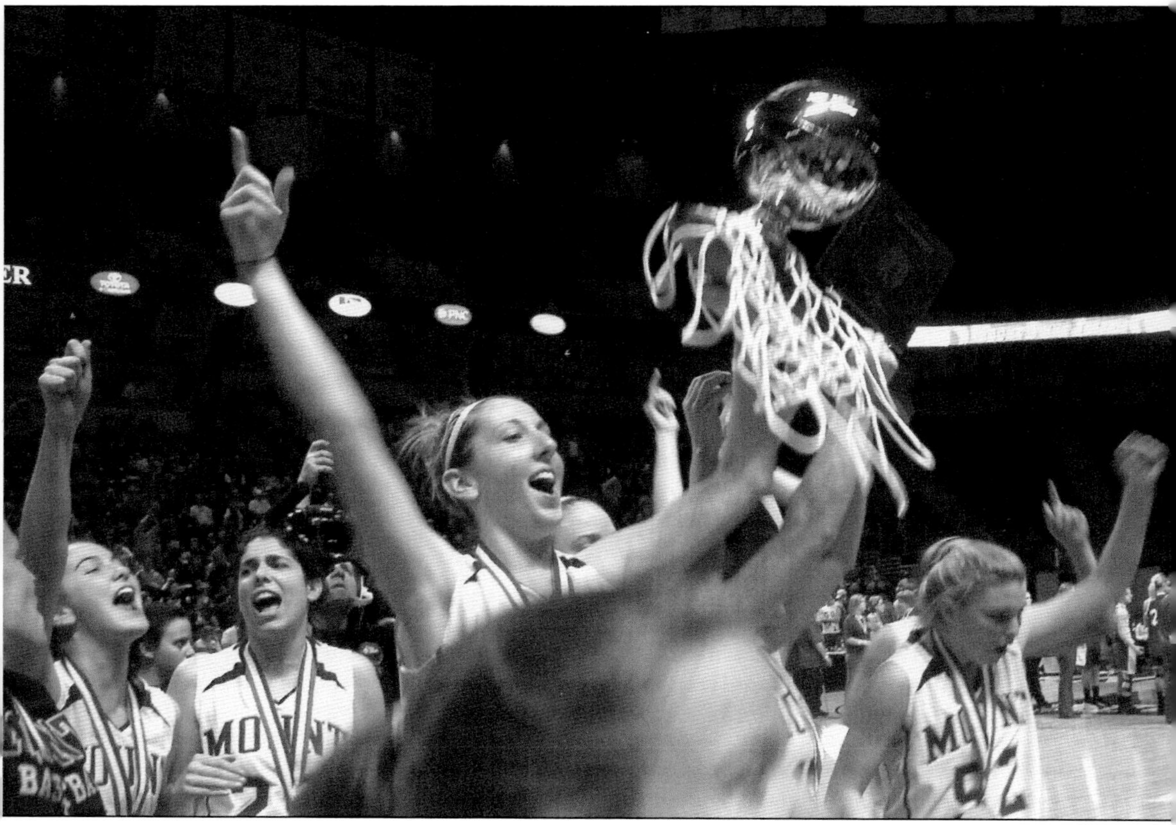

In March 2008, the Mount Magic basketball team won the PIAA Class AAA state championship game at Pennsylvania State University, toppling Erie's Mercyhurst Prep, 53-43. It was the Mount's first state championship and drew three busloads of students to Happy Valley. The Magic, under coach John Miller, finished the season 29-3 overall.

Five

MUSIC AND THE ARTS

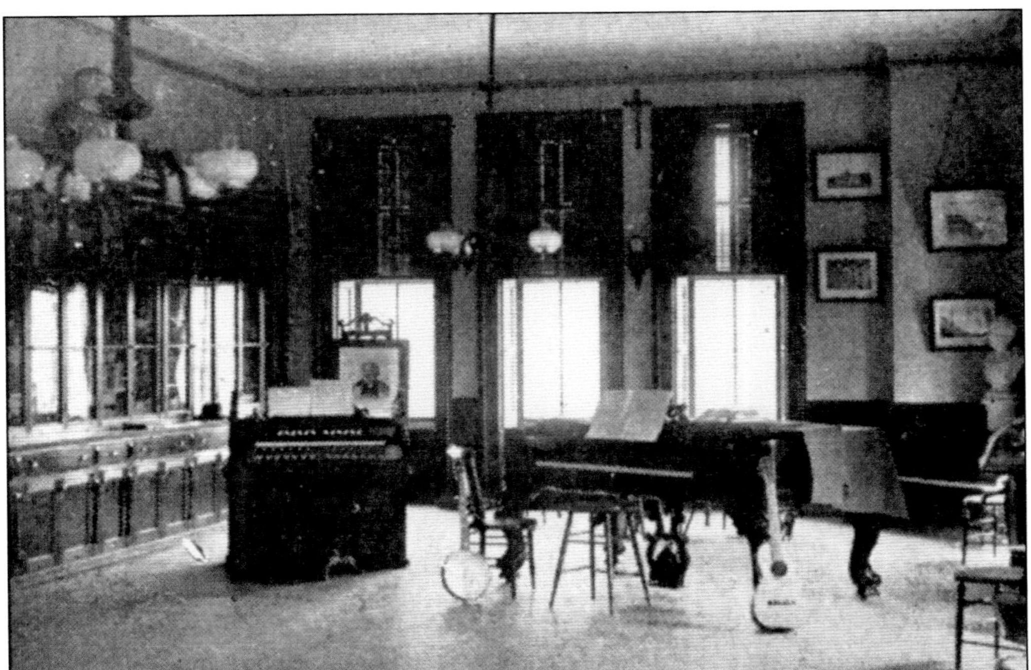

When Bishop John Neumann presided at the first commencement of Mount Saint Joseph Academy, he was delighted in the ability of the new school to produce such a first-rate program of music and drama. One of the Mount's earliest records details the moving of a piano from the library in 1875 (above), which the girls wanted for the recreation hall. The tab was $20.

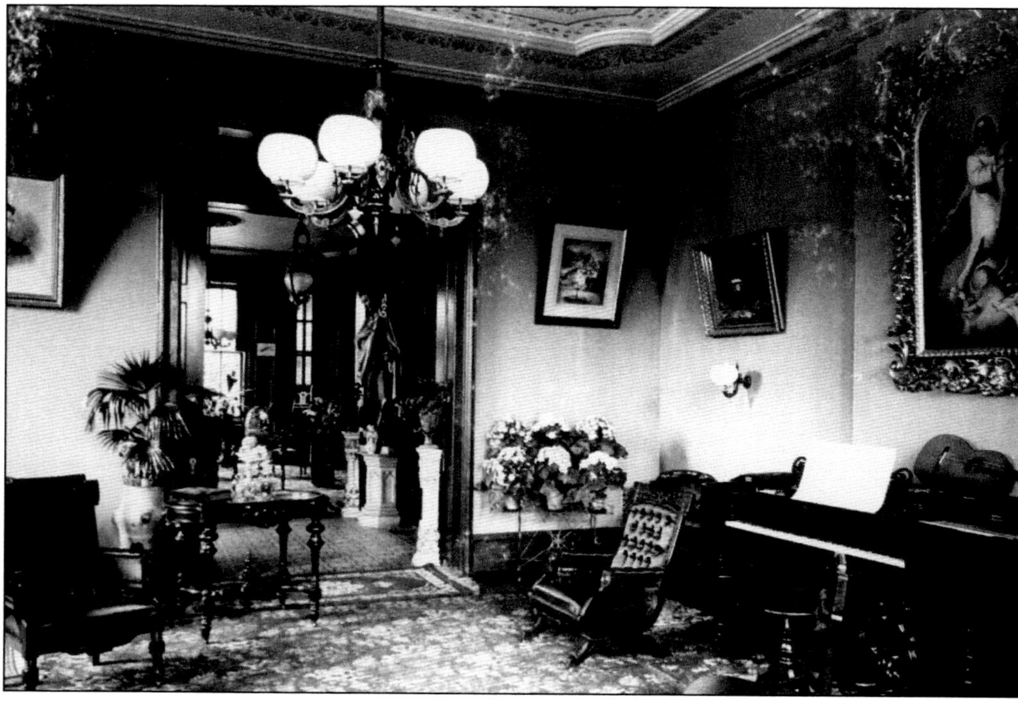

Between 1859 and 1883, two of the six headings in the Mount's curriculum were instrumental music and religious music, and melodies rang throughout the corridors. In 1890, organ and guitar pupils practiced in individual rooms. Before 1900, harp was an elective, for which an additional fee was charged. Instruments were not limited to the music room, as this 1875 view of the parlor shows. After the new academy opened in 1903, the music continued to resonate. In 1918, the school orchestra played for the first time in public, and it was common to hear the orchestra performing in the auditorium under the chapel. This auditorium was also used for other musical and theater performances.

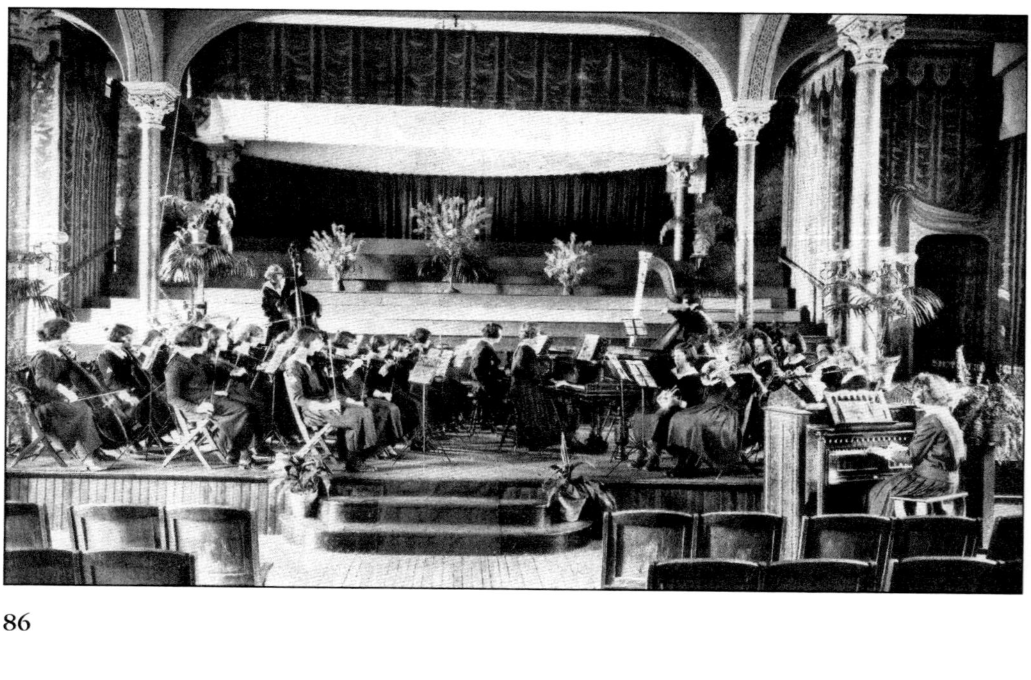

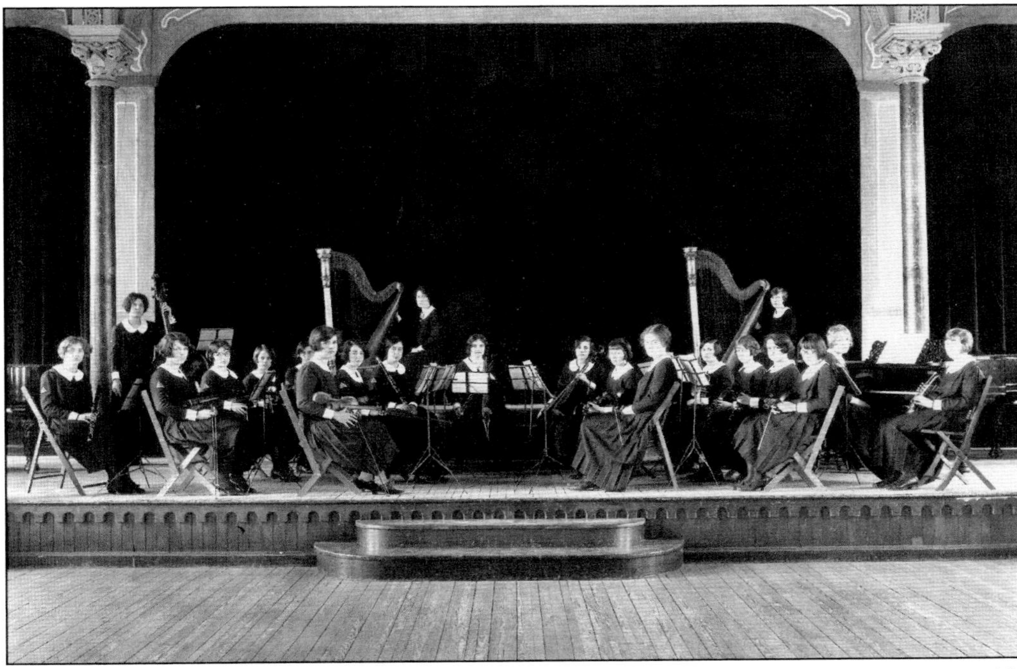

Instruments in the orchestra included pianos, organs, guitars, and harps. Through ensemble work, students became skilled in both concentration and synchronization. The work of the school orchestra attracted a great deal of interest from the Philadelphia Orchestra and vice versa; the girls made regular trips to see the Philadelphians at the Academy of Music. Since the Sisters of Saint Joseph could not attend nighttime performances, Mount conductor Benjamin D'Amelio arranged for them to attend afternoon rehearsals. In these photographs, the Mount's orchestra performs in the auditorium in the 1940s and poses in the rotunda of Saint Joseph's Hall.

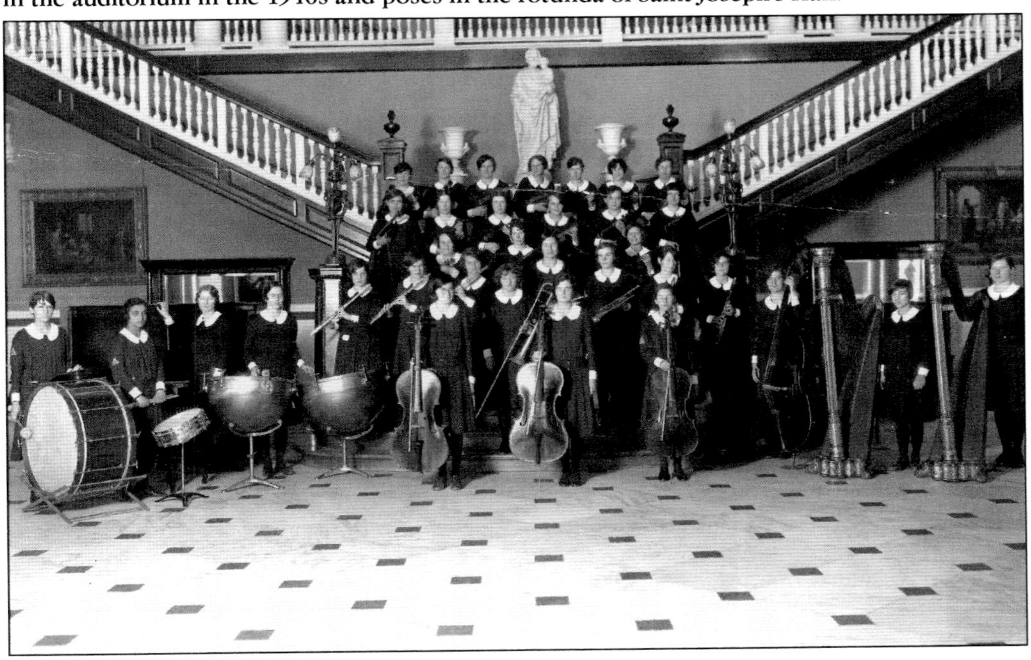

Mount St. Joseph's Academy,

CHESTNUT HILL,

Thursday, June 25th, 1874.

Programme.

LA CHASSE, - - - ORGAN AND FOUR PIANOS,
Misses M. Murphy, M. Nixon, E. Greene, K. Murphy, M. Tischner,

SALUTATORY, - - Composed by Miss J. Whitcomb,

WELCOME OF THE SEASONS, - - - CHORUS,
ACCOMP. - - - - - - TWO PIANOS,
Misses M. Mathieu, E. Taylor, R. Barr', S. McGee,

WHITE ROSE POLKA, - - - - FOUR PIANOS,
Misses L. Mathieu, Fitzpatrick, McLerney, Mealey, Gardner,
Tompkins, Holt, Gibbs, Apeldorn, M. McNickle,
McGinty, McGowan.

DREAMS OF MY HOME, - - - - QUARTETTE,
Misses R. Barr', L. Tingley, M. Jennings, E. Greene,
ACCOMP. - - - - - Miss M. Mathieu,

ÆSTAS, LATIN ODE, - - - - - Miss A. Heard,

MARCHE DU PROPHÈTE, - - - - - FOUR PIANOS,
Misses Greene, Whitcomb, Taylor, Tischner, Burke, Healey,
A. McNickle, Tingley.

LA CHASSE AUX PAPILLONS, - - - - CHORUS,
ACCOMP. - - - - - - Miss J. Whitcomb,

MEMORY, - - - - - Composed by Miss A. Biers,

ERIN IS MY HOME, - - - - - Miss M. Murphy,
ACCOMP. - - - - - Miss K. Murphy,

During Mount Saint Joseph Academy's era as a boarding school, the girls performed shows for their parents' weekend visits. These were lively productions—operettas, dramas, melodramas, and tableaus—and programs were created as keepsakes. Mother St. John Fournier wrote many of the plays.

Programme.

OVERTURE,—"Poet and Peasant," . . TWO PIANOS,
Misses M. Nixon, E. Greene, M. Taylor, A. Biers,

SALUTATORY, ... Miss M. Murphy,
Composed by Miss M. Harrity,

NATIONAL SONG, ... CHORUS,
ACCOMP. . . . Misses E. Greene, A. Lawlor,

SCHUBERT'S SERENADE, . ORGAN and TWO PIANOS,
Misses J. Fitzgerald, K. Nowlan, M. Nixon,

FAIRY BOWERS, ... CHORUS,
ACCOMP. . . . . . Miss M. Mathieu,

THE ADOPTED CHILD,

Misses M. Harrity, M. Gardner,

MARCH, ... THREE PIANOS,
Misses M. Tischner, R. Barr', A. Heard, A. Durney, E. Taylor,
T. Burke, M. Stinson, M. McDonald, A. McNickle,

O RESTLESS SEA, ... TRIO,
Misses A. Biers, E. Maguire, M. Nixon, R. Barr', E. Greene,
ACCOMP. . . . . Miss M. Tischner,

THE SISTERS, . . . Misses J. Whitcomb, K. Nowlan,

THE MUSICAL FAMILY, - . By the Little Misses,
ACCOMP. . . . . . Miss L. Mathieu,

SILVER TRUMPETS MARCH, . . FOUR PIANOS,
Misses A. Lawlor, K. Nowlan, M. Murphy, J. Whitcomb,
M. Harrity, M. Mathieu, J. Fitzgerald, A. Durney,

THE LITTLE SHAMROCK, , ... GUITAR,
Misses M. Gardner, K. Deal, M. McGowan, K. Clark,

LE RETOUR DU PRINTEMPS, . . . CHORUS,
ACCOMP. . . . . Miss J. Whitcomb,

CASTA DIVA, ... PIANO and ORGAN,
Misses A. Biers, R. Barr'

TUSCAN GIRLS CROWNING THE SEA,

QUEEN, ... Miss M. Murphy.
SEA-NYMPH, ... " M. Tischner,
MAIDENS, . {Misses M. Taylor, M. McDonald, K. Nowlan,
M. Stinson, A. Lawlor, M. Mathieu,

SCHOTTISCHE, ... THREE PIANOS,
Misses L. Mathieu, K. Deal, L. Fitzpatrick, E. Holt, A. Young,
S. Pelouze, M. McGowan, M. McNickle, M. Gardner,

PROPERZIA ROSSI, ... Miss A. Heard,
"Properzia Rossi," a female artist, celebrated for her misfortunes, though more for her proficiency in sculpture, painting and music, died of a broken heart, just as Pope Clement VII had invited her to Rome, to show his admiration for her masterpiece in the Church of San Petronio, at Bologna.

O JESU, O PASTOR, ... QUARTETTE,
Misses M. Taylor, A. Biers, K. Nowlan, M. Nixon,
M. Jennings, E. Greene, M. Murphy, M. Mathieu,
ORGAN ACCOMP. . . . . Miss J. Fitzgerald.

DISTRIBUTION OF PREMIUMS.

FAREWELL SONG, (Words by Miss A. Lawlor,) CHORUS,
ACCOMP. . . . Misses M. Murphy, M. Harrity,

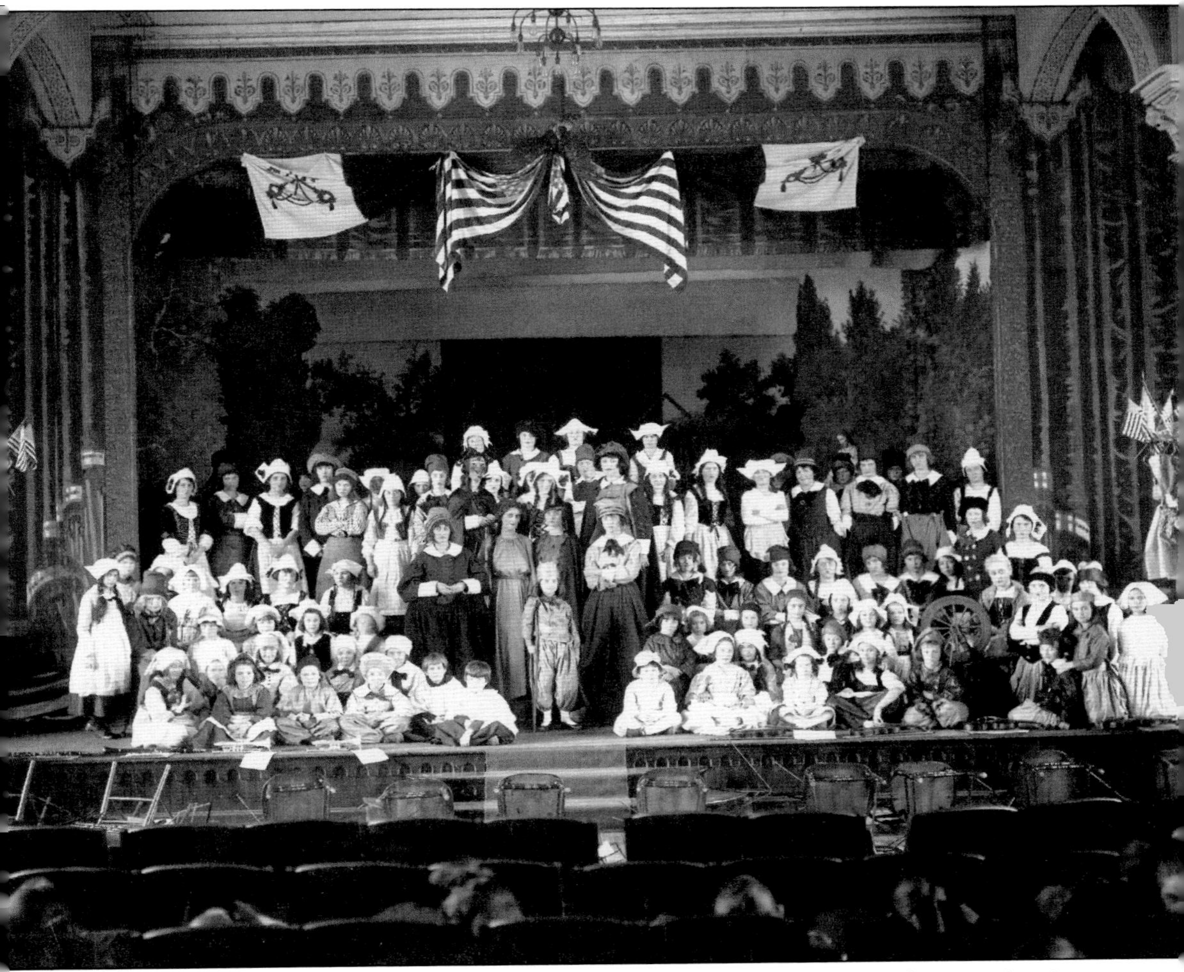

Dramatic productions took on a cultural flair in the early 1900s, with students performing plays in French, Latin, and German. In 1912–1913, *Barbe Blue* was a popular production. In 1932, German students traveling under sponsorship of the German Consulate presented an old medieval miracle play, *Der Tod*, in their native language. Early shows at the Mount often included young students from Norwood Academy and Fontbonne Hall. This show took place in 1937.

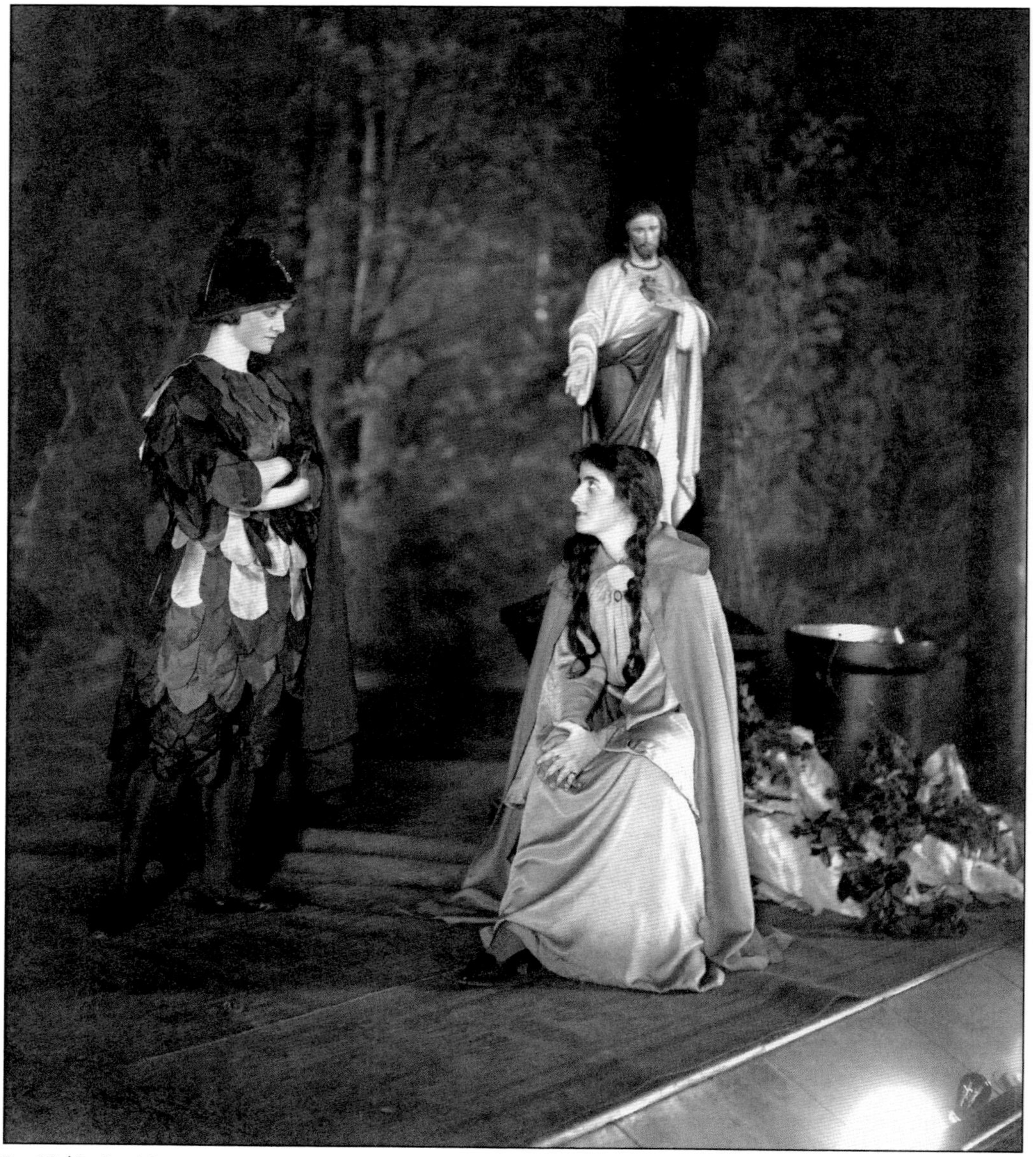

In 1940, Sr. Mary Gervace organized a dramatic society known as the Acadram to produce a Christmas play, operetta, and May Day festival production. This photograph shows one of the earlier Acadram performances. In the late 1960s, the Acadram show was performed for Mount students at an assembly, with one performance only. Today, Acadram, moderated by Jean Korey, has a dedicated group of participants and rehearses four times a week for six weeks, with three performances over one weekend.

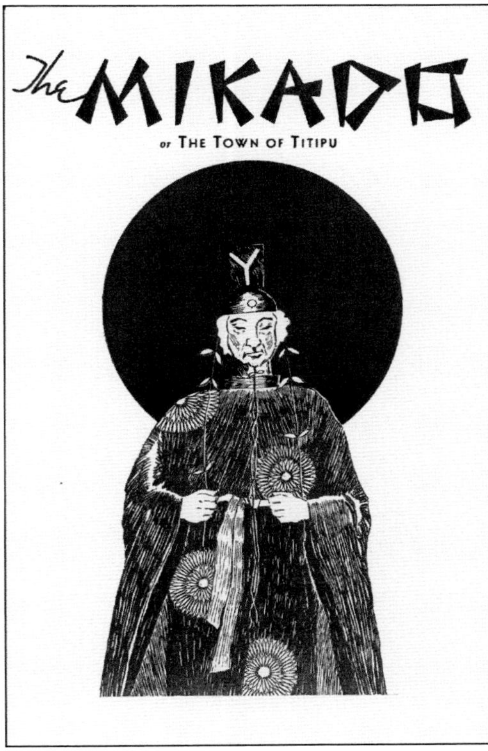

These show programs were created for Mount musical theater performances. *The Mikado* was performed in the auditorium under the chapel when the Mount was in Chestnut Hill. In 1953, Mount girls presented a shortened version of the show on the *Young Pennsylvanians* radio program. *Peter Pan* was performed in 1985 in the 600-seat Fournier Auditorium.

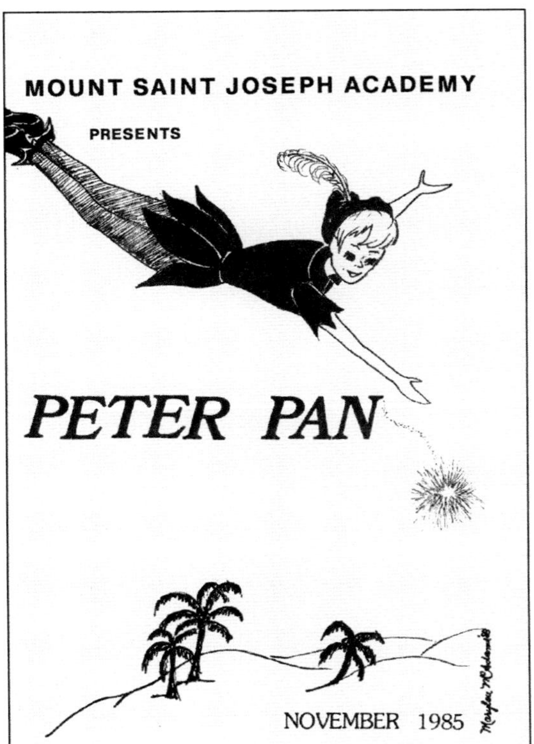

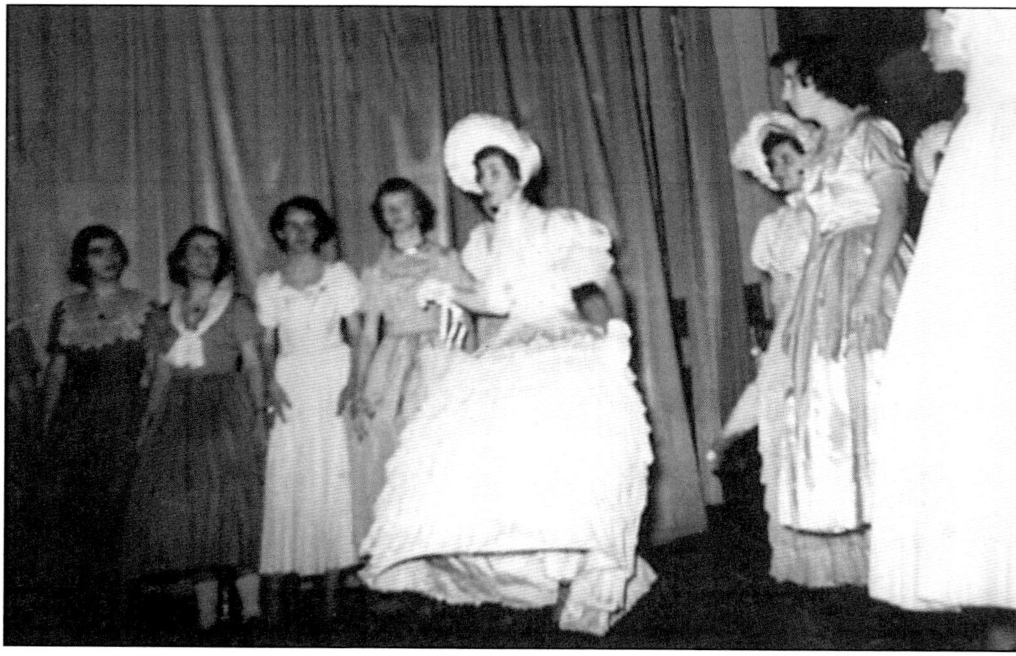

Musical theater became increasingly popular, and the girls began to perform famous shows, such as *Blossom Time* (above), which was the second-longest-running Broadway musical of the 1920s. This 1950 production was directed by Sr. Marie Therese. After the Mount moved to Flourtown, the annual musical has been one of the most anticipated fall happenings, with sell-out crowds on November performance weekends. For this 2004 production of *Les Miserables* (below), Renee Veneziale '86 (who played Eponine in the first national touring company of *Les Mis*) returned to her alma mater as a member of the audience at the November 14 performance. She joined the cast in their traditional circle before the start of the show. (Above, courtesy of Lorraine Sukalski McGlynn '52.)

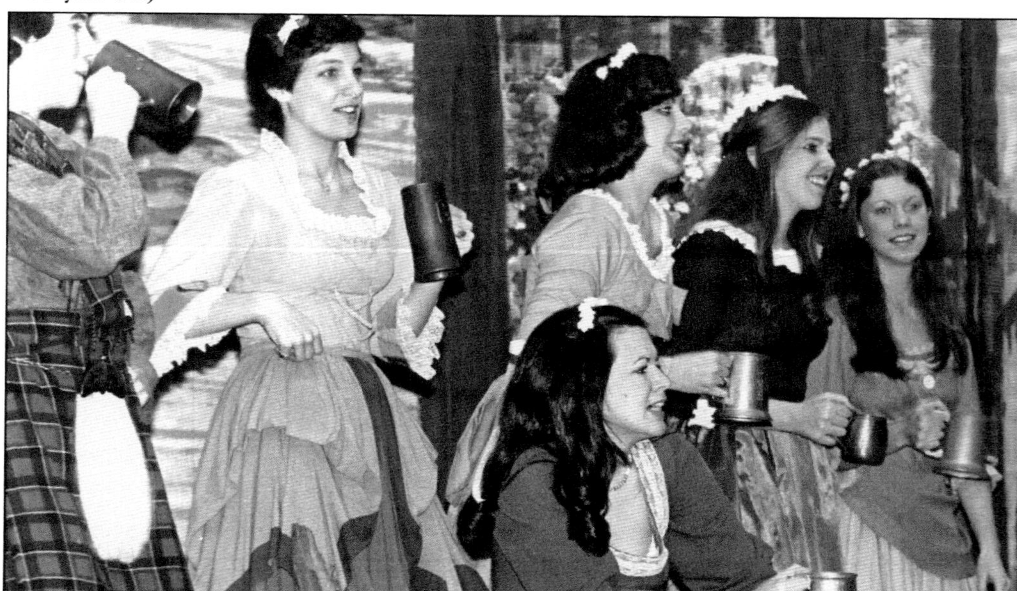

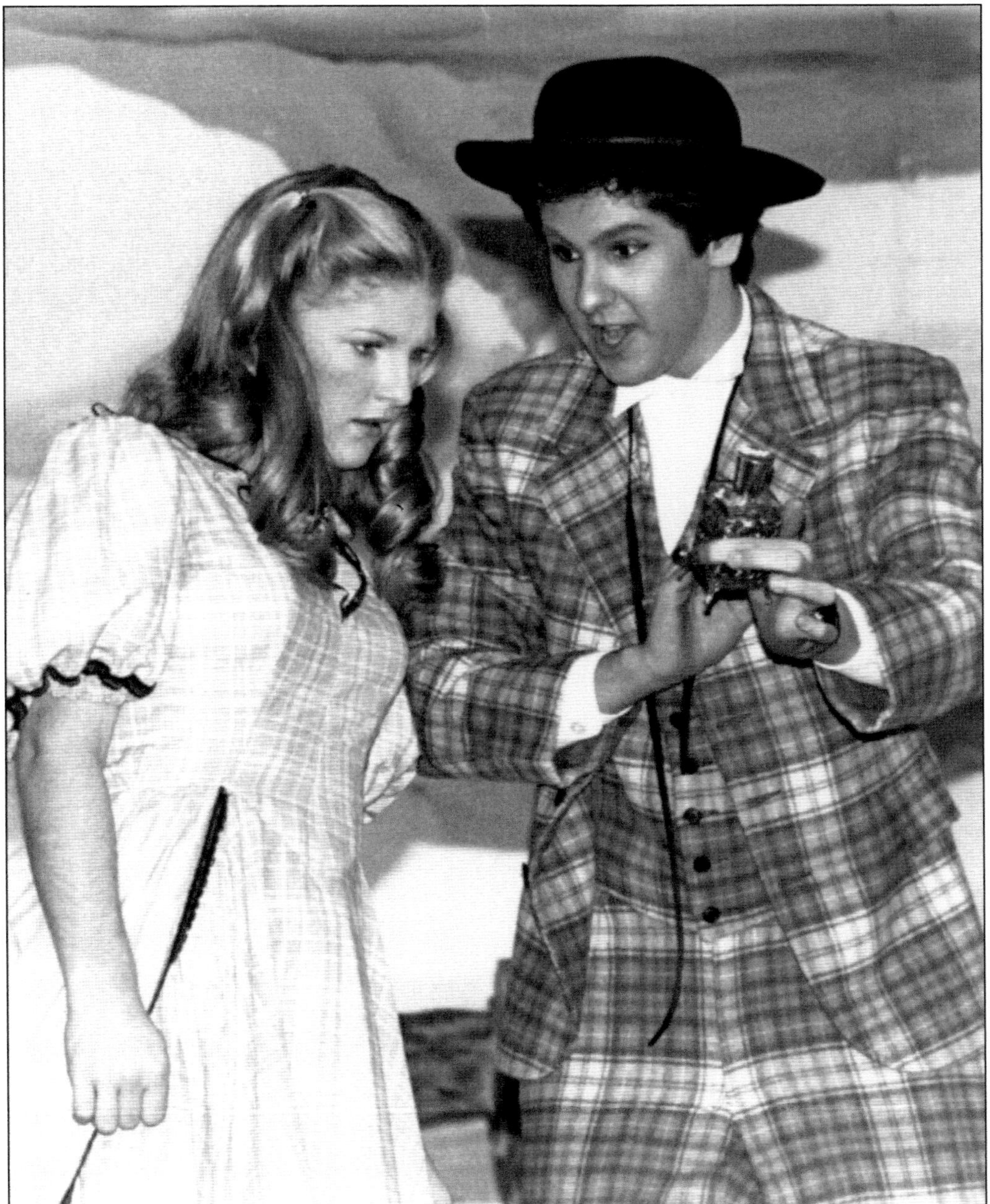

In 1980, the Mount staged *Oklahoma!* In the earlier days, one of the challenges of an all-girls' school was casting male parts. Until actors from nearby brother schools were enlisted for the male roles, as shown here, Mounties played both male and female roles. One of Mount's strengths is the arts, and the school awards piano, voice, and art scholarships each year.

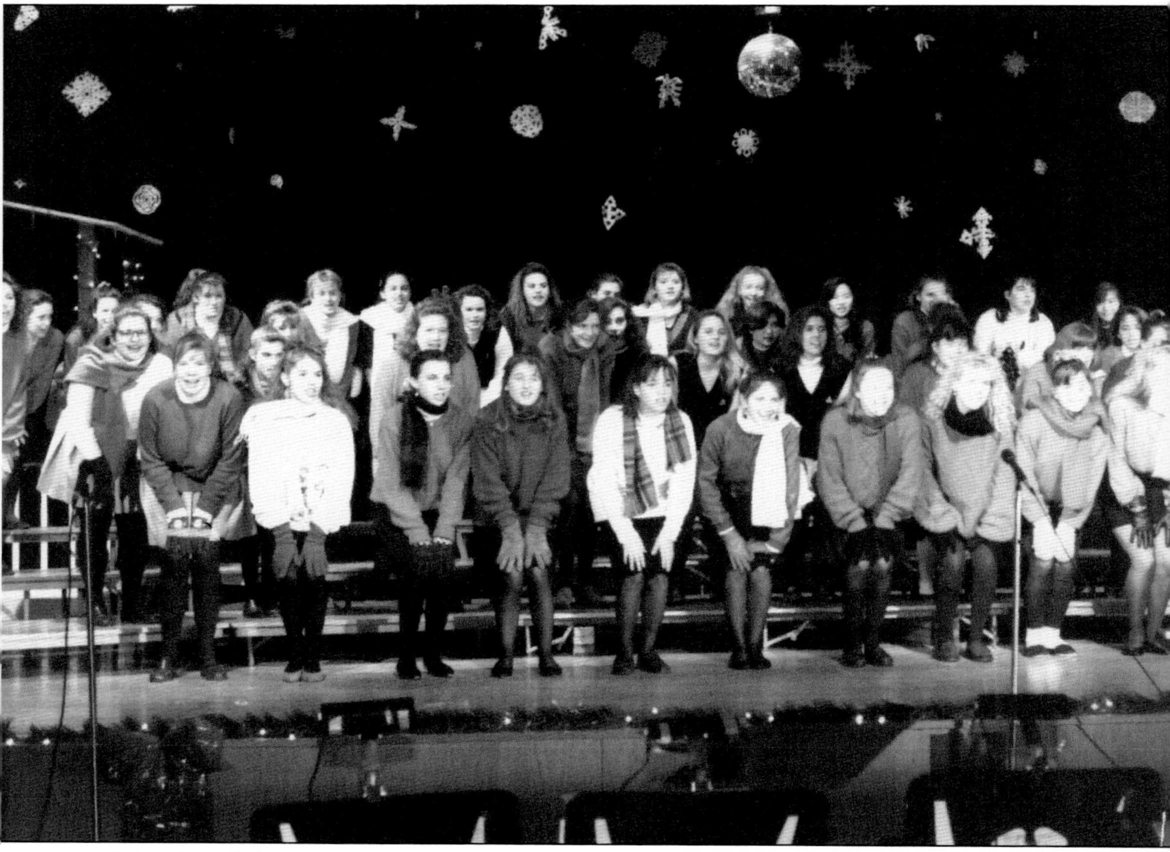

The Glee Club was organized by Sr. Regina Dolores in 1940. This group kept up the tradition of vocal music by singing the mass for Baccalaureate Day and performing on *The Catholic Hour*. Among the Glee Club's performances is the school's annual Christmas show, shown here in the early 1990s.

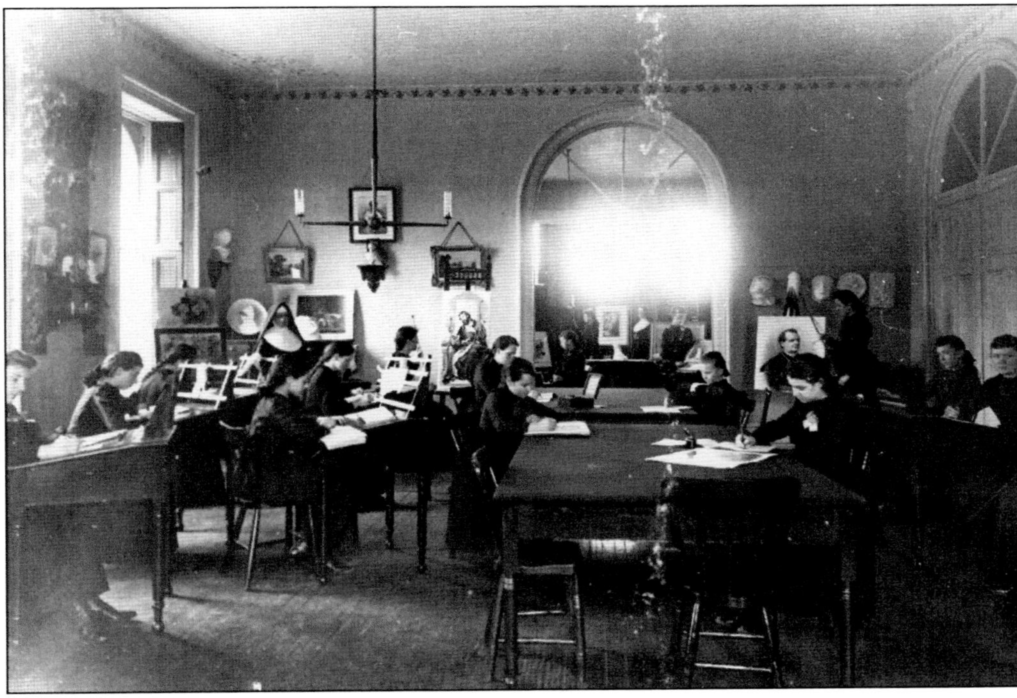

In this 1893 photograph, students attend an art class in the drawing room. Courses included oil painting, painting in watercolors and pastels, and drawing.

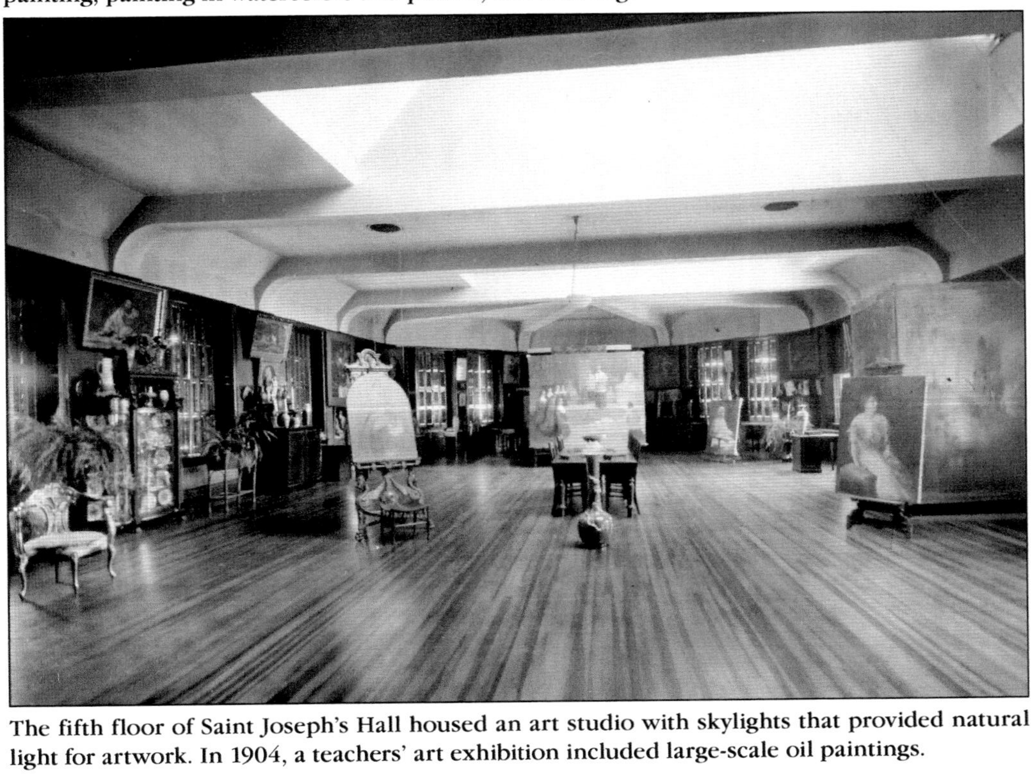

The fifth floor of Saint Joseph's Hall housed an art studio with skylights that provided natural light for artwork. In 1904, a teachers' art exhibition included large-scale oil paintings.

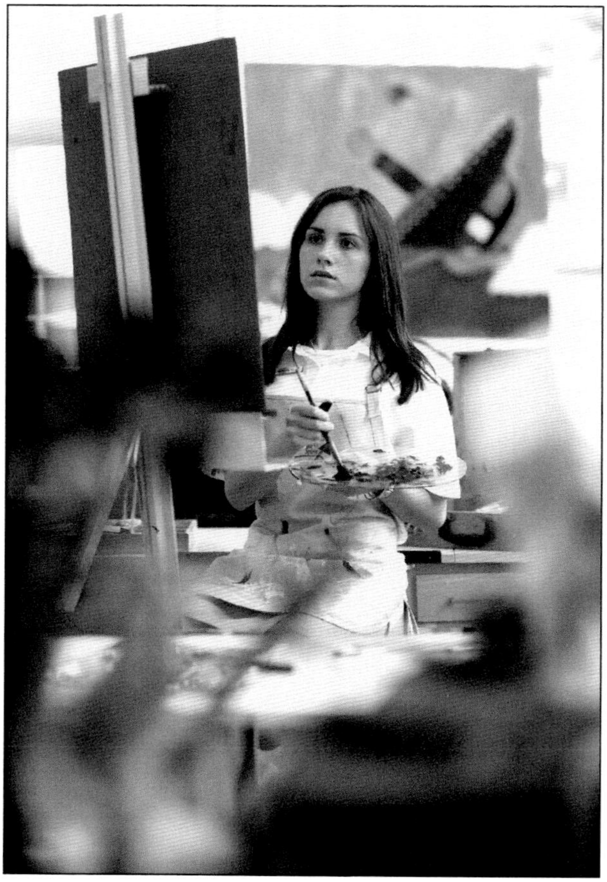

In 2003, the art and theater rooms were renovated and expanded. Today this area includes an airy painting and drawing room, a computer classroom equipped with 25 computer graphics systems, separate rooms for ceramics and a kiln, and an enlarged classroom for theater arts. Art classes at the Mount include design basics, color theory, painting, three-dimensional design, commercial design, art history, print media, and advertising. The case outside the art room displays the range of the students' work for passersby.

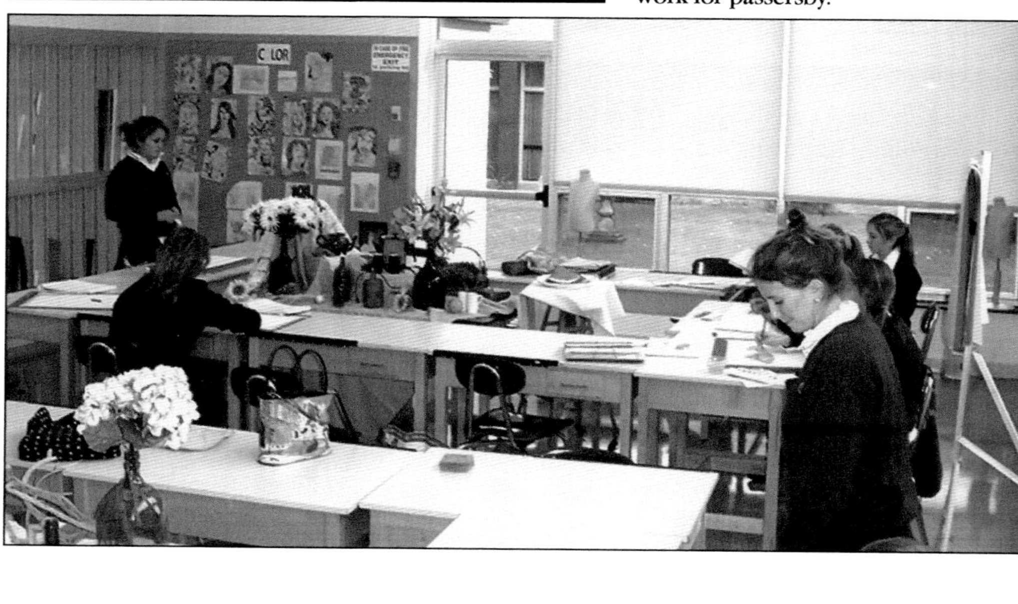

Six

Mount Traditions and Celebrations

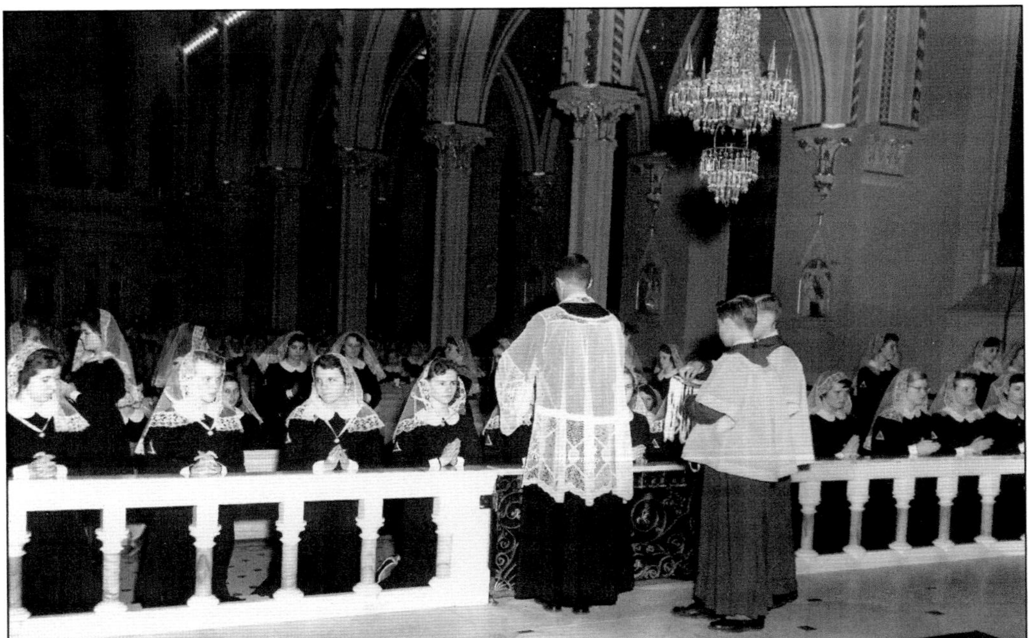

For more than 100 years, the Sodality of the Children of Mary, organized in 1866 by Mother Xavier Walker, was one of the most important aspects of spiritual life. Mounties of the 1940s and 1950s recall attending a January retreat in the convent chapel. After four months' preparation, the aspirants were received into the sodality and given the Medal of Mary. St. Joseph appeared on the reverse.

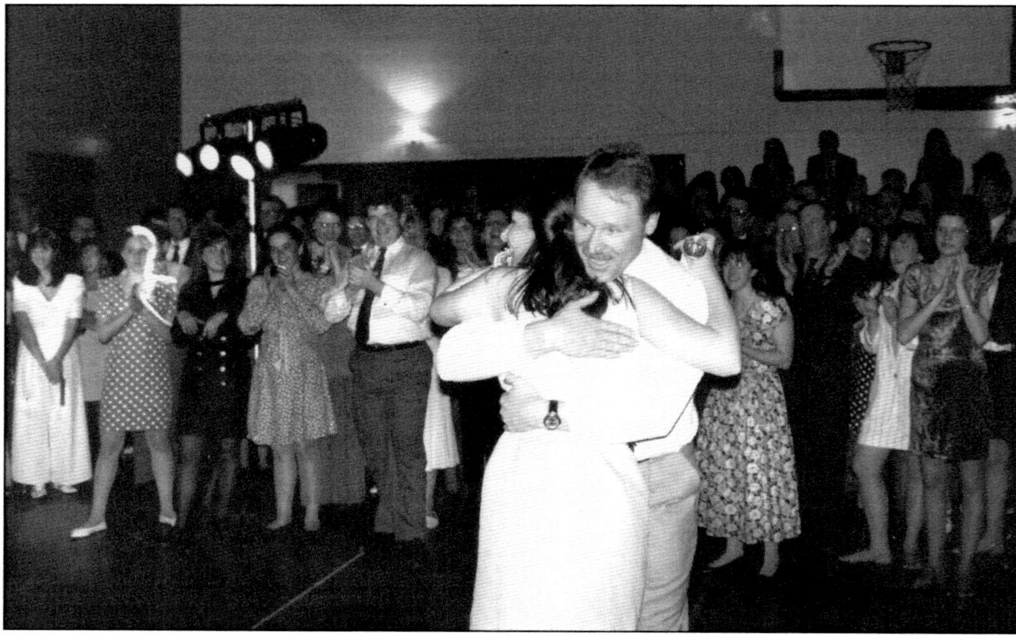

The father-daughter dance began in 1961 at Flourtown Country Club. Mothers attended in 1962, making it a threesome at Cedarbrook Country Club. By 1982, it was back to girls and dads only, in the gymnasium in March. This photograph dates from about 1993. The moms have their own event—the mother-daughter fashion show—each January.

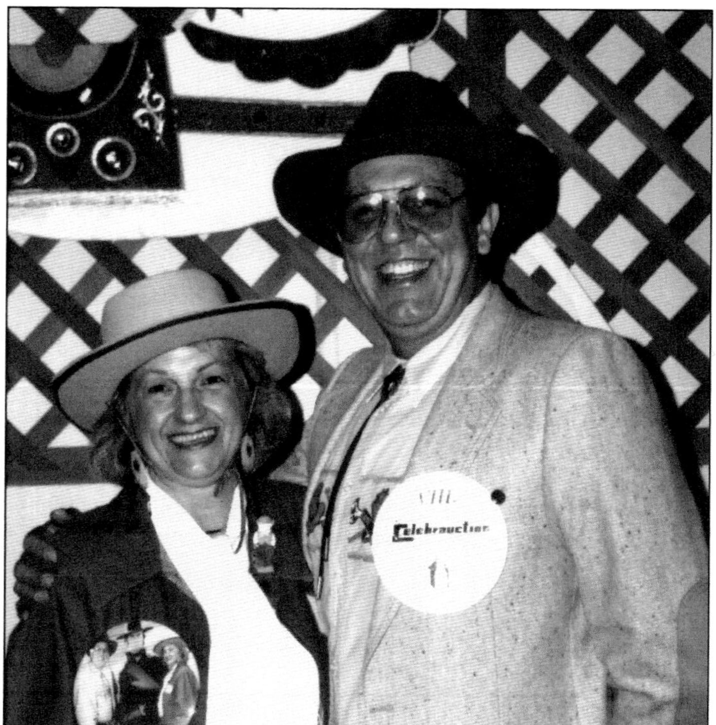

As the Mount marks its sesquicentennial, Celebrauction, the school's signature event and fund-raiser, celebrates its 25th anniversary. Chaired by parents of current students, Celebrauction brings together the entire Mount community for a black-tie-optional night of dinner and auctions (1992 saw a rodeo theme) in the gymnasium, emceed each year by William F. Comly and Son. In 1985, the most expensive item, a trip to Puerto Rico, sold for $950. The highest price in recent years was a $13,000 Napa Valley excursion. More than $300,000 was raised in 2008.

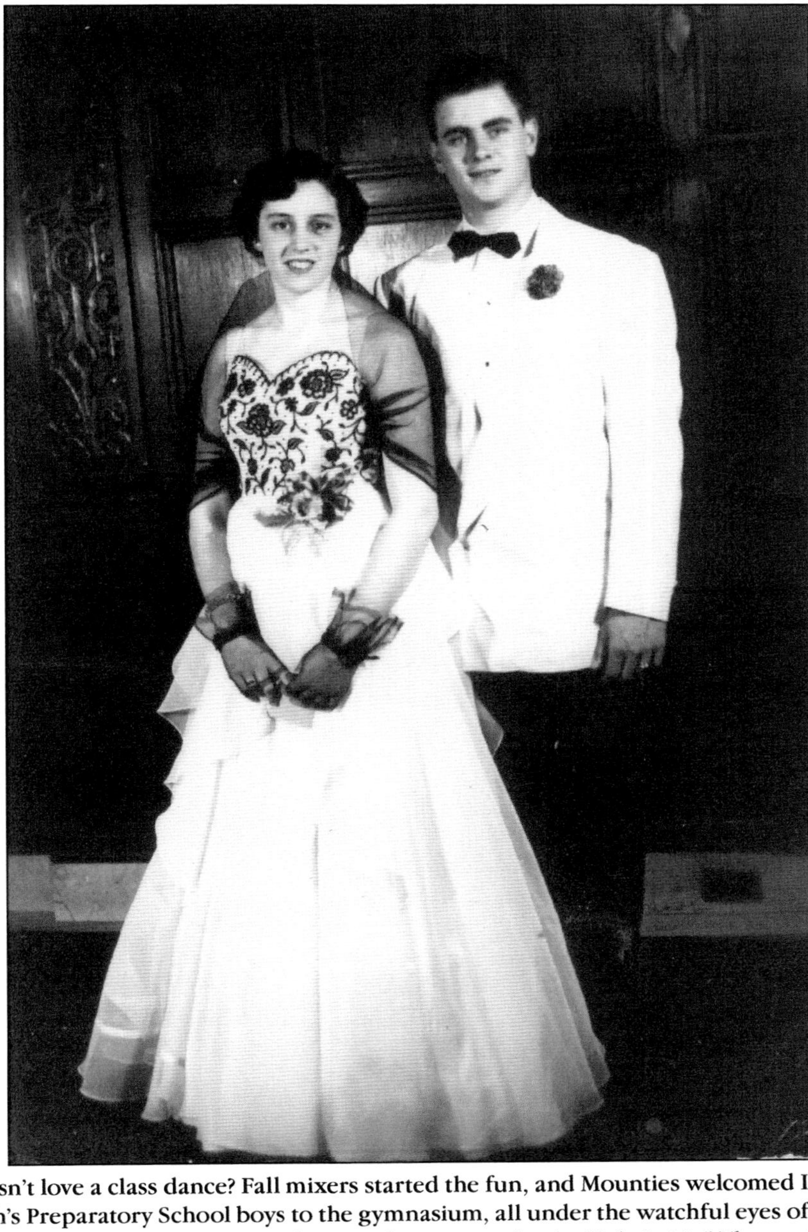

Who doesn't love a class dance? Fall mixers started the fun, and Mounties welcomed LaSalle and St. Joseph's Preparatory School boys to the gymnasium, all under the watchful eyes of the Sisters of Saint Joseph, who encouraged students to "leave room for the Holy Spirit." The semiformal for the underclassmen—the Soph Hop—was first held in Fontbonne in 1978. By the 1980s, themes for the gym dance ranged from "Stairway to Heaven" to "In Your Eyes" (with a special dedication to the chaperones, "Don't Stand So Close to Me"). January tea dances were popular in the 1940s and were held in the rotunda, allowing the sisters to watch from five balconies above. During World War II, the *Sheaflette*, a student-operated newspaper, lamented at the "shortage of men" for the tea dance. An editorial encouraged the establishment of a blind date bureau, which said it could not guarantee the looks of Tyrone Power, the dance floor wizardry of Fred Astaire, or the personality of Orson Welles, but would do its best to supply dates from "surplus brothers, cousins and friends."

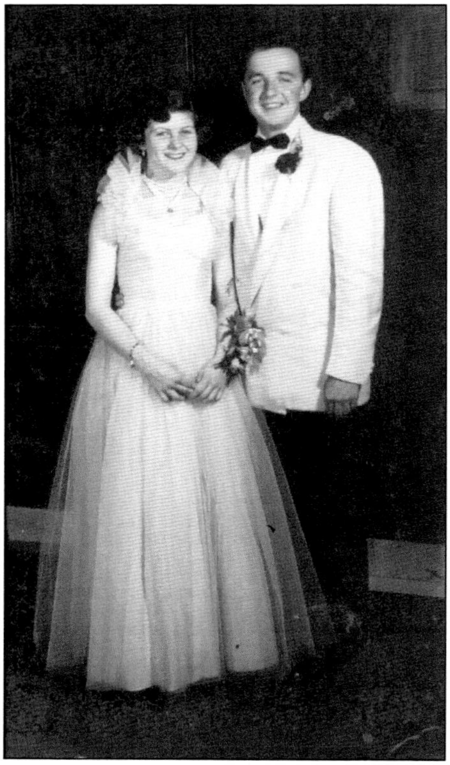

Surely there is no greater highlight than the prom. In the 1940s, both the junior and senior proms were held at the Barclay Hotel on Rittenhouse Square (below). By 1967, the seniors gathered at Flourtown Country Club for prom, and Inn of the Four Falls for the post-prom party, both with live bands. The Academy of Music hosted the class of 1969's senior prom, with a post-prom at Flourtown Country Club.

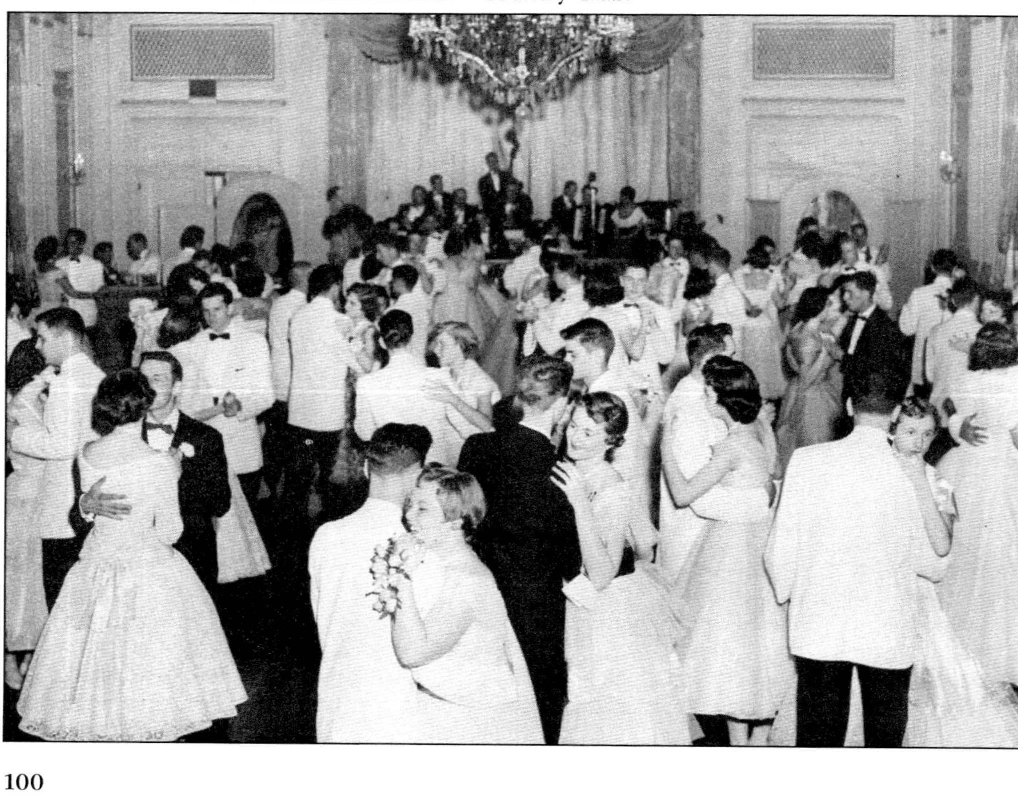

By 1983 (at right is Angel Stout '83), Whitemarsh Valley Country Club hosted many a junior and senior prom. The Jefferson House hosted the class of 1990's senior prom. Prom themes of the late 1980s and 1990s included "Wonderful Tonight," "Eternal Flame," "And We Danced," and "I've Had the Time of My Life." Today the junior and senior proms are held at Whitemarsh. Receiving lines were a staple of all Mount dances since at least the 1940s. Members of the class of 1990, shown below at their junior prom at Whitemarsh Valley Country Club, had the chance to practice their manners as they introduced their dates to principal Sr. Mary Dacey (right, at rear) and administrators. Dates' names and schools were registered in advance, and Mountie parents attended a mandatory pre-prom meeting.

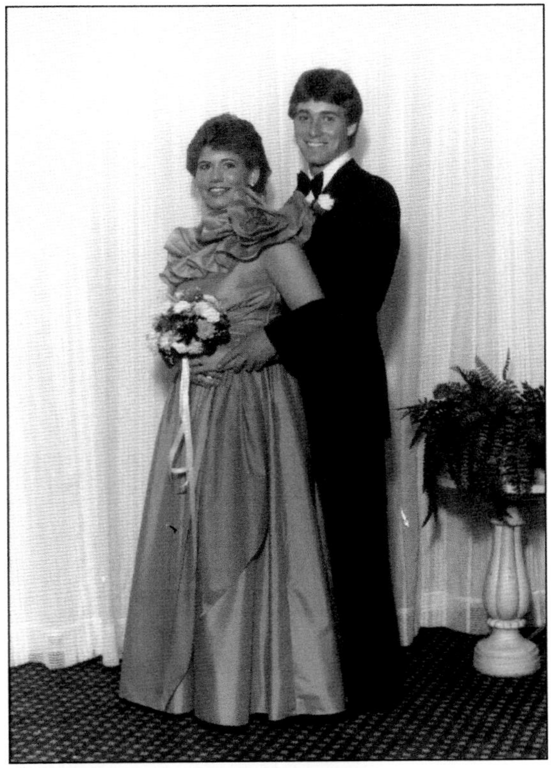

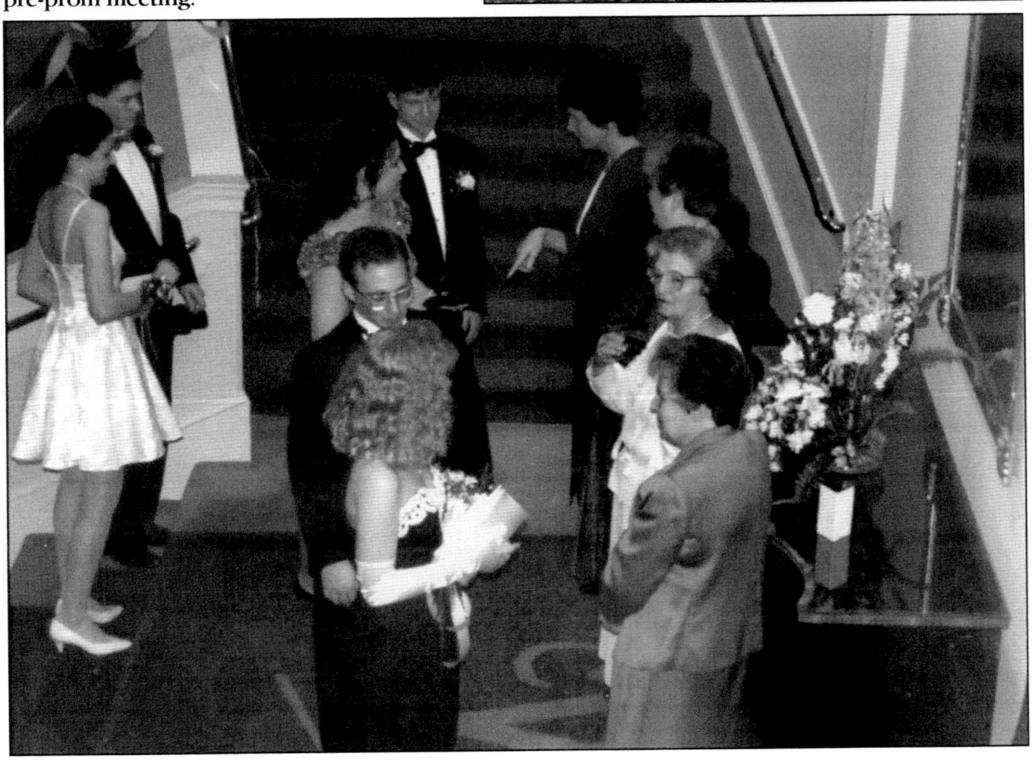

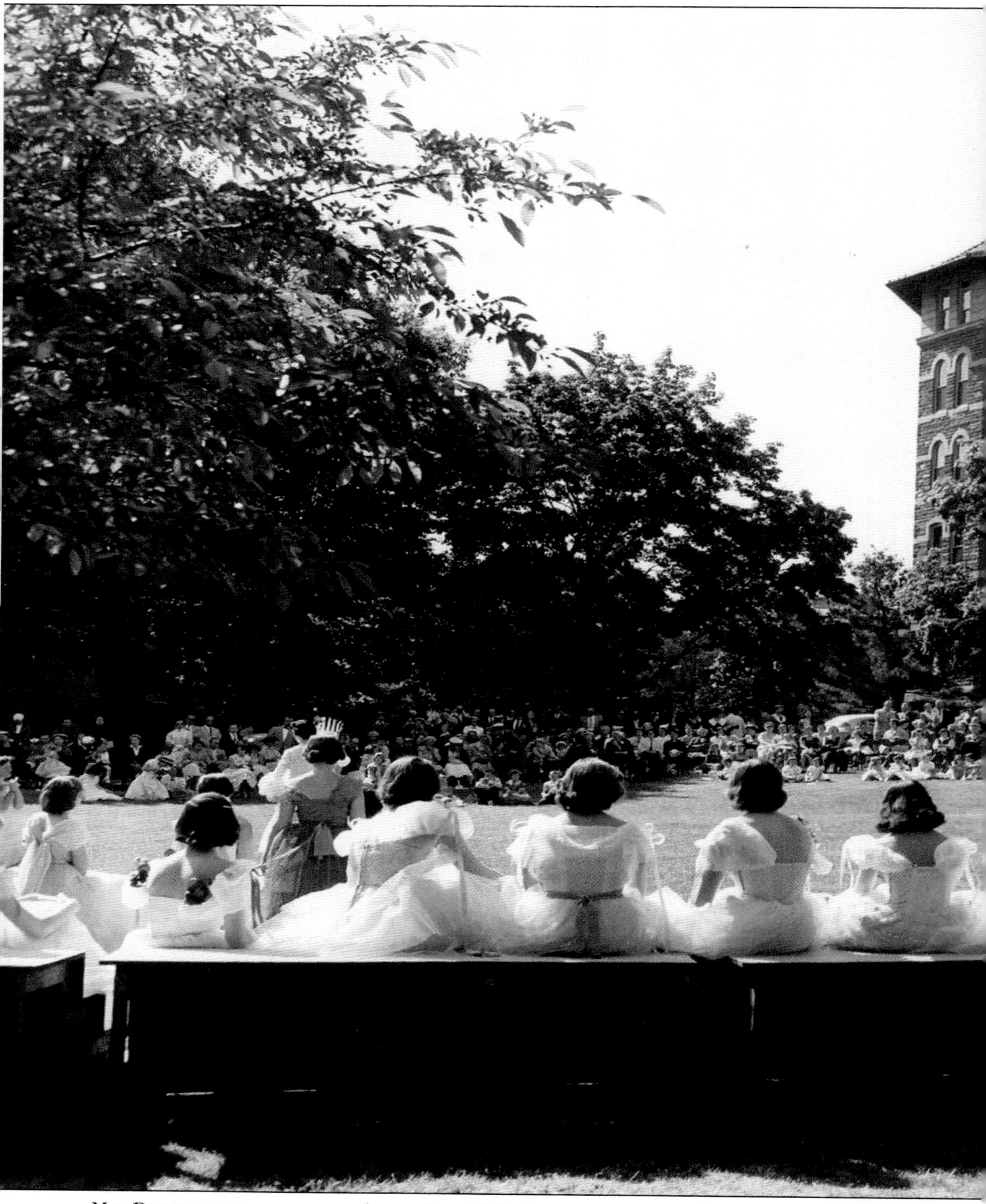

May Day queens were crowned as early as 1867. Parents were invited to the annual celebrations, which included a procession in honor of Our Lady and picnics on the front lawn, in this 1950

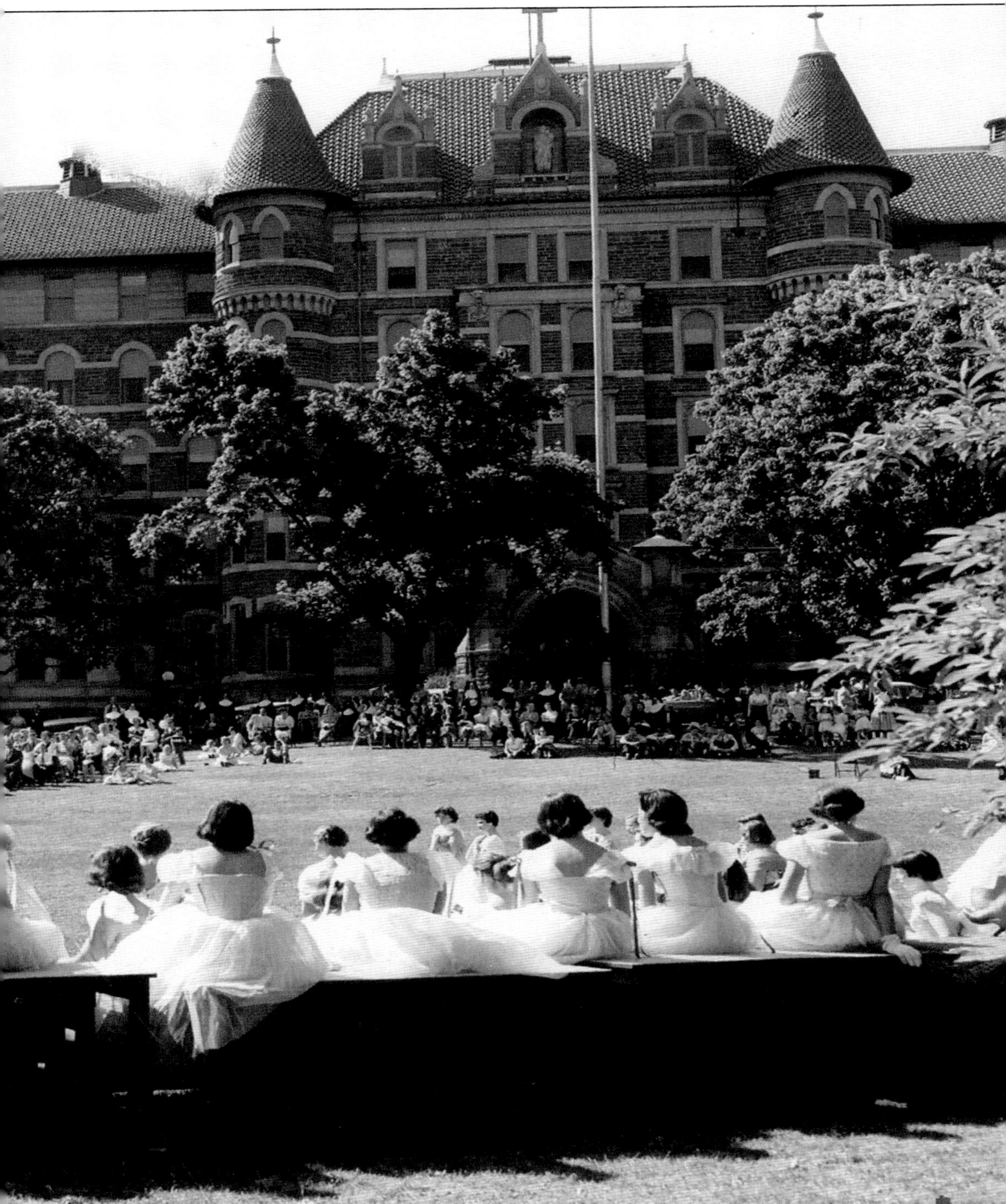

photograph. In 1945, the seniors began wearing their white commencement dresses and white shoes. When it rained, May Day festivities moved inside to the rotunda.

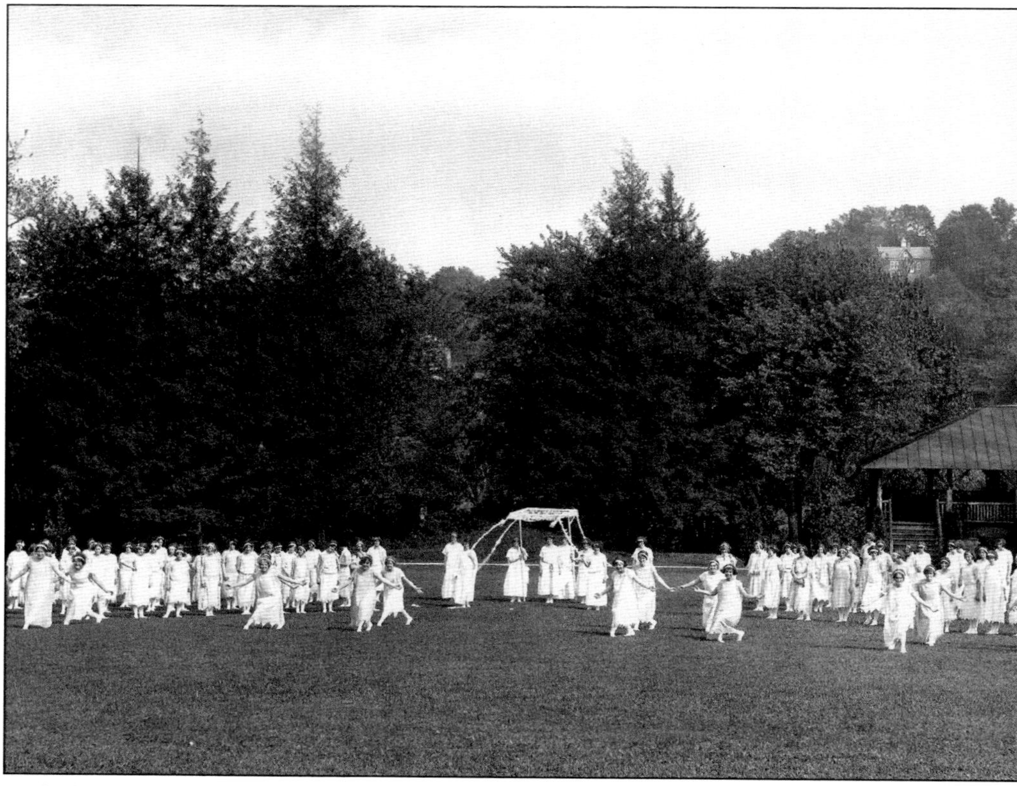

Each class presented a maypole dance, as seen in the above photograph from 1930. By 1954, the Marian Year, the students formed a living rosary, shown below. A May Queen was crowned, and students processed to the Our Lady of Lourdes grotto. The custom of having the student council president crown the Blessed Mother at the grotto was introduced about 1947.

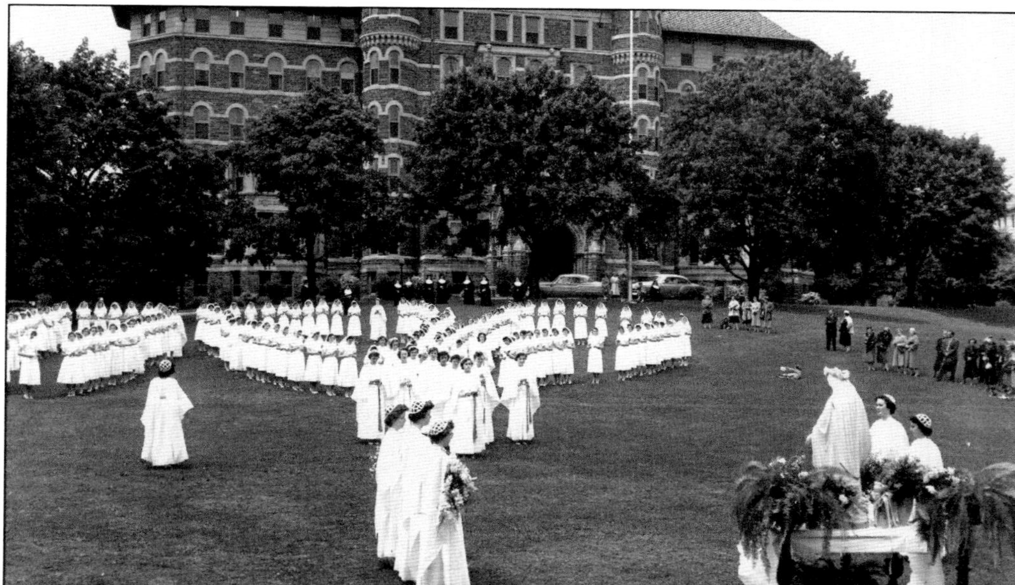

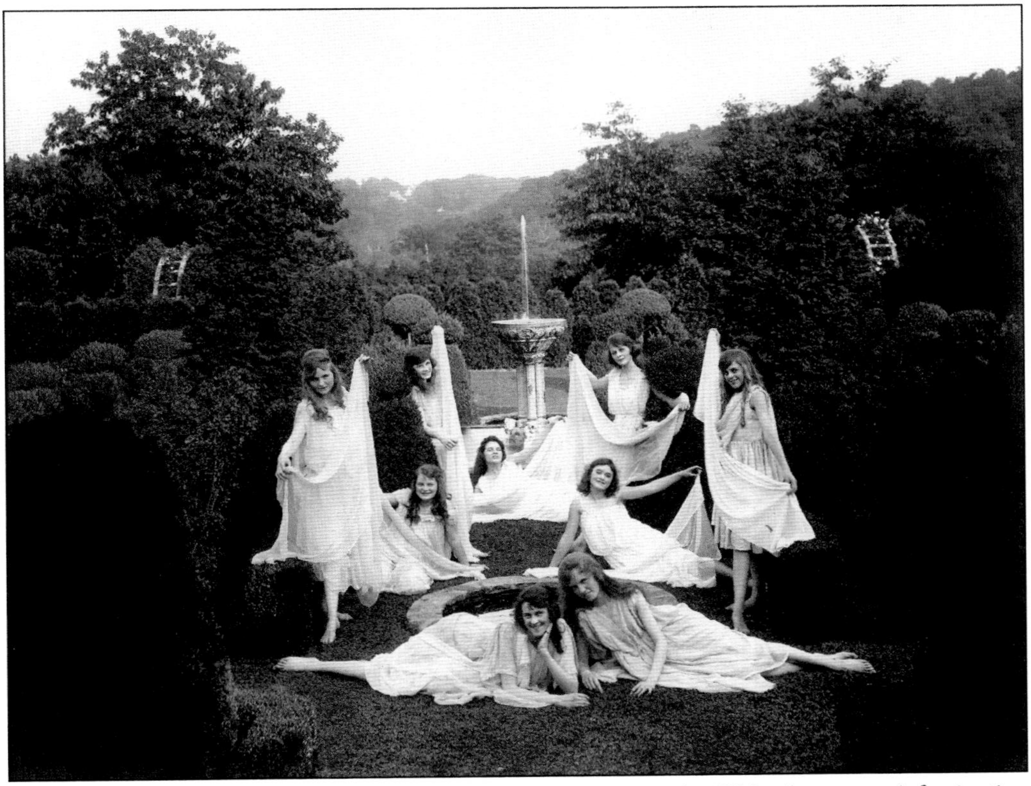

By the early 1900s, dancing lessons were offered as an elective. In the 1930s, the country's fascination with dancing was reflected in May Day, as modern interpretive dance was incorporated into the festivities. Here, the 1930 May Day court frolics by the fountain and pool.

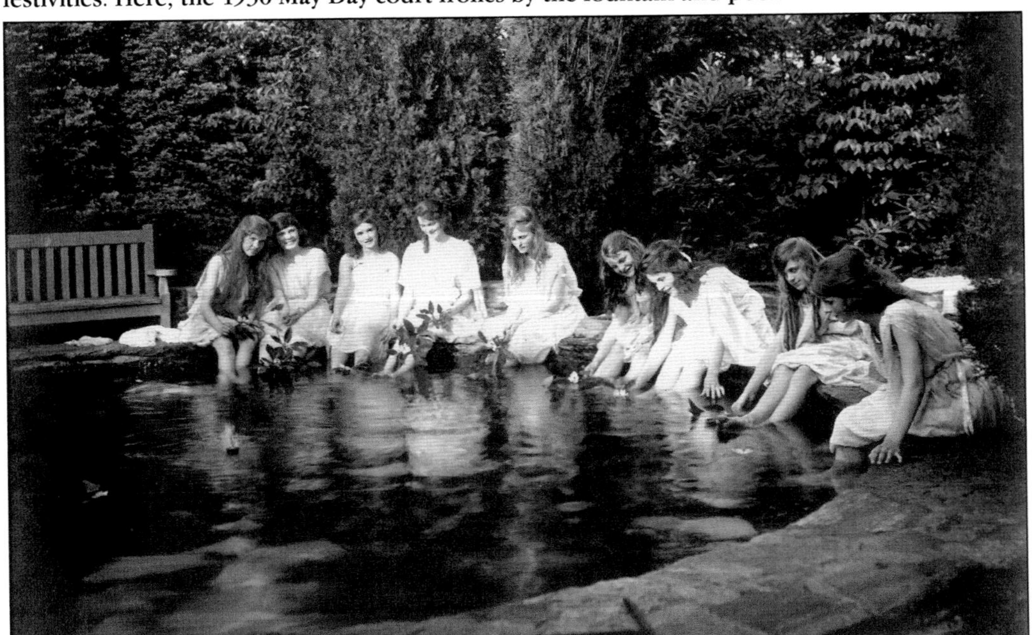

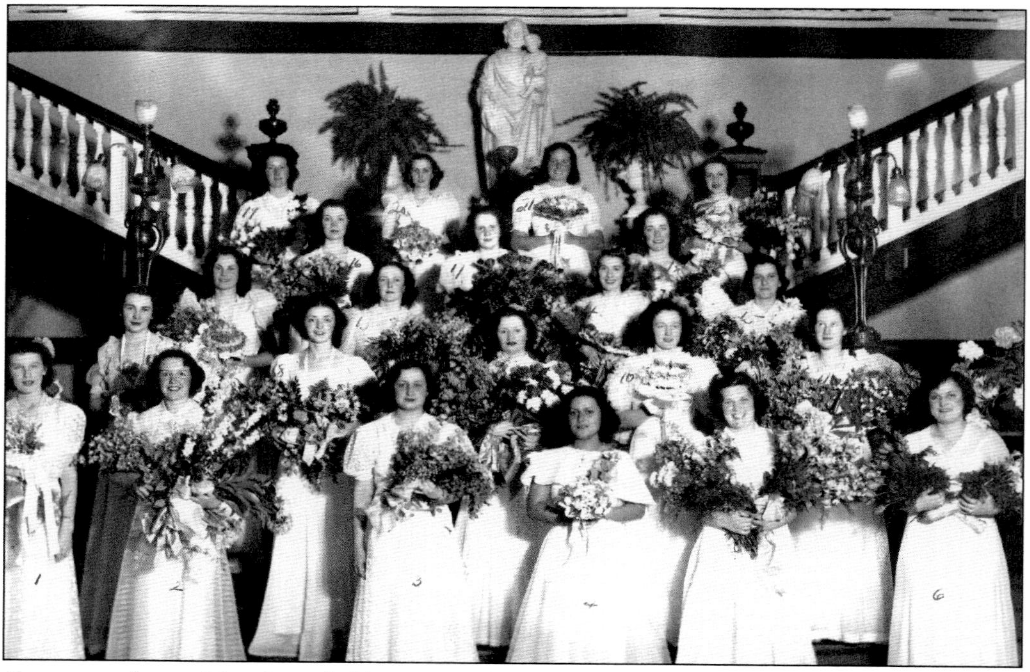

Above, members of the class of 1937 pose in their graduation dresses after mass on the Bishop's Stairs inside the rotunda. Baccalaureate ceremonies originated in 1914, with a farewell talk or benediction closing out the year. By 1919, seniors wore fancy dresses and bridal veils. Before 1918, the class valedictorian at commencement was the girl who had attended the Mount the longest. In 1918, it was decided that "the girl most capable should compose the valedictory and the one best able should deliver it"—a joint effort that involved a faculty-judged speaking contest. Below, the class of 1944 gathers for its farewell photograph.

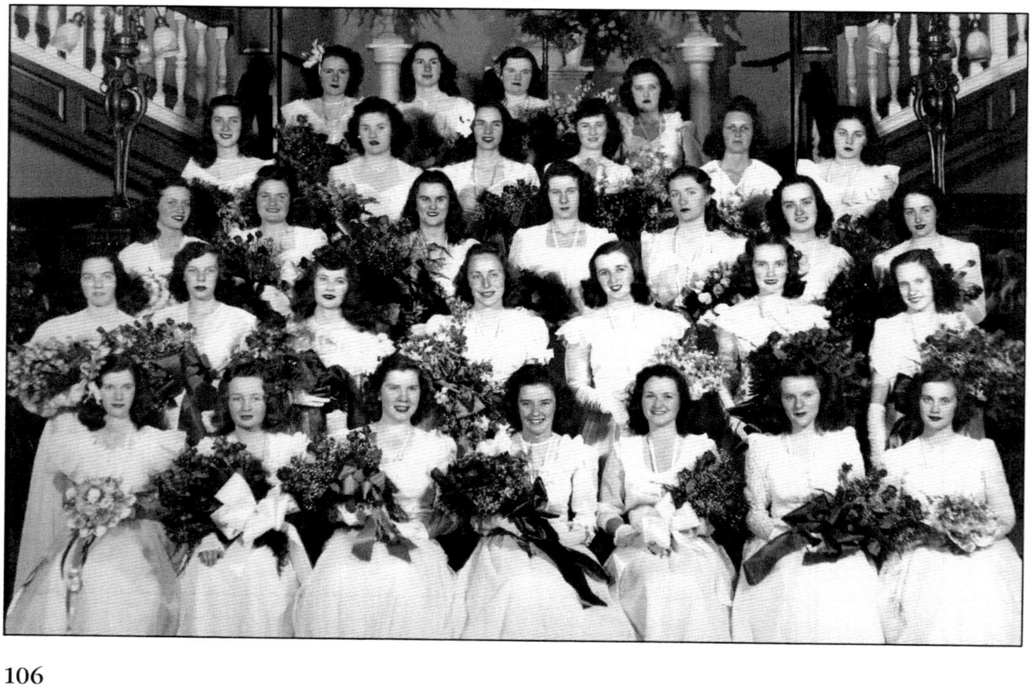

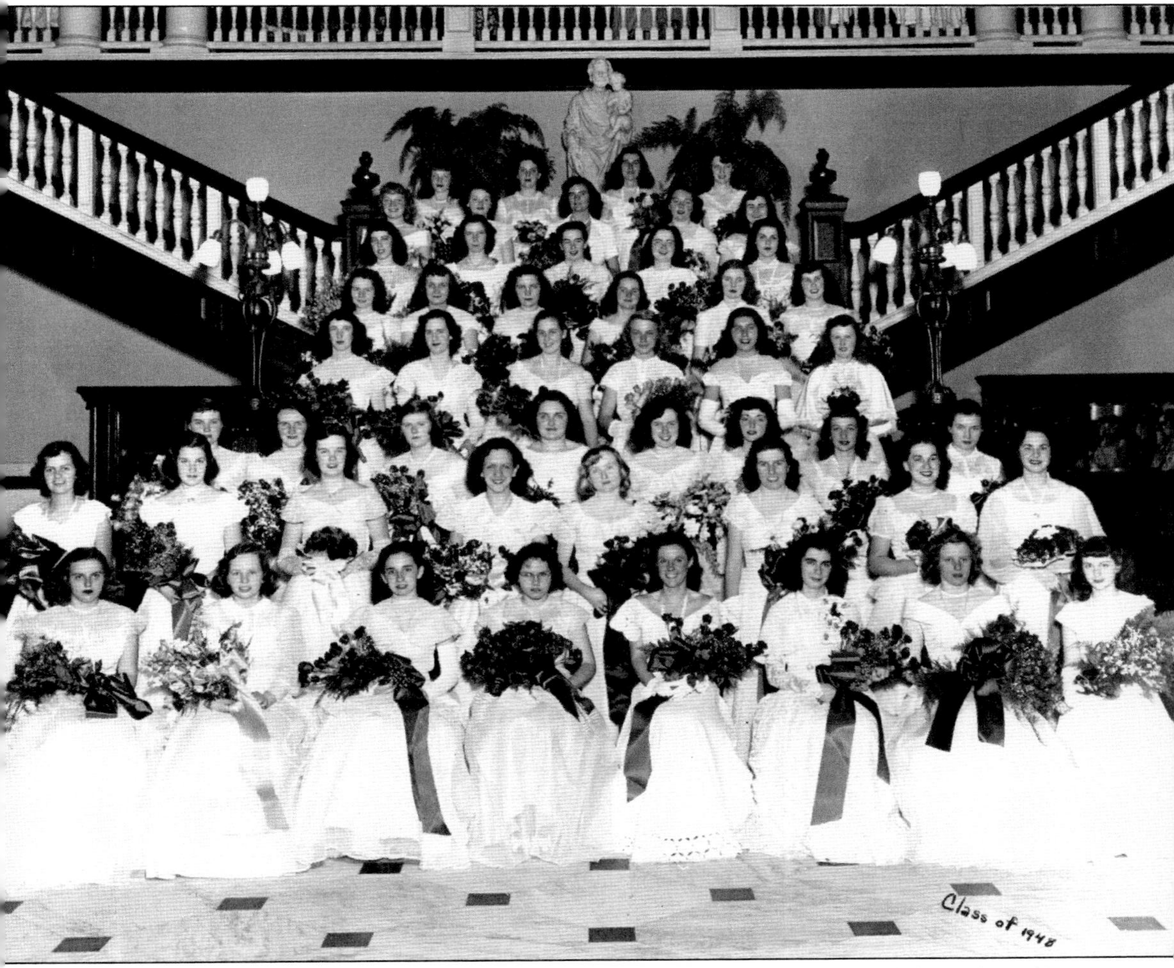

The academy's orchestra, organized in 1916, played at graduation from 1918 until the early 1940s. Members of the Philadelphia Orchestra acted as directors, while a corps of music teachers taught the instruments and led practices. Among the members of the class of 1948, shown here, are (first row, second from left) Adele Bateman Donahue, honorary alumnae board member; (second row, far left) Mary Merz Berko, honorary alumnae board member and current member of the school's board of directors; (seventh row, third from left) Mary Ellen Carroll Brown, alumnae executive board member.

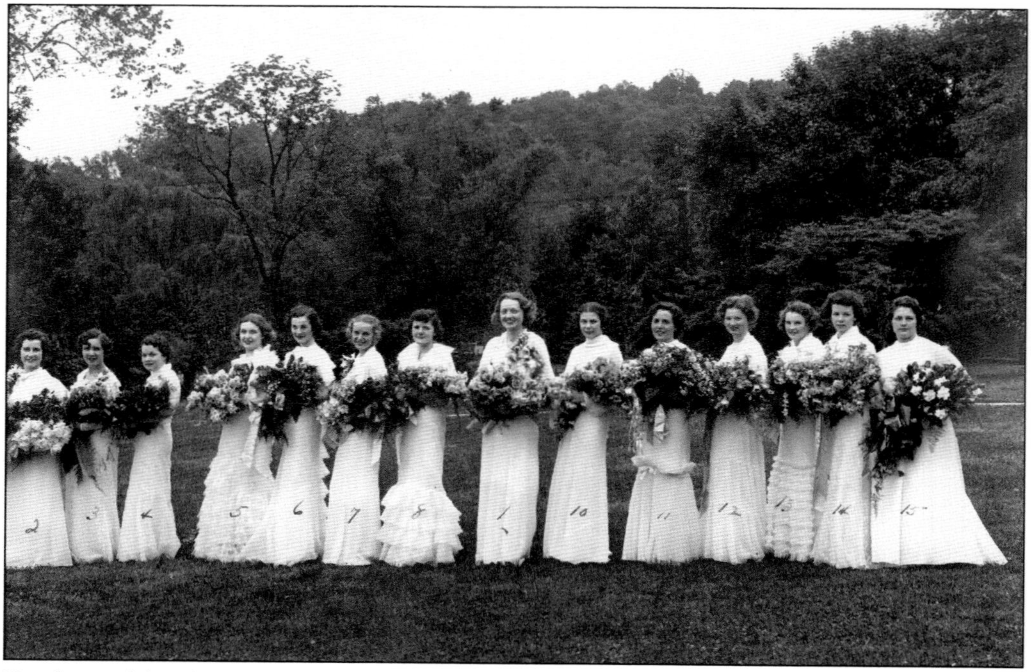

Members of the class of 1935 pose outdoors in their fashionable white dresses. Below, the class of 1953 wears the traditional white and pale yellow flowing gowns and gold Juliet caps. Mount Saint Joseph graduates have been wearing these gowns since 1896. They are an adaptation of the Delsarte gown, adopted in the late 19th century as part of the teachings of Francois Delsarte, whose system of physical culture called for participants to wear a loose-fitting, Grecian-inspired gown for gymnastics, singing, and rhythmic exercises and dance. The 1896 graduates chose to wear their new white and yellow gowns for a Delsarte concert and again for commencement. The tradition continues to the present day.

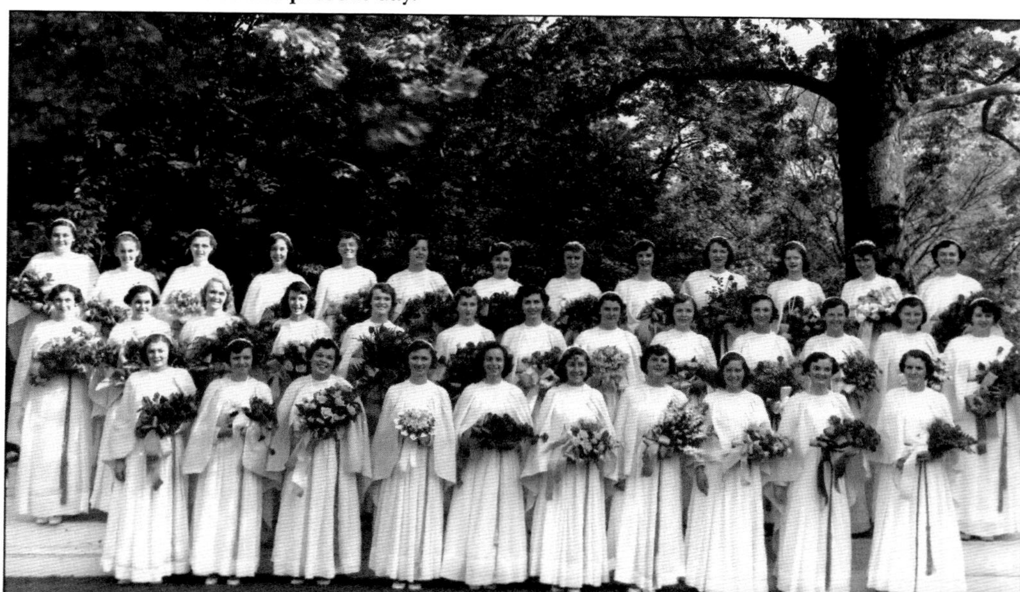

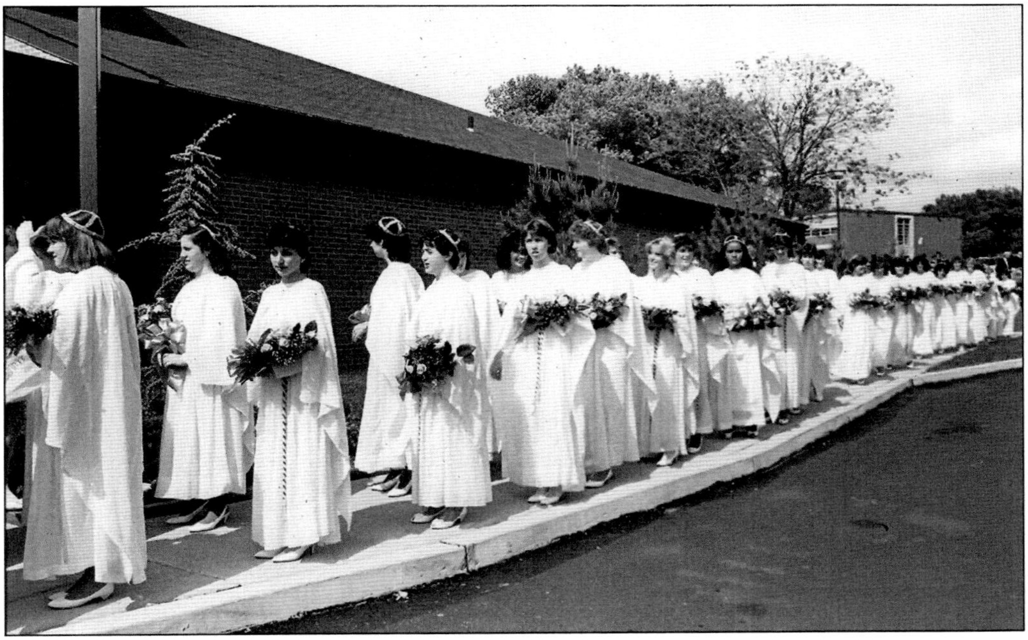

The location of graduation has changed through the years. The school auditorium hosted graduates in the early 1980s. From 1985 to 1988, graduation was celebrated at either St. Genevieve's in Flourtown or, as shown here, at St. Philip Neri in Lafayette Hill. As evidenced in this early 1990s photograph below, students from 1989 to present graduated from Immaculate Heart of Mary in Andorra and received bouquets of yellow roses.

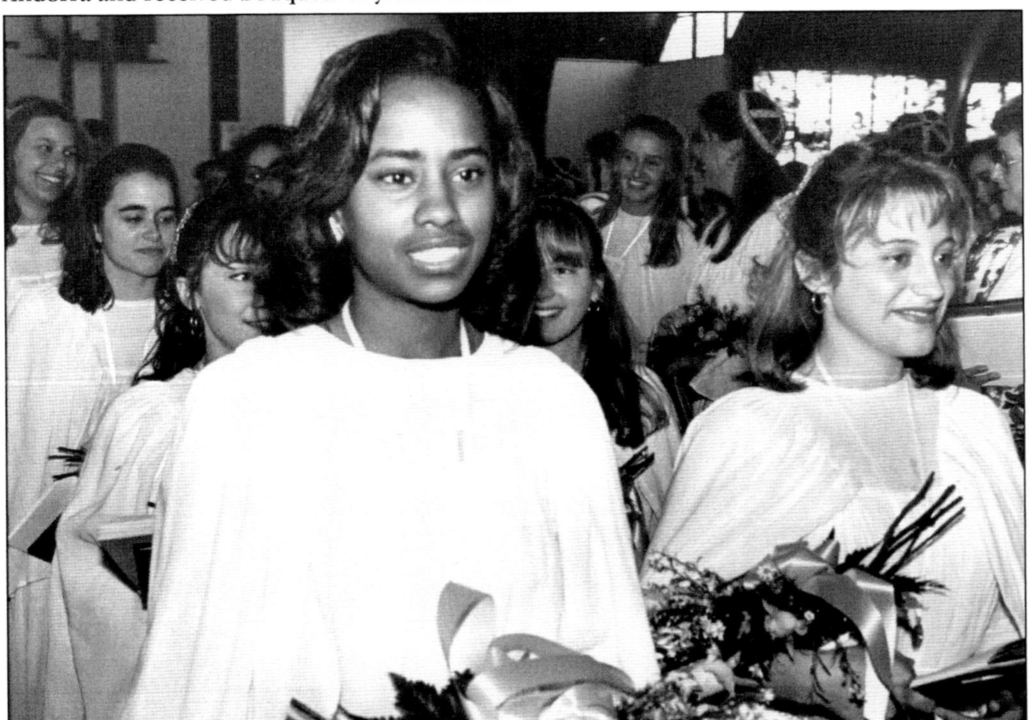

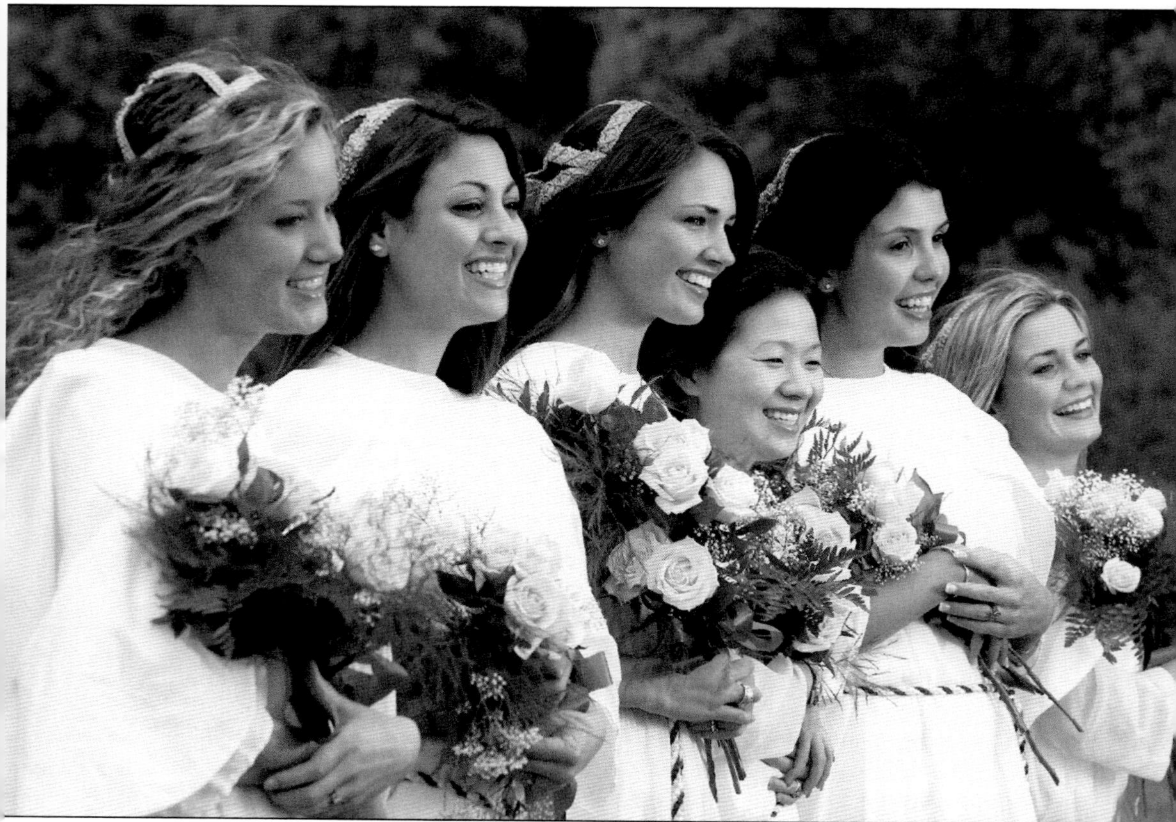

Seniors began receiving class rings in 1919. Juniors received class pins beginning in 1930, but the bestowing of class pins can be traced to the class of 1904. That same class also developed the first school song. Rev. Joseph Moran, assistant rector of Our Mother of Consolation in Chestnut Hill, helped the girls adapt words to a melody from the musical comedy *The Prince of Pilsen*. Today's "Alma Mater" harkens all Mounties to rally 'round the school colors—purple, white, and gold.

Seven

The Alumnae Association

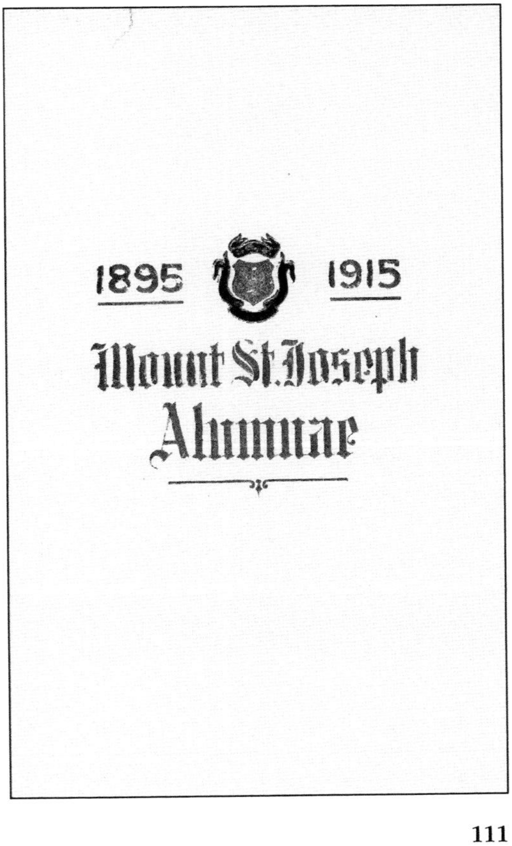

The Mount Saint Joseph Alumnae Association began in 1895, the year of the silver jubilee of St. Joseph. Directress Mother St. Ephrem issued invitations to all former graduates to meet at their alma mater on June 13, where a musical program and festivities were held. The formation of the alumnae association was proposed and approved by the great number of alumnae in attendance. On this day, the Sisters of Saint Joseph welcomed their "harvest home . . . bearing sheaves."

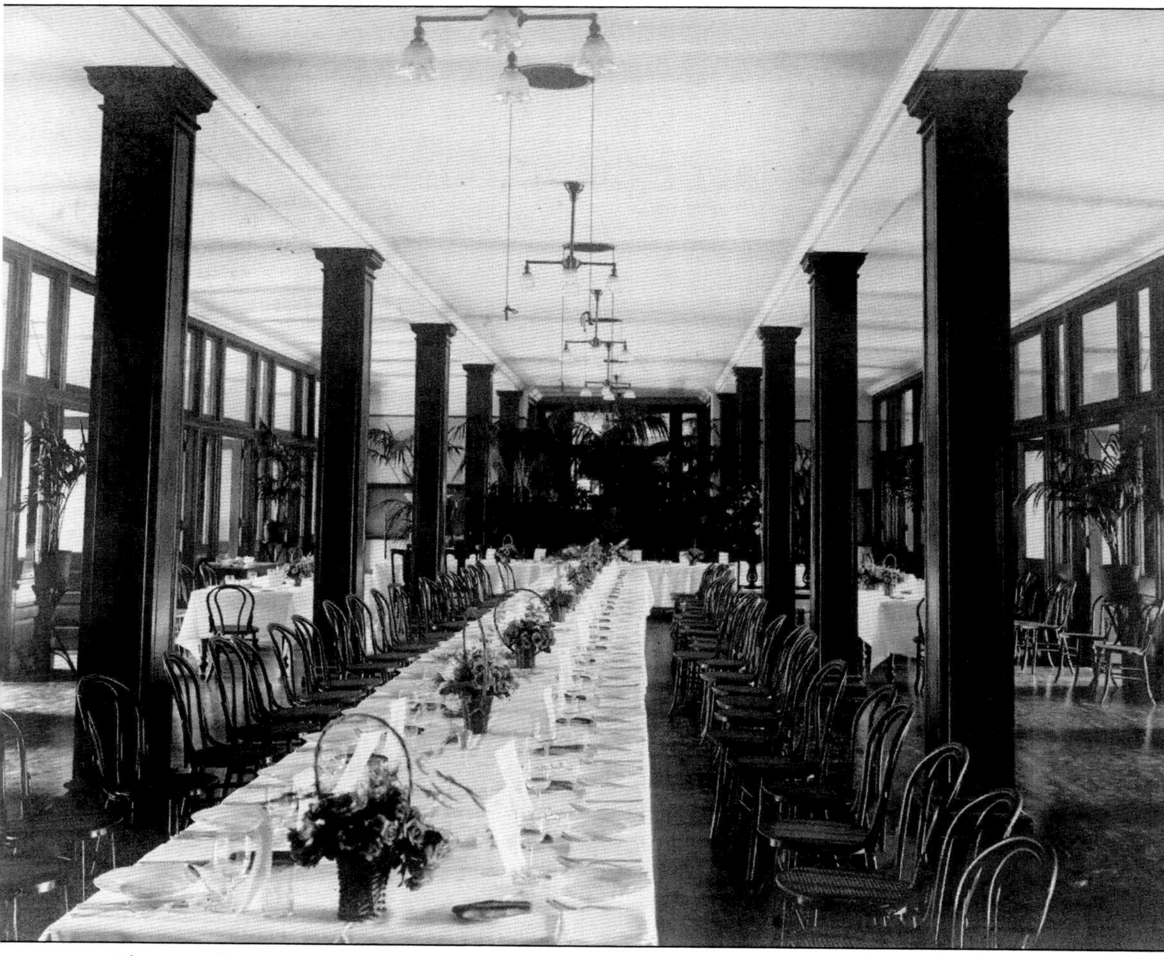

Alumnae Day is an annual social reunion that dates back to the association's founding. Initially reunions were held in May, with the Sisters of Saint Joseph hosting the alumnae at a banquet held in the music corridor of Saint Joseph's Hall, upstairs to the left of the rotunda (above). Today Alumnae Day is held in mid-April at the Mount. Graduates from Saint Joseph's Hall meet in the old building for lunch, followed by a mass at the Flourtown campus and reunion-year class receptions.

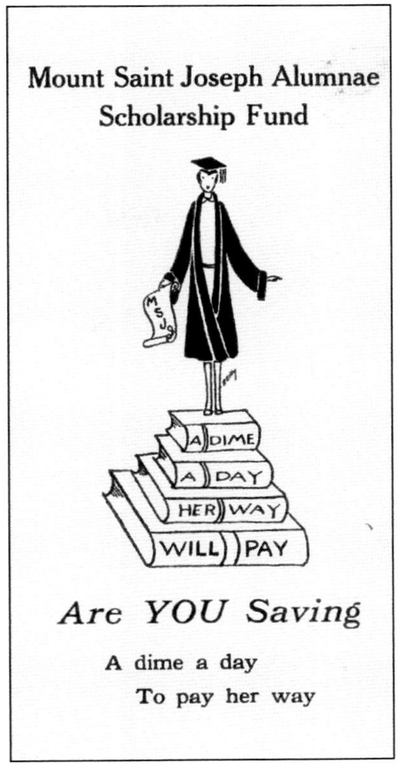

As stated in its by-laws, the objectives of the Mount Saint Joseph Alumnae Association are threefold: "to promote the moral and intellectual culture of its members; to extend and maintain their social relations with one another; and to advance in every way the interests of their alma mater." Service has been an integral part of the alumnae association's mission. In 1927, the association initiated a scholarship fund to benefit students. Through the generous donations of alumnae, the association provided a $1,000 scholarship to Mount Saint Joseph College to benefit an academy girl, and the gift was presented at the June 4, 1928, commencement. Since the 1970s, Mount alumnae have offered a scholarship to a deserving daughter or sister of an alumna.

Mount Saint Joseph
Chestnut Hill
Philadelphia

Dear Friends of the Alumnae:

Nearly a year has passed since the inauguration of the drive for a Mount Saint Joseph Alumnae Memorial Scholarship. Its progress has been very satisfactory. The method adopted—saving a dime a day—aroused general interest, and met with the unqualified approval of our members.

The majority returned their pledge cards, promising to contribute the stipulated quota. A few, not waiting until the end, have made very generous donations.

You may recall that April 26, 1928, feast of Our Lady of Good Counsel, Patroness of the Alumnae, was the date set for the termination of the drive.

With less than three months intervening, it is most important for each one to redouble her efforts in order that we may successfully complete the work set before us and have this scholarship take its place beside the other praise-worthy achievements of Mount Saint Joseph Alumnae.

Katherine K. Bohem, *Ex-Officio*
Regina M. Gilligan, *Chairman*
Kathleen Lee Diamond, *Treasurer*
Rosemary McNally, *Secretary*
Florence M. Bell, *Chairman of Captains*
Margaret Carroll, *Assistant Chairman of Captains*

February 1, 1928.

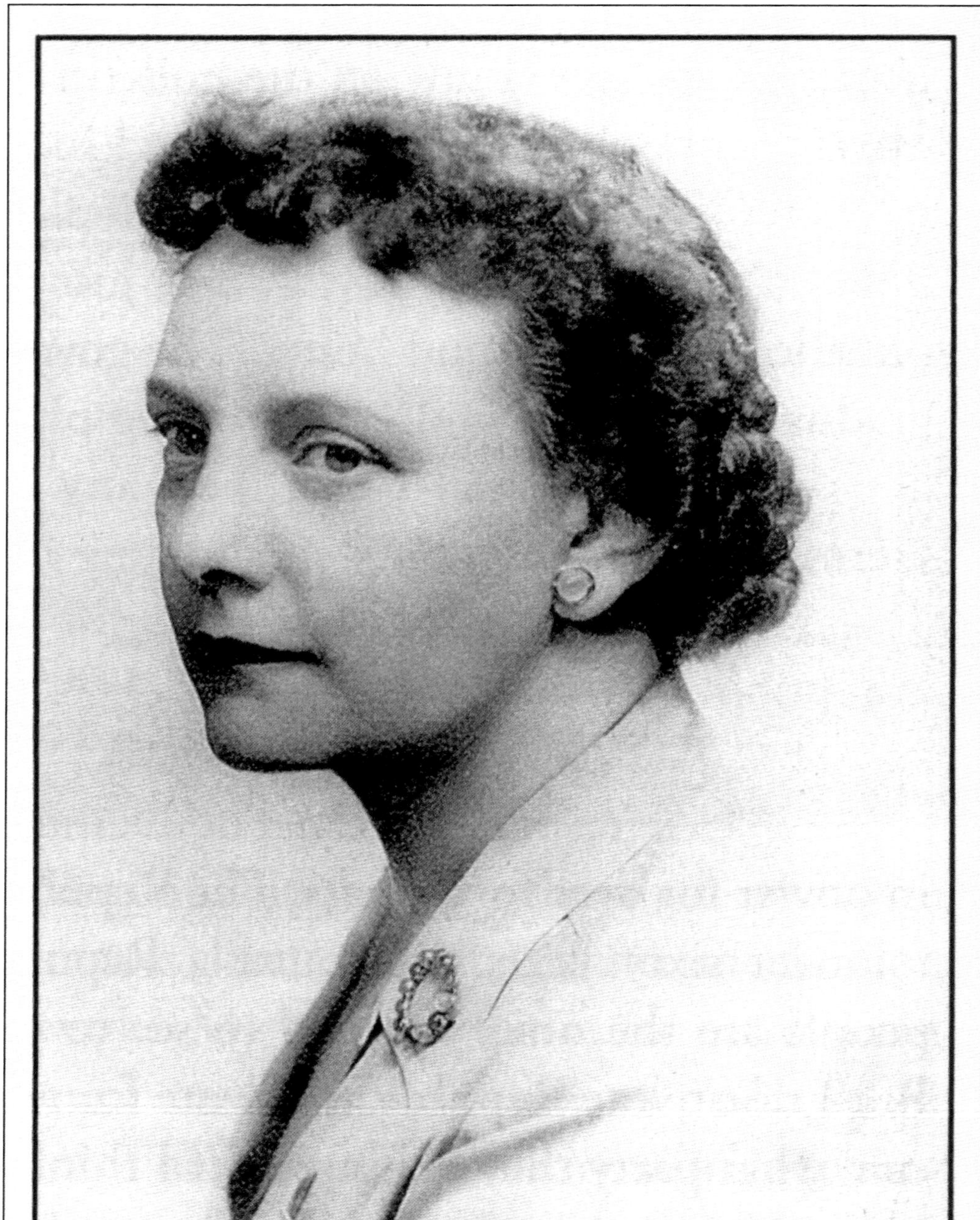

Rosemary McNally '17, served as president of the Mount Saint Joseph Alumnae Association from 1942 to 1946. In honor of her commitment, dedication, and service to the Mount, the alumnae association established the Rosemary McNally '17 Alumnae Award, presented annually on Alumnae Day to an alumna who has distinguished herself through consistent dedication and outstanding service to Mount Saint Joseph Academy. (Courtesy of the McNally family.)

ORDER OF EXERCISES

10.00 A. M. ....Conference
11.15 A. M. ....Conference
12.00 Noon ....Luncheon
2.00 P. M. ....Question Box
3.00 P. M. ....Way of the Cross
4.00-5.00 P. M. ....Holy Hour

Retreatants who wish to wear veils in the Chapel are requested to bring them.

Train leaves Broad Street Suburban Station at 8.24 A. M., arriving at Chestnut Hill Station at 8.54 A. M., connecting with the City Line Bus "X" at 8.59 A. M. Buses run every 18 minutes thereafter.

You are earnestly urged, in deference to the Sisters who must plan accordingly, to make your reservation not later than Thursday, March 31, 1938, to

Miss Rosemary McNally,
5800 Greene Street,
Germantown, Philadelphia, Pa.

When the Mount was still in Chestnut Hill, the Mount Saint Joseph Alumnae Association sponsored annual retreats or "days of dedication," for alumnae, who returned to the convent chapel with their white veils for a day of reflection and spiritual renewal.

COMMITTEE

Miss Rosemary McNally, *Chairman*

Mrs. Walter B. Gibbons
Miss Eleanor M. Morris
Mrs. John P. Meehan
Mrs. Arthur Richard Bell
Mrs. Thomas J. Clary
Mrs. James P. Meaney
Miss Anne Dolaway
Miss Anne Keenan
Mrs. John Heffren
Miss Winifred Brady
Miss Mary Roberta McNally
Miss Dorothea M. Barry
Miss Elizabeth Murphy
Mrs. James Cassidy
Miss Marguerite M. Hayes
Miss Mary McManus
Miss Elizabeth Schultz
Miss Mary K. Loughery
Miss Mary Elizabeth Welsh
Miss Nancy F. Bradley
Miss Marie E. Stillmun
Miss Mary B. Edel
Miss Sarah O'Connell
Miss Frances Glynn
Mrs. Francis J. McDevitt
Miss Mary Anne Cleary
Miss Stella May Da Costa
Miss Elizabeth M. Burgoyne
Miss Bernadette M. Obert
Miss Catharine A. O'Donnell
Miss Isabel Ronon
Miss Margaret Mary King
Miss Ann Winifred McGrath
Miss Margaret Mary Kelly
Miss Margery G. Stroebele
Miss Marie W. Betz
Miss Marie Therese McGarrity

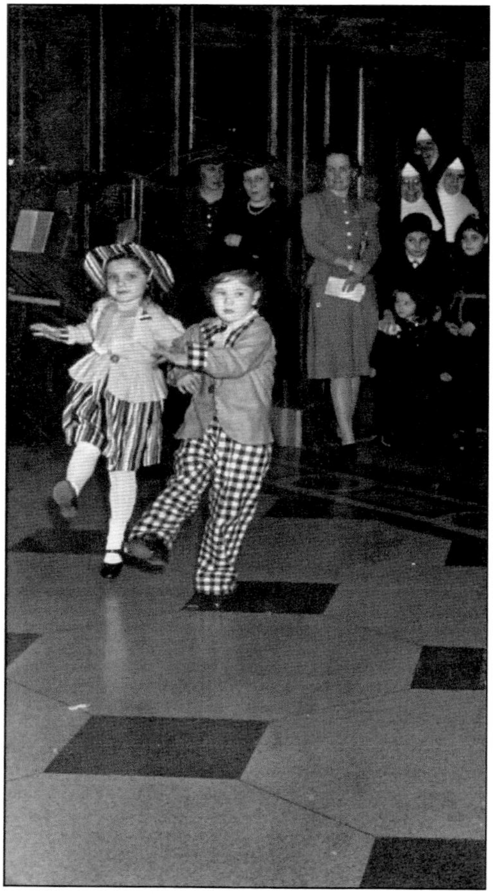

Children's Day, a popular event inaugurated in 1931, provided annual fall entertainment for alumnae children. At the earliest parties, the children were entertained with movies, marionettes, and magicians. In later years, the children from Fontbonne Hall provided the entertainment. In 1943, the seniors, under the direction of Sr. Austin Marie, became responsible for the event and the entertainment, and each year they produced an original skit based on a popular attraction.

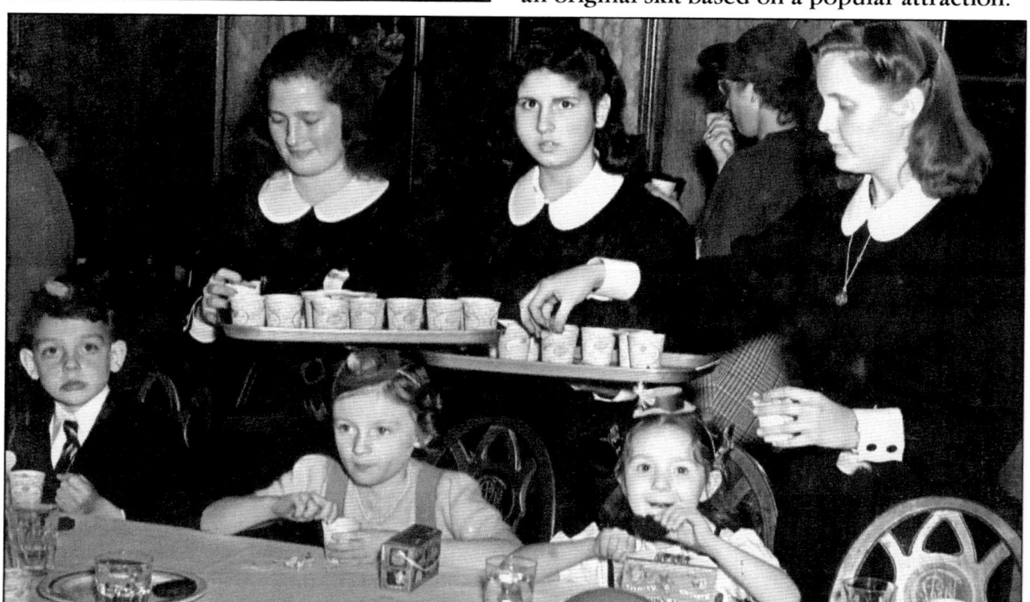

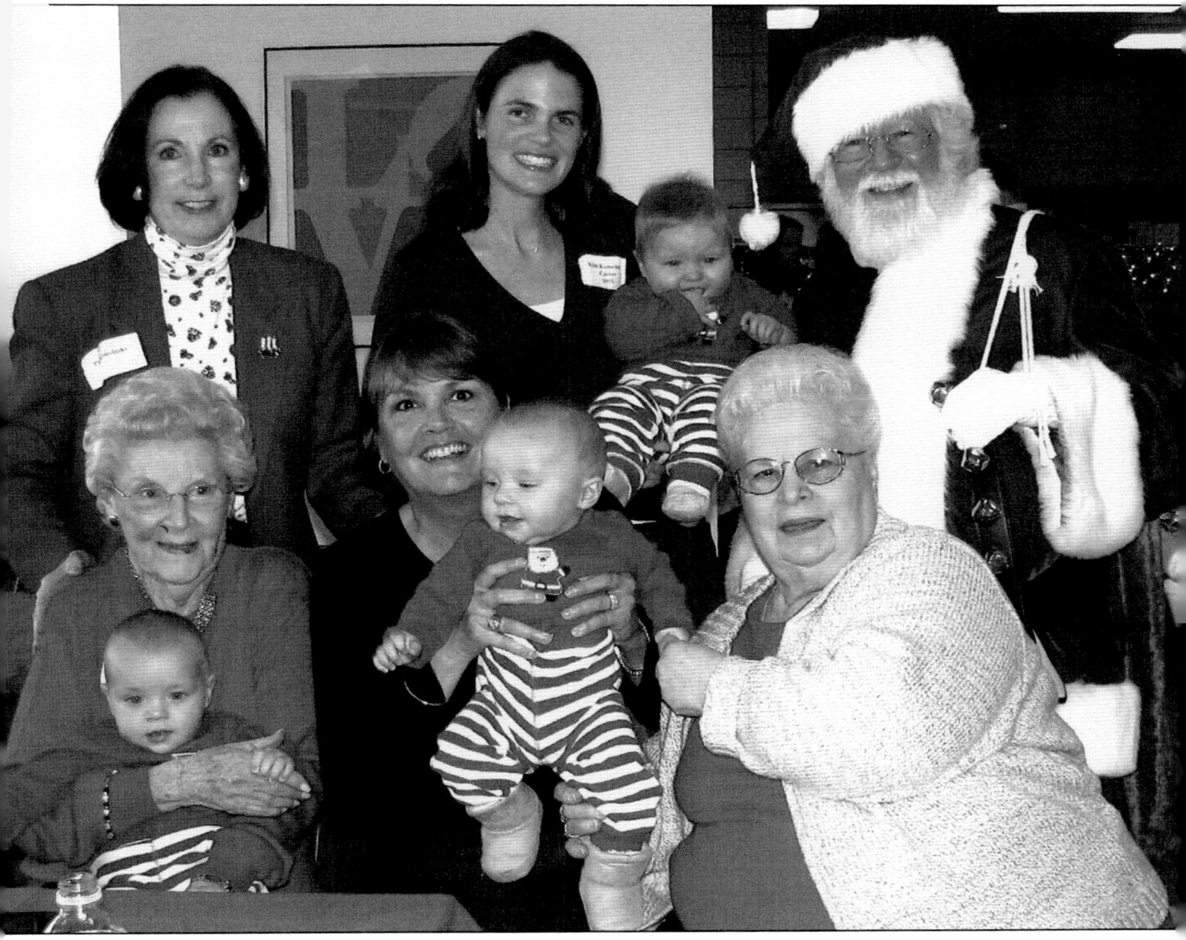

The tradition of entertaining alumnae children continues today with Lunch with Santa, the Mount Saint Joseph Academy Alumnae Association's popular family event. On the first Saturday in December, approximately 300 alumnae families and friends, spanning generations, return for a luncheon, arts and crafts, and a visit with Santa Claus. A magician or puppeteer entertains throughout the afternoon.

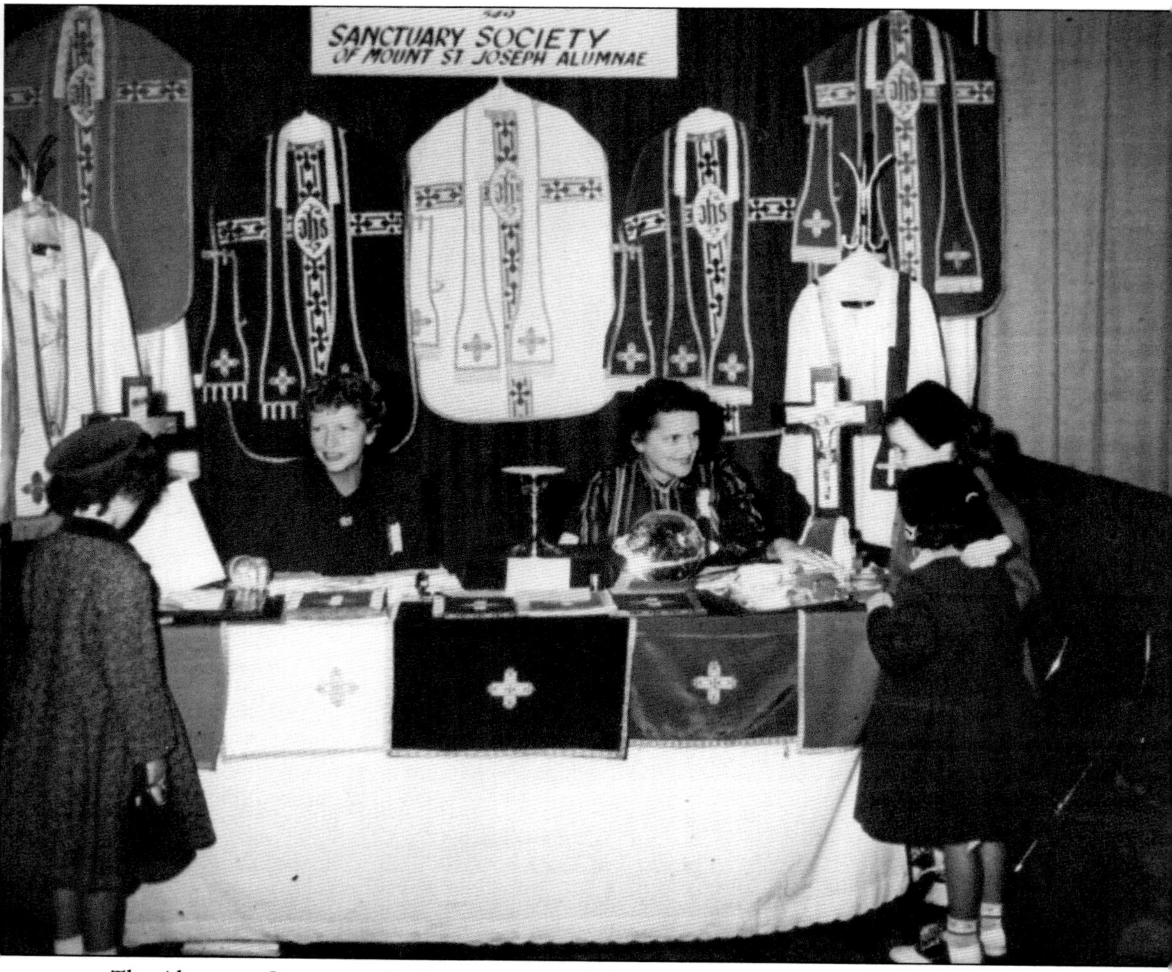

The Alumnae Sanctuary Society, a group of alumnae members who met once a week to sew for the missions, was organized in 1914 after Mother Mary Joseph, the Mount's directress, and appealed for vestments for the poor missionaries of the west and south. Katherine Hanratty and six alumnae, including Mary McNally (class of 1894), offered to repair old vestments in the stack room of the library. The Sanctuary Society later sewed vestments and altar linens for local and foreign parishes and priests in need, with alumnae memorializing or honoring loved ones through donations. Each Tuesday in the early to mid-20th century, the members would gather in the sewing room of the Old Mount to hem and embroider vestments; later they convened in Fontbonne Lounge. On Alumnae Day, the Sanctuary Society acknowledged the donations that benefited parishes and priests near and far.

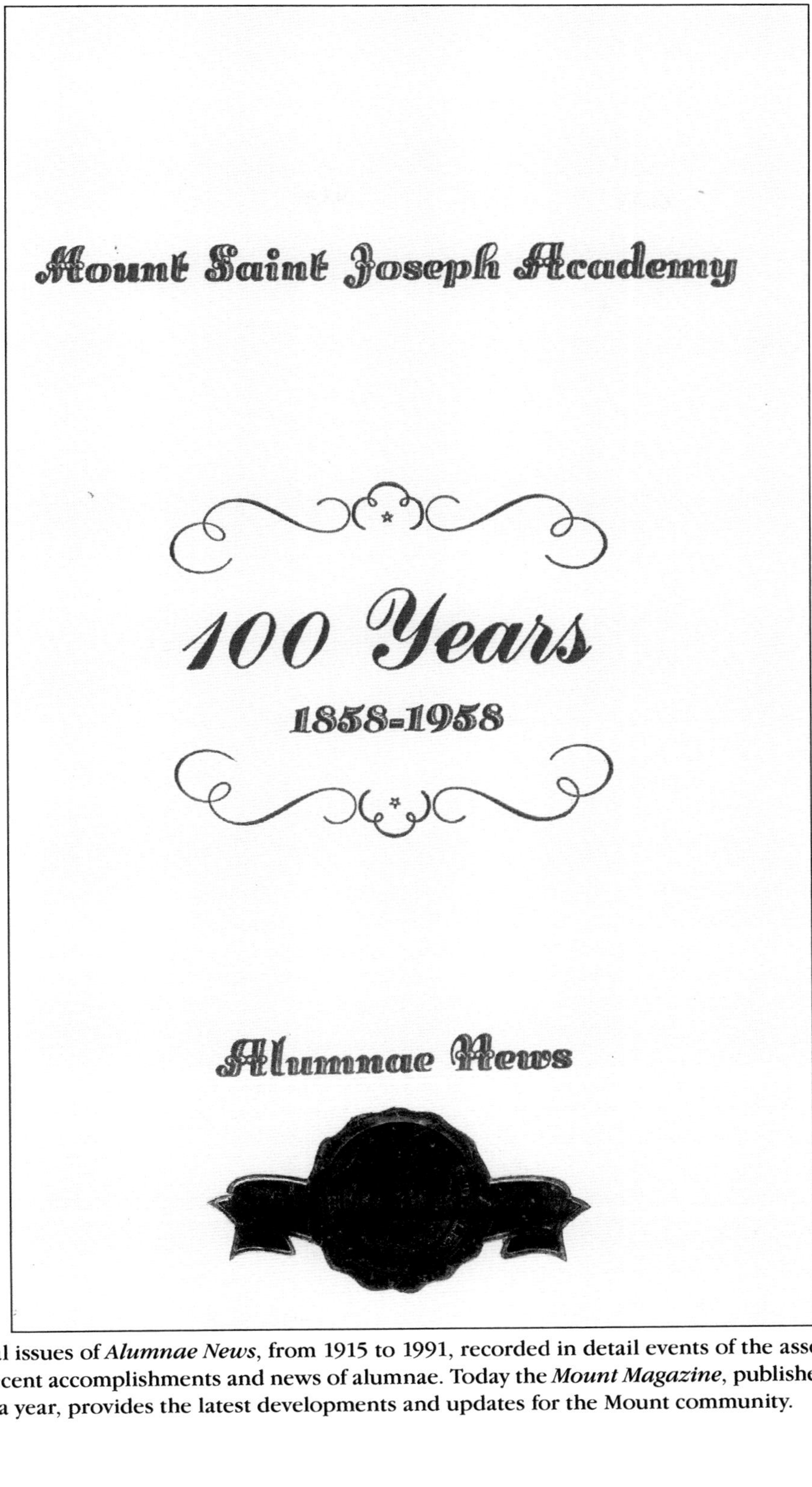

Annual issues of *Alumnae News*, from 1915 to 1991, recorded in detail events of the association and recent accomplishments and news of alumnae. Today the *Mount Magazine*, published three times a year, provides the latest developments and updates for the Mount community.

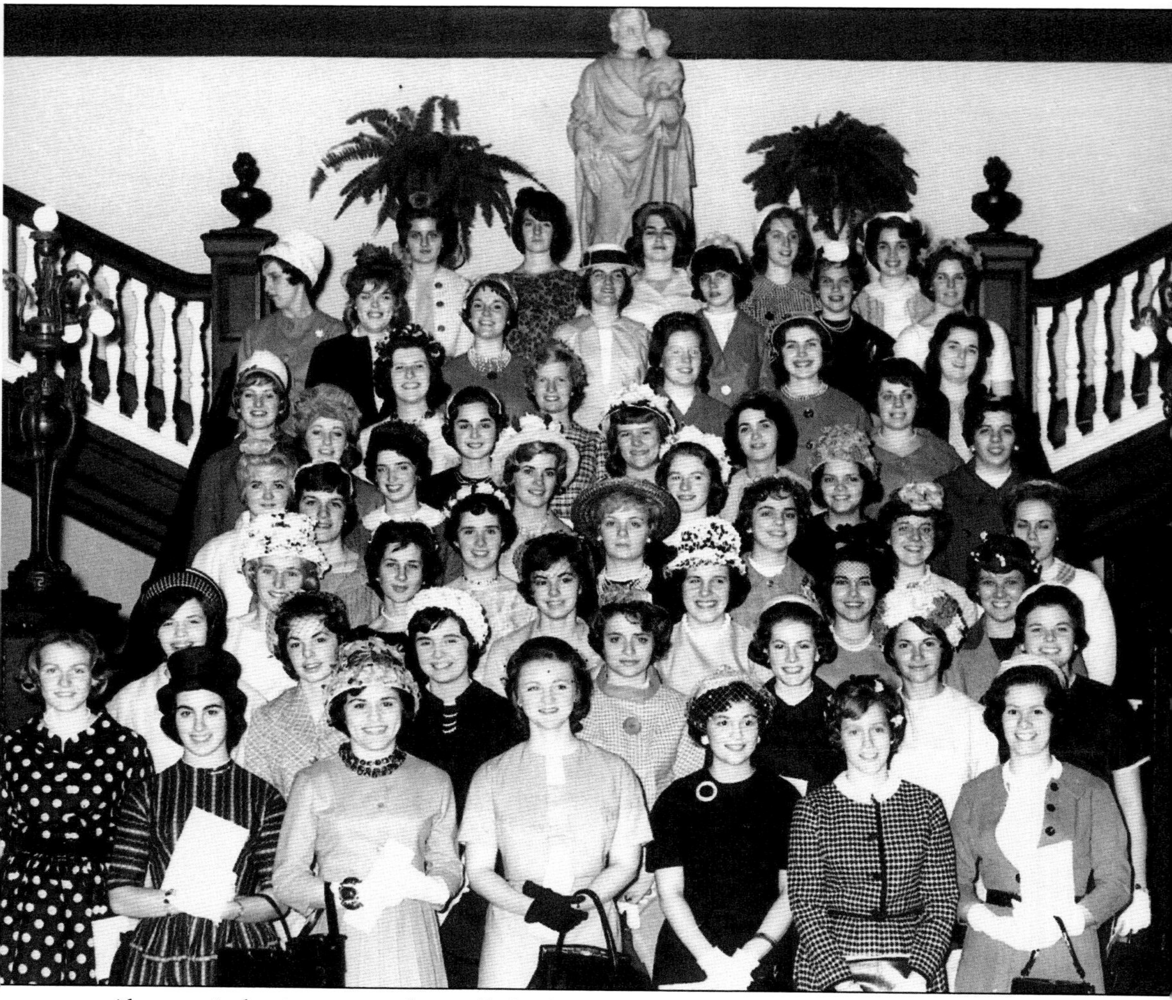

Alumnae induction was traditionally held on the Sunday after Easter, before graduation. Senior girls donned their best hat and gloves to be welcomed into the Mount Saint Joseph Alumnae Association by the reverend mother of the Sisters of Saint Joseph in the east parlor of Saint Joseph's Hall. The class of 1961 (above) was the last graduating class to be welcomed in the parlor before the Mount's move to Flourtown. Today, alumnae induction is jointly conducted by the president of the school and the alumnae association in Fournier auditorium. Recognizing the generational legacy of the academy, graduates receive induction pins distributed by alumnae mothers or grandmothers of the graduating class.

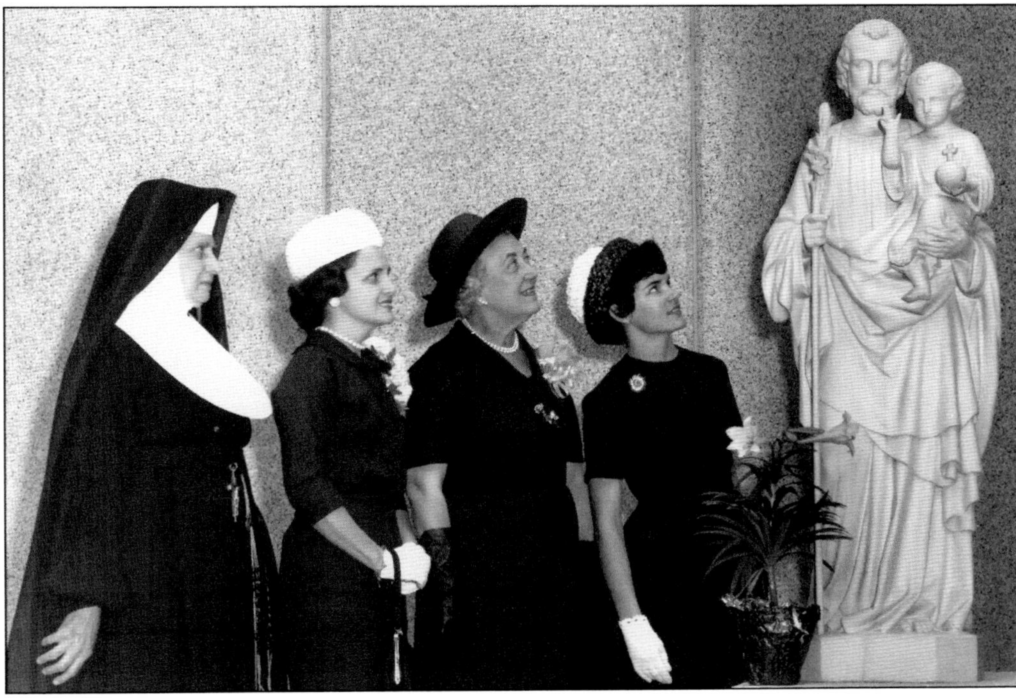

Over the years, the Mount has graduated many women of distinction. The Honorable Kathryn O'Hay Granahan '14, treasurer of the United States, attended the annual alumnae reunion on April 21, 1963, at the academy in Flourtown. At the statute of St. Joseph are pictured, from left to right, Mother M. Sylvester, principal; Kathleen Rhoads Waters '52, president of the alumnae; Kathryn O'Hay Granahan; and Marilyn T. Cattie, president of the graduating class of 1963.

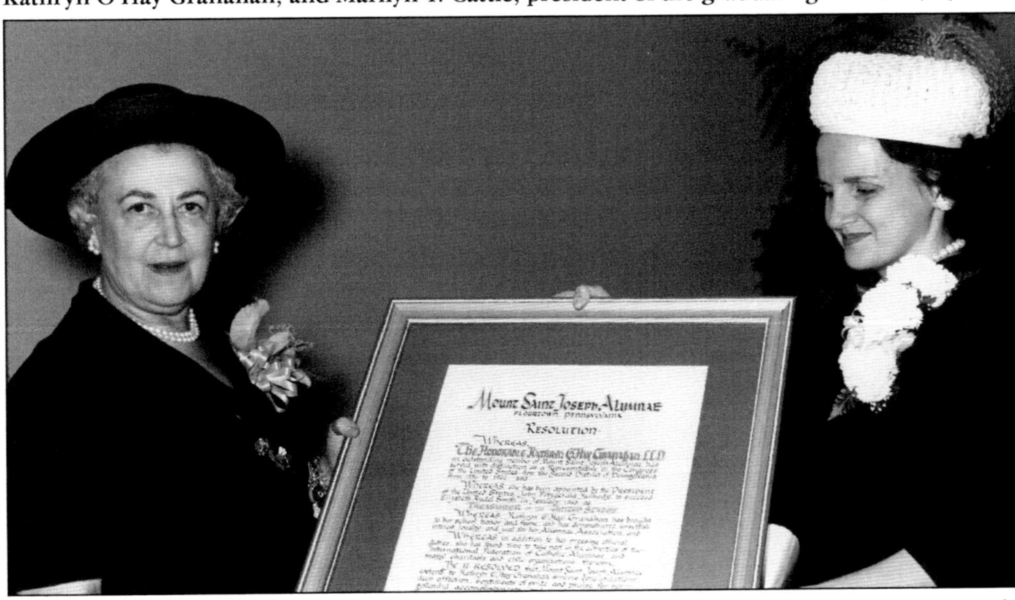

Granahan was elected to Congress in 1956, serving as Philadelphia's first congresswoman in the Second District. In 1963, Pres. John F. Kennedy appointed her as U.S. treasurer. In this photograph, Waters presents Granahan with an honorary membership on the Mount alumnae board.

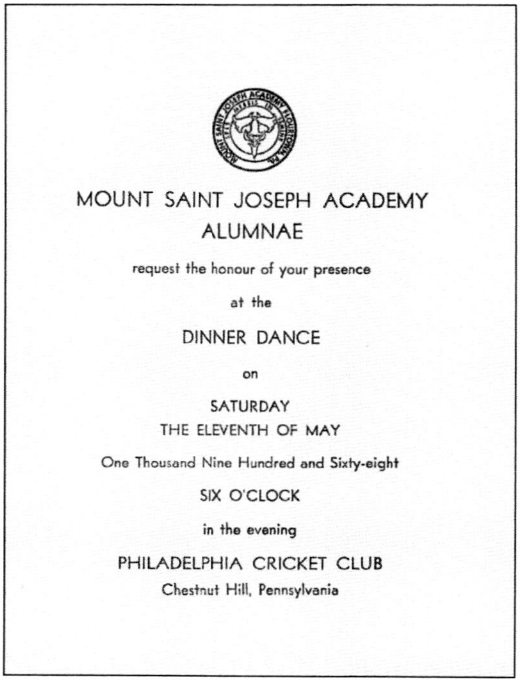

MOUNT SAINT JOSEPH ACADEMY
ALUMNAE

request the honour of your presence

at the

DINNER DANCE

on

SATURDAY
THE ELEVENTH OF MAY

One Thousand Nine Hundred and Sixty-eight

SIX O'CLOCK

in the evening

PHILADELPHIA CRICKET CLUB
Chestnut Hill, Pennsylvania

From the 1930s through 1960s, many social functions were sponsored by the Mount Saint Joseph Alumnae Association, including dinner dances, teas, and bridge parties, the proceeds of which were presented in the form of a "gift check" to the academy on Alumnae Day. These events entailed hard work and dedication on behalf of the alumnae committees. Below are Rosemary Toohey '48 and Helen Branagan '48, cochairs of the March 17, 1956, tea dance, selling raffle tickets for the drawing of a Bermuda holiday cruise.

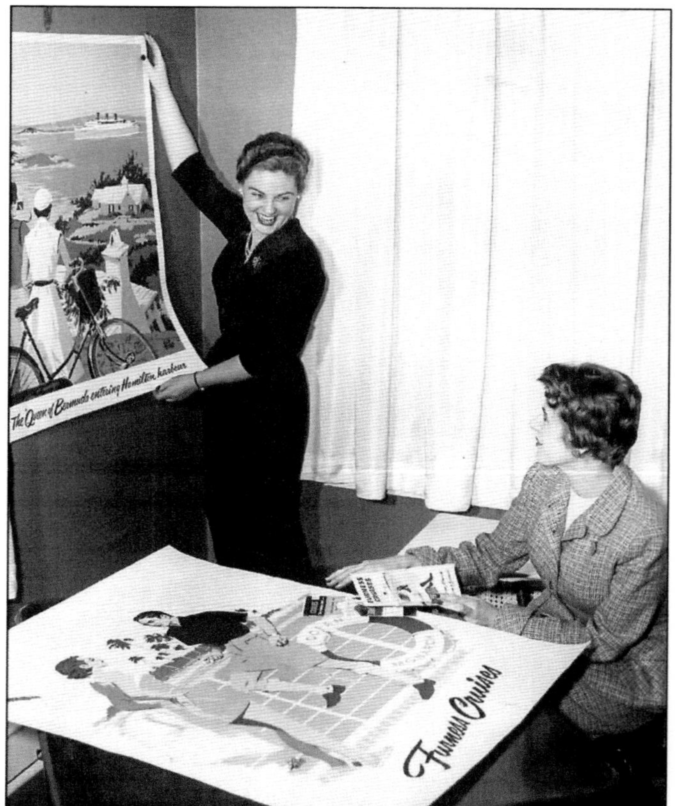

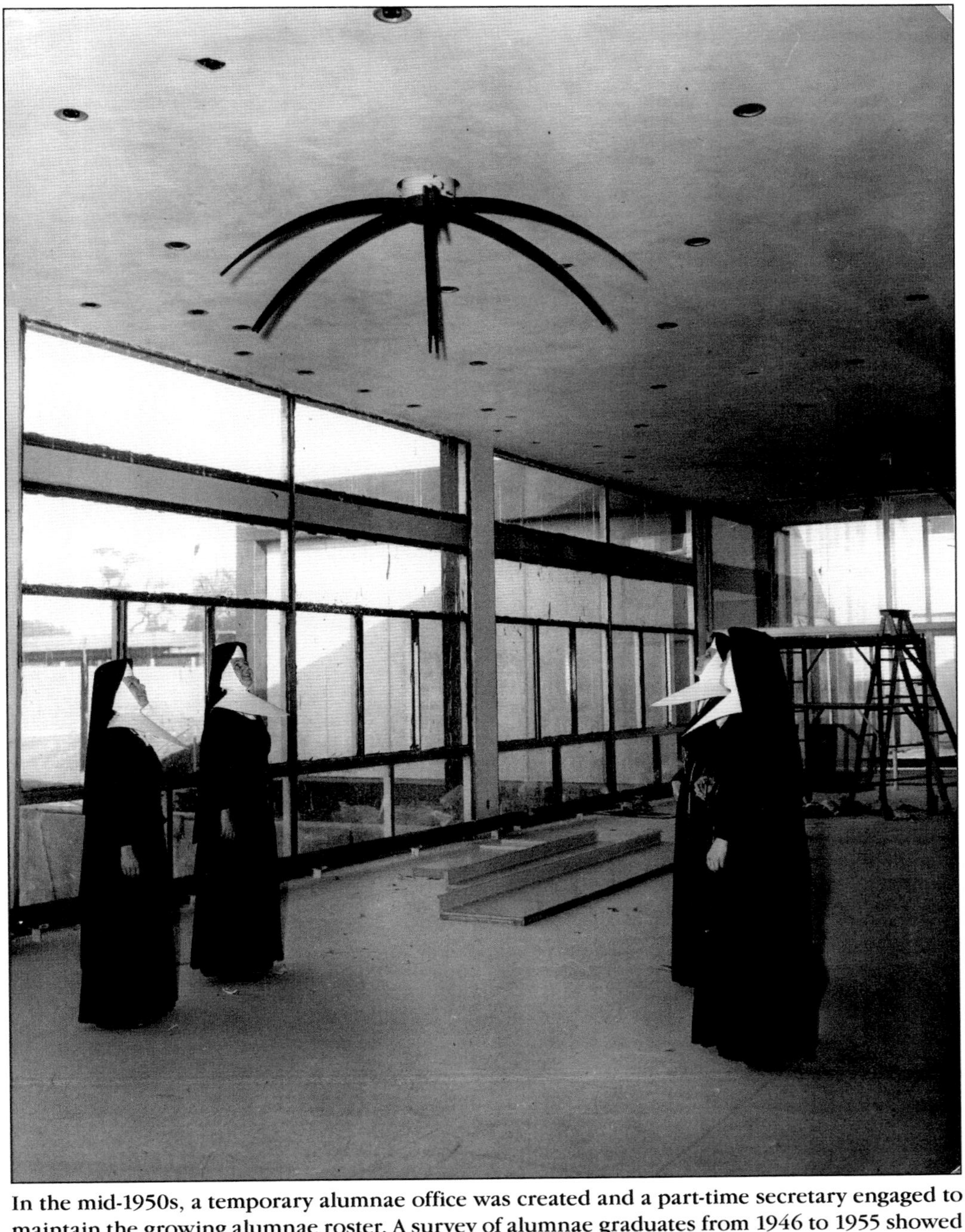

In the mid-1950s, a temporary alumnae office was created and a part-time secretary engaged to maintain the growing alumnae roster. A survey of alumnae graduates from 1946 to 1955 showed 53.5 percent in college, 19.8 percent at work, and 6.5 percent at home. When the school moved to Flourtown, an alumnae room was built. In this 1961 photograph, the Sisters of Saint Joseph appear in awe of the room's modern design.

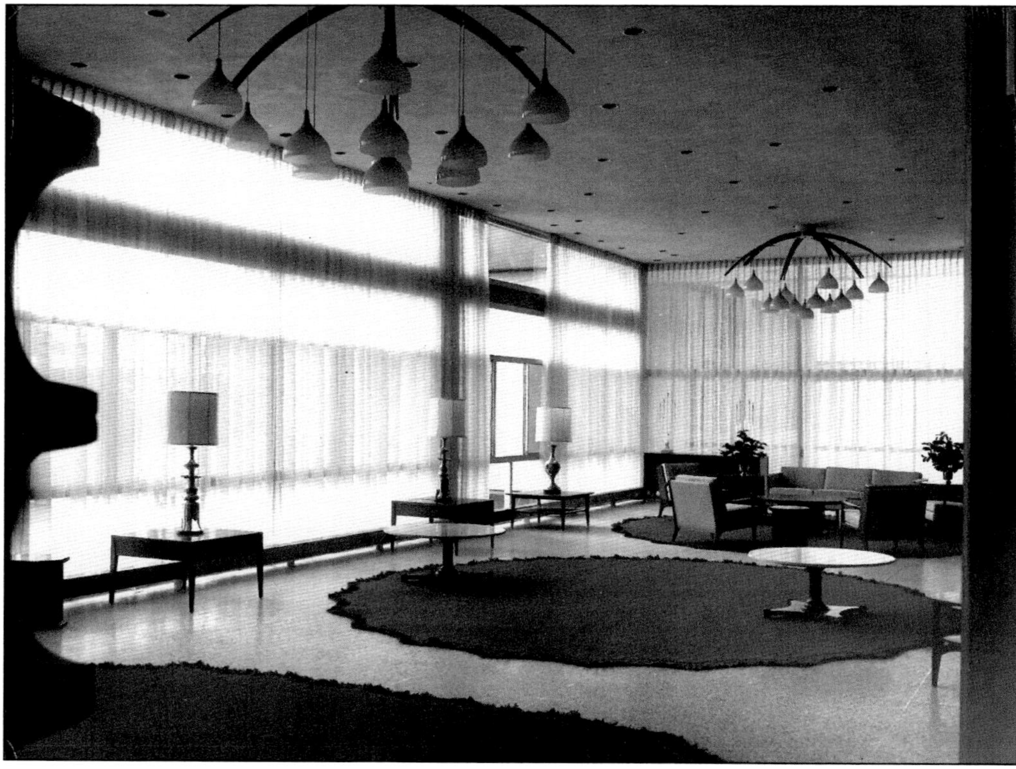

By the early 1980s, the alumnae room needed an updated space to accommodate the growing alumnae base. In 1982, principal Sr. Mary Josephine Larkin commissioned Barbara Doloway Michie '55 to design and remodel the alumnae room. Today, the beautiful alumnae room hosts alumnae board meetings and school and alumnae receptions and events.

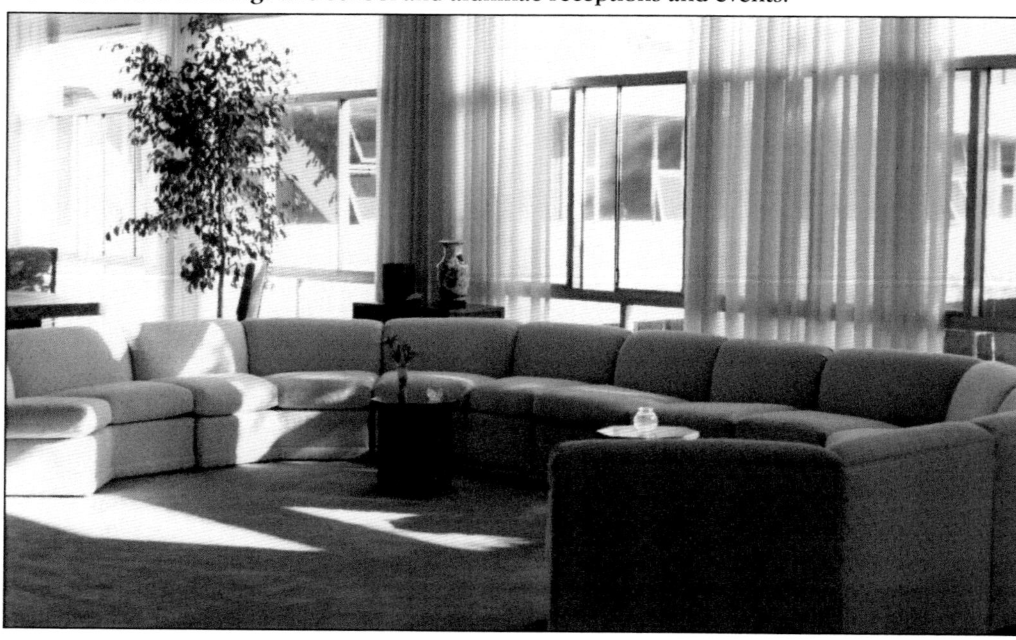

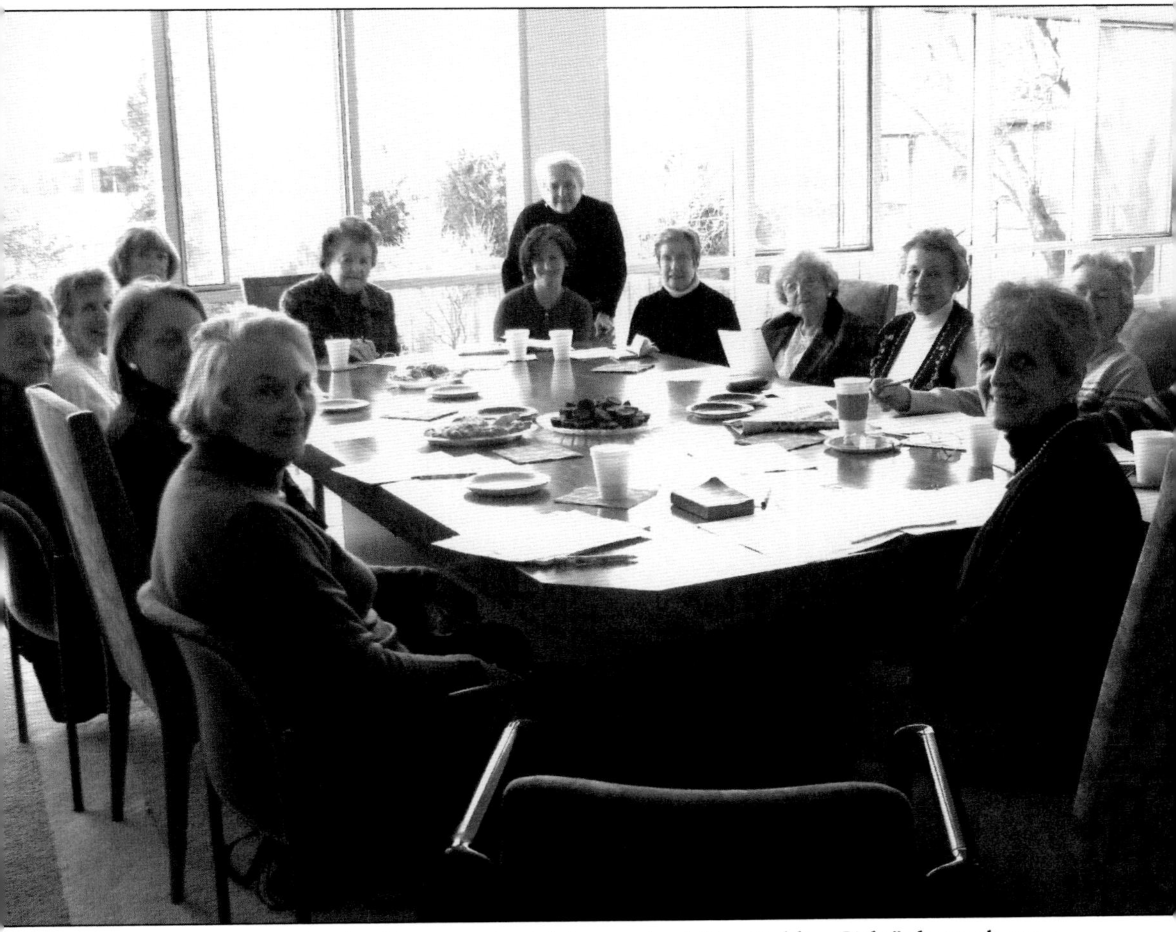

In 2000, Mary Merz Berko '48 (foreground, right) organized "the Golden Girls," those alumnae who graduated from the Mount 50 or more years ago. It was a successful attempt to preserve the history and camaraderie of generations of alumnae. The Mount Saint Joseph Alumnae Association hosts a Golden Girls luncheon each September, and those 50-year graduates are recognized at Alumnae Day each spring. In this photograph, members of the Golden Girls planning committee meet in the alumnae room to discuss forthcoming events.

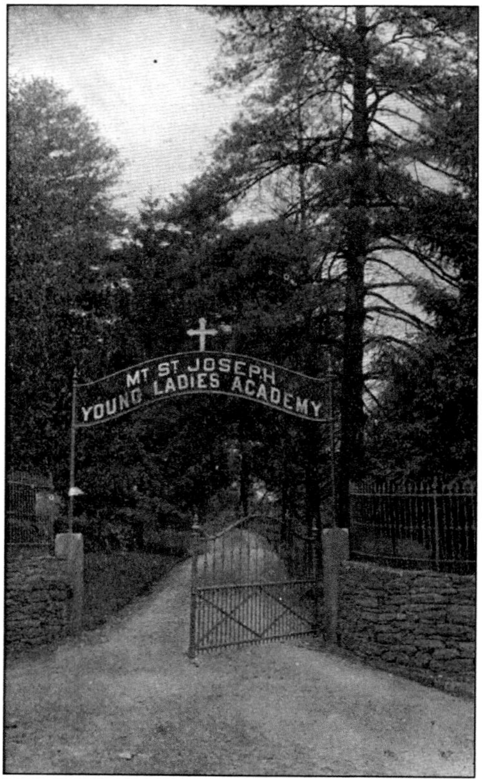

The 1915 *Alumnae Record* begins, "In one of the most beautiful suburban sites of a great city . . . stands a noted institution which represents education life in its best form, the education of the mind and of the spirit, Mt. St. Joseph Collegiate Institute, Chestnut Hill, Philadelphia. Situated amid all the woodland beauty of hill and vale, beneath the changeful loveliness of arching skies, its leafy campus framed in living green by gleaming waters of the Wissahickon . . . the Sisters of St. Joseph, with gentle guidance and zealous counsel, have educated and instructed the numberless pupils entrusted to their care, and year after year, cohorts of girl graduates have gone forth with morning faces to meet the challenge of the world. It is from among this great army of her former children that alma mater numbers her Alumnae."

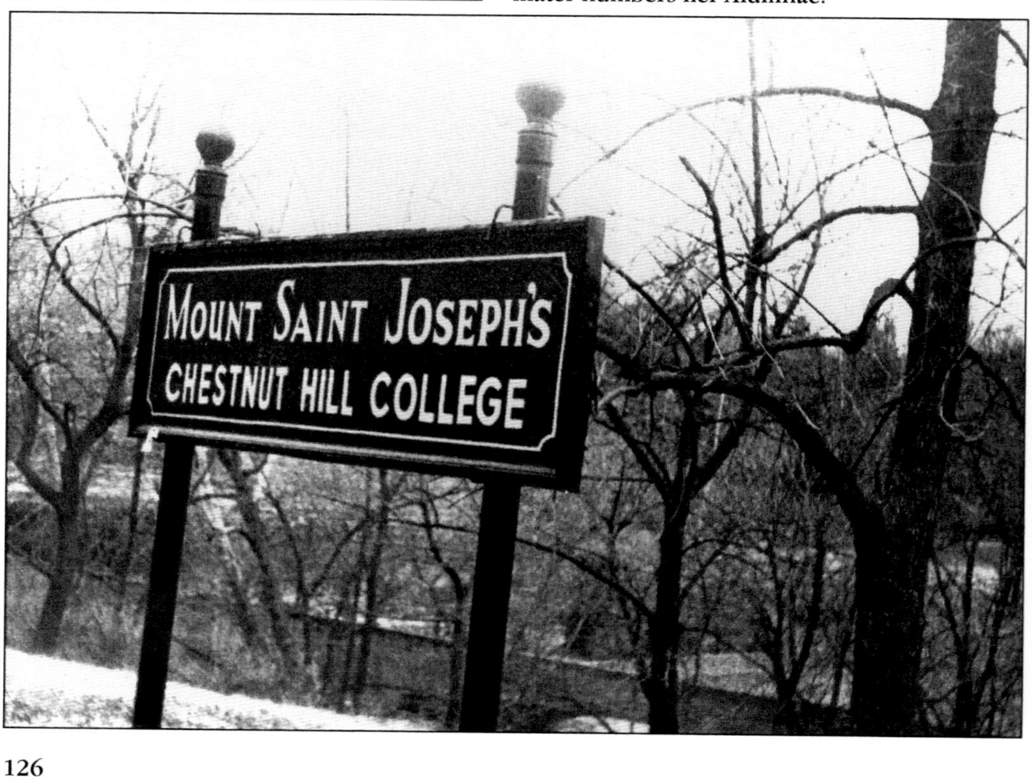

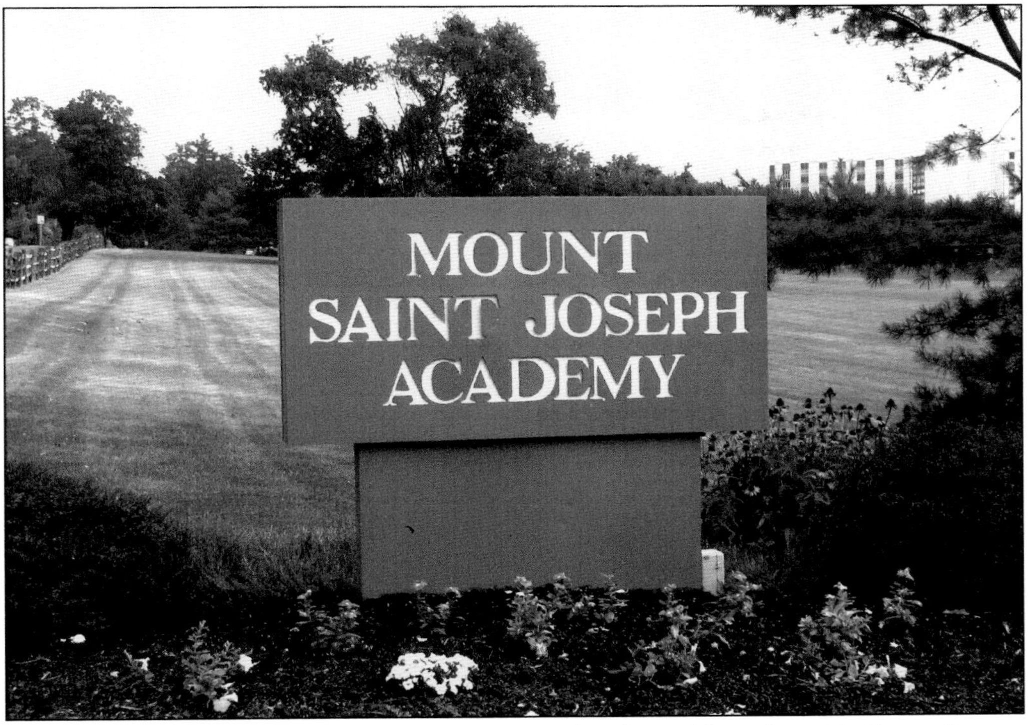

In the words of the first historian of the Mount, "The glory of Saint Joseph's Mount lies not in buildings great, sparkling rivers, verdant meadows or wooded hill . . . she prizes first and best her Alumnae who have gone forth with her seal impressed deeper on their hearts than on their diplomas."

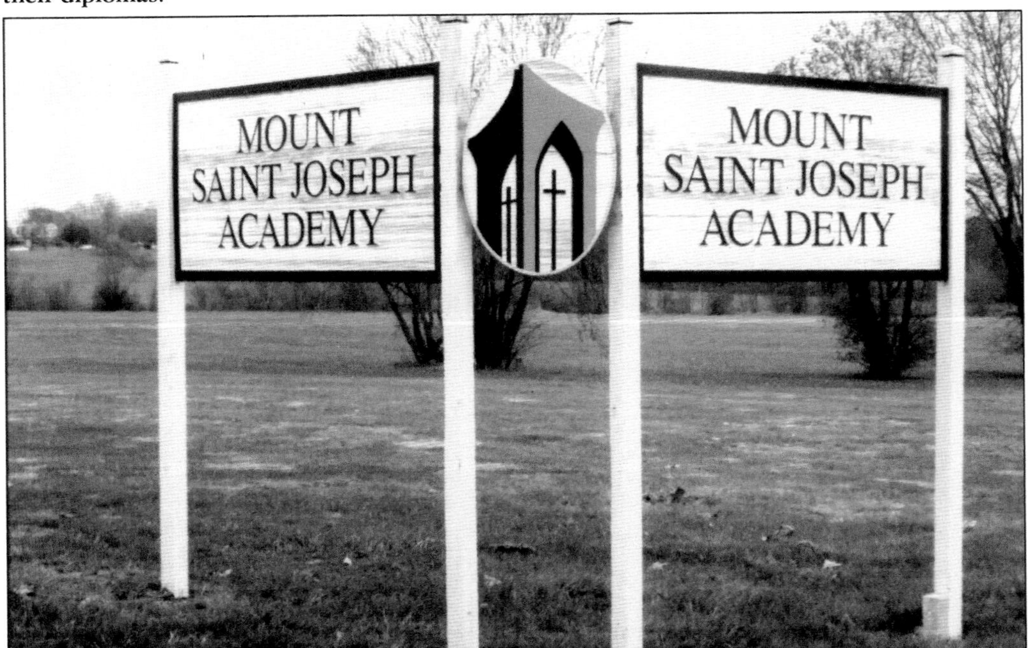